Drought and Aid
in the Sahel

About the Book and Author

The 1968-1974 drought in the Sahel was an unprecedented catastrophe for the region, causing extensive crop failures, loss of human and animal populations, political instability, and the destruction of social and cultural structures. The response of the world to the catastrophe began with food aid donations from the Western nations and led to the formation of two cooperative organizations--Comité permanent Inter-états de Lutte contre la Sécheresse dans le Sahel (CILSS, formed by the Sahel states) and the Club du Sahel (formed by donors and the Sahel countries). These organizations have attempted to help the Sahel attain regional food self-sufficiency and to make the region less vulnerable to drought. The recent recurrence of drought in the last three years, however, raises questions about the wisdom and the suitability of the developmenet strategies being pursued and the impact of foreign aid. Dr. The book Somerville analyzes the successes and failures of the development strategies, aid to the region, and the efforts of Sahelians and donors in overcoming drought and underdevelopment.

Carolyn M. Somerville is assistant professor of political science at Hunter College.

Drought and Aid in the Sahel

A Decade of Development Cooperation

Carolyn M. Somerville

Westview Press / Boulder and London

Westview Special Studies on Africa

This Westview softcover edition was manufactured on our own premises using
equipment and methods that allow us to keep even specialized books in stock.
It is printed on acid-free paper and bound in softcovers that carry the
highest rating of the NASTA, in consultation with the AAP and the BMI.

Published in 1986 in the United States of America by Westview Press, Inc.;
Frederick A. Praeger, Publisher; 5500 Central Avenue, Boulder, Colorado 80301

Library of Congress Cataloging-in-Publication Data
    Somerville, Carolyn M.
    Drought and aid in the Sahel: a decade of development cooperation.
    (Westview special studies on Africa)
    Includes index.
    1. Sahel--Economic policy. 2. Economic assistance--
Sahel. 3. Droughts--Sahel. 4. Famines--Sahel.
I. Title. II. Series.
HC1002.S65 1986   338.966   86-5635
ISBN 0-8133-7087-6

Composition for this book was provided by the author.
This book was produced without formal editing by the publisher.

Printed and bound in the United States of America

 The paper used in this publication meets the requirements of the
American National Standard for Permanence of Paper for Printed
Library Materials Z39.48-1984.

6   5   4   3   2   1

A tous les Saheliens
qui ont tellement souffert
et qui souffrent encore

Contents

Tables

Preface

The road to writing a book does not begin the
moment the author sets pen to paper. The writing
of a book is a process of experiences through
which one explores an issue more profoundly. For
me, this process began in 1973 when I spent a year
in France. While there I formed very valuable and
long-lasting friendships with Africans from the
Sahel region. This encounter sparked an interest
to learn more about the African continent and its
people.

Upon my return to the United States I enrolled in a graduate school program which introduced me to the issues of development and underdevelopment. Fortunately, graduate advisors pin-
pointed an area of research for my dissertation
which combined these personal experiences and
intellectual interests. To complete the research
initally I spent six months in the Sahel and in
Paris in 1980 and returned for two weeks in the
summer of 1982. The recurrence of drought in the
Sahel in 1982-85 led me to make an additional trip
to Paris in 1985 in order to update material for
this book.

This work, then, grew out of a long-standing
interest in certain intellectual themes and research issues: development and underdevelopment,
forms of international cooperation, the structure
of international organizations and the role of aid
in development. In the Comité permanent Inter-
états de Lutte contre la Sécheresse dans le Sa-
hel(*)--CILSS--and its parallel donor group, the
Club du Sahel, all of these issues converge. This

book is a case study of this one African regional organization, its response to the particular historical event which signalled its existence--the 1968-1974 drought and famine in West Africa, and its relevance as a model for international cooperation.

As an instrument of regional cooperation, CILSS is unlike other groups. Though it bears some parallels to traditional concepts of regionalism, there are three fundamental differences. It was formed in 1973 to provide a regional response to a specific event--the 1968-1974 drought and resultant famine in the Sahel. With a membership composed of the nine most affected nations, (Burkina Faso, Cape Verde, Chad, Gambia, Guinea-Bissau, Mali, Mauritania, Niger, and Senegal), CILSS defined an agenda which concentrated its activities in the rural and least developed sectors of the regional economy. In doing so, it departed from the usual strategy of regional organizations (which focus on the promotion of industrial trade and development) and endorsed the conclusion of the many scholars who agree that agricultural development is a prerequisite to economic development.

A firm linkage to the donor community in the form of the Club du Sahel further distinguishes this regional cooperative scheme. The Club du Sahel is a loosely-structured organization of any countries or agencies interested in the development of the Sahel. Linkage to donor agencies has not been a conventional approach to Third World regionalism; the Club du Sahel was specifically organized to generate donor support and donor resources for Sahelian development.

For ten years, CILSS and the Club du Sahel have worked to build Sahelian-regional and Sahelian-donor cooperation towards the achievement of self-sustaining economic development. In joining with the donor community to promote common goals, CILSS has been a privileged recipient of a considerable amount of official development assistance from the donor community. The per capita ODA to the Sahel has surpassed the levels given to Asia and all other Sub-Saharan African countries. Additional benefits have been a better understanding of the Sahelian environment and the con-

straints on its development, and the articulation
of sectoral and policy analyses at both the national and regional levels.

Despite these important contributions, however, the region is further from the goal of self-
sustaining economic development than it was ten
years ago. An unintended by-product of donor aid
has been increased dependency: food self-sufficiency has declined to the lowest levels in decades and the reliance on food aid and food imports has become an enduring feature of the political economy of the Sahel. Development aid has
not always been used to promote productive endeavors. As often as not, it has been used in
balance of payments support, budgetary support and
other non-productive activities. It could be said
that the increase in development assistance to the
region has contributed to a growing debt burden
facing several of the Sahel nations.

The CILSS/Club du Sahel arrangement fits into
the general historical pattern of South-South and
North-South cooperative theory. The fundamental
differences, however, and the implication of these
differences warrant closer study. In the chapters
that follow I will describe and analyze the growth
of regional cooperation within the Sahel, cooperation between Sahelians and donors, and the impact
of ten years of the CILSS/Club du Sahel framework
for development in the region.

Chapter 1 provides an introduction to the
political economy of the Sahel. Chapter 2 examines the problem of drought in the region. A
comparison of the 1968-1974 drought and the recent
drought of 1982-1985 will be made and Chapter 2
will end with an analysis of relief efforts during
both droughts.

Chapter 3 discusses CILSS in the context of
South-South cooperation to demonstrate how CILSS
differs from other African cooperative schemes.
In addition, North-South cooperation between donors and Sahelians will be examined. The question
will be asked: Are North-South and South-South
efforts within the CILSS/Club du Sahel framework
complementary or contradictory? Are they responding to shared or separate goals?

In Chapter 4 the structure of CILSS will be
described. The functions performed by CILSS and

the evolution and expansion of its operations since the early years will be presented in detail. Chapter 4 can be skimmed or skipped by those readers whose interests do not require such a detailed accounting of CILSS´ administrative and functional organs.

Chapter 5 looks at the support donors and Sahelians have offered CILSS to enable it to carry out its goals. Have donors and Sahelians responded to CILSS´ needs and requests in a manner which ensures institutional growth and continuity?

In Chapter 6 the support for CILSS projects is analyzed. Which projects have donors and Sahelians prefered to support? Are there types of projects which do not attract donor or Sahelian support? Is there a pattern of support which can be related to areas of donor expertise, donor expectations of development, short-term domestic interests of the donors, or short-term domestic political considerations of the Sahelian governments?

The final chapter analyzes the impact of CILSS and the Club du Sahel on development efforts. The recurrence of drought and famine in 1982-1985 raises questions about the effectiveness of CILSS and the efforts of the Sahelians and the donors to overcome the degradation of the Sahelian environment. Have CILSS´ goals been attained. Are CILSS´ goals, in fact, attainable through this regional cooperative effort? What benefits and costs derive from the CILSS/CLub du Sahel framework? Can the CILSS/Club du Sahel framework be reproduced in other regional contexts?

Carolyn M. Somerville

*In the English translation the name is Permanent Interstate Committee to Combat Drought in the Sahel.

Acknowledgments

Although the writing of this book was the work of one individual, many others contributed to the final product. For providing the funding to help me to conduct the research I am especially indebted to the Compton Foundation, the Center for Research on Economic Development at The University of Michigan, and the Research Foundation of the City University of New York.

A number of individuals provided critical and constructive comments along the way--Harold K. Jacobson, Miroslav Nincic, and Ali A. Mazrui took time out from their busy schedules to provide guidance and insight. Mervat Hatem, Evans Young, David F. Gordon, and Pearl T. Robinson offered thoughtful and encouraging feedback during the writing process. A special thanks goes to Michael Champion who helped solve my computer problems. I am especially grateful to Terry Plater who helped me to edit this work.

To my friends and colleagues at Hunter College and my friends from The University of Michigan I deeply appreciate all the support, help, encouragement, and camaraderie. Without the aid of the Club du Sahel, CILSS, and USAID, the research would never have been completed. The personnel of these institutions generously opened their files and allowed me to ask many questions. Particularly helpful were Mr. Aly Cisse, Mme. de Lattre, Arthur M. Fell, Abdou Salam Drabo, Alioune Sall, and Willie Saulters.

A special thanks goes to my family: my husband, Arthur; my mother and father, Dorothy and Albert; and my sister, Paula. They have all put up with so much and have remained so supportive as only family will do. Finally, I must acknowledge two individuals, Aimee Kron and Joel Samoff, whose profound influences shaped and altered my life in ways unknown to both.

C.M.S.

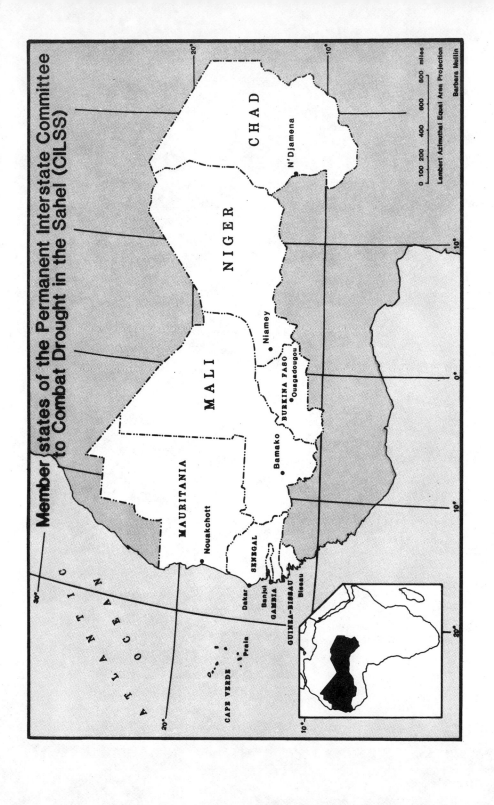

Member states of the Permanent Interstate Committee to Combat Drought in the Sahel (CILSS)

1

Introduction:
The Political Economy
of the Sahel

Since 1981, media images of a human tragedy
without parallel in modern Africa have served to
remind the world of the precariousness of life.
While drought has been a familiar and recurrent
feature in the African environment, never in
recorded history have its effects touched so many
countries at once. In the great drought of 1968-
1974, the 16 affected countries spanned the
northern part of Africa from west to east and
included: Cape Verde, Senegal, Gambia, Mali, Mauritania, Burkina Faso, Chad, Niger, Benin,
Nigeria, Central African Republic, Libya, Sudan,
Somalia, Djibouti and Ethiopia. The current
drought (1982-1985) has touched many more countries: Madagascar, Malawi, Mozambique, Tanzania,
Togo, Angola, Cameroon, Equatorial Guinea, Guinea-
Bissau, Kenya, Lesotho, Uganda, Zambia, and Zimbabwe as well as most of those affected by the 1968-
1974 drought. In all, 26 African nations have
been touched by drought and famine since 1982.
Media has focused much of its coverage on
East and Southern Africa where Western--and especially American--concerns about the Marxist regimes of Ethiopia and Mozambique have hinged on
the fresh opportunities for political and diplomatic change. Drought and famine in Mozambique, no
doubt, played a role in that government's accord
with the South African government. In 1984, after
two consecutive years of drought and the
successful efforts of the South African backed
opposition group, the Mozambique National
Resistance (MNR), in thwarting relief deliveries

1

to affected regions of the country, the Mozambican government was compelled to sign a non-aggression pact, the Nkomati Accord. In signing the Accord, Mozambique calculated that South Africa would halt its support and financing of the MNR destablization campaign. This would allow aid relief to reach the drought affected areas of the country. While MNR destablization efforts have not ended, the Accord has led to the establishment of a new relationship between Washington and Maputo. Washington viewed the signing of the Accord as an indication of Mozambican willingness to move away from the Socialist bloc. The Reagan Administration has provided Mozambique with drought and military aid (1).

In the Horn of Africa, drought in Ethiopia has exposed that nation to some of the contradictions of aid agreements. The need for large amounts of food aid, unfulfilled by the Eastern bloc, has been met by Western donors. This participation has given the Western donors the opportunity to exercise some influence, even if only to demonstrate the limits of Ethiopia´s alliance with the Soviet bloc. Western donors witness to the corruption of the Ethiopian government in its mishandling of aid shipments--including documented instances of profiteering--have publicized these findings (2). Media reports of the government´s treatment of refugees from Eritrea, Ogaden, and Wallo provinces have helped to generate support for these groups. If political and diplomatic points have been made in recent years by Western donors in East and South Africa, far less attention has been paid to the human consequences of drought and famine recurring in other regions of Africa, particularly the Sahel (3).

Ten years ago the Sahel was the focus of attention paid to the African drought and its victims. The media was captured by the tragedy and because of its coverage, multilateral and bilateral aid poured into the region. Aid donors pledged to help get the Sahel back on its feet economically. What happened to that pledge? After millions of dollars in aid to the Sahel, why did another major disaster occur?

To a certain extent, drought has been a natural phenomenon recurring periodically in Africa.

Its effect--famine--however, is symptomatic of a larger problem facing the continent: underdevelopment and dependency. A combination of factors, some internal and some external to Africa, has left their economies devasted.

EXTERNAL FACTORS

Beginning in the 1970s, the industrialized countries, beset by major economic problems such as growing recession and unemployment, were forced to institute readjustment policies. To counter adverse conditions, the developed nations reduced their demand for imports, thus affecting African economies. As demand for African commodities dropped, Africa's share of the world output of these products also dropped. Between 1961 and 1982 the annual average production of oils and oilseeds in Africa registered tremendous declines (4). For example, production of groundnuts as a percentage of the world's total dropped from 85 percent in 1961-1963 to 18 percent in 1980-1982. During the same period production of cereals as a percentage of the world's total fell from 4.1 percent to 2.5 percent (5). What is particularly disturbing about Africa's declining exports is the fact that these products account for a major portion of foreign exchange earnings.

A second outcome of the stagnating world economy during the 1970s and the 1980s was the sharp drop in prices for African commodities. As demand for African exports took a downward turn, the price paid for Africa's raw materials dropped also. According to World Bank estimates, the prices of African commodities such as groundnuts, phosphate, and uranium rose sharply in the mid-1970s and then fell precipitously (6).

What is clear from Table 1.1 is the extent of the vulnerability of Third World exporters of non-fuel products in the global market place. While the price for their exports declined significantly, the price of needed imports of fuel and manufactured goods rose dramatically. For African oil importers, terms of trade deteriorated about 8 percent from 1970-1980 (7). As the World Bank indicates, this loss of purchasing power is

3

TABLE 1.1
Index of World Terms of Trade
(Index: 1978=100)

	1978	1980	1982
Price of raw materials (except oil)	100	126.4	95
Price of petroleum products	100	238.6	252.2
Price of industrial exports	100	126.5	117.8

Source: OECD/Club du Sahel/CILSS La dette extérieure des pays du CILSS (Paris: OECD, 1985), p. 6.

most likely permanent (8).

For most of the Sahel West Africa the same pattern of declining terms of trade occured. Between 1970 and 1982 the Sahel´s average annual terms of trade grew at negative rates.

With the exception of Mauritania and Niger whose sales of iron ore and uranium, respectively, improved slightly from 1981 to 1982, the countries of the Sahel region experienced a downward shift in their terms of trade. The steepest decline--30 percent between 1981 and 1982--was registered by Gambia.

Since World War II African exports have suffered a comparative disadvantage in the world market place. To compound the economic difficulties, two major oil price hikes resulted in a fivefold increase in the price of oil in the 1970s (9). Though the Sahel´s consumption of fuel imports is low, the steep and sudden rise in the price of petroleum did have some influence on the region. Energy imports as a percentage of merchandise exports jumped from 38 percent in 1960 to 71 percent in 1981 in Burkina Faso; from 6

percent to 23 percent for Niger during the same
period; and from 8 percent to 77 percent for
Senegal (10).

TABLE 1.2
Terms of Trade for the Sahel
(Index: 1980=100)

	1970	1979	1981	1982
Burkina Faso	133	113	106	97
Chad	81	100	103	99
Gambia	141	122	126	88
Mali	118	107	107	102
Mauritania	175	101	92	97
Niger	169	112	82	89
Senegal	100	110	101	89

Source: World Bank, Toward Sustained Development
in Sub-Saharan Africa (Washington, D.C.: World
Bank, 1984), p. 67.

TABLE 1.3
Merchandise Trade Growth Rate
(in percentages)

	Exports (1970-1982)	Imports (1970-1982)
Burkina Faso	9.1	6.7
Chad	-8.6	-3.6
Gambia	-1.7	6.4
Mali	6.6	6.6
Mauritania	-0.1	3.0
Niger	20.8	11.0
Senegal	-1.8	1.3

Source: World Bank, Toward Sustained Development
in Sub-Saharan Africa, p. 63.

5

The combination of oil shocks, stagnant export demand, and declining terms of trade left the Sahelian economies grossly out of balance. As can be seen in Table 1.3, export growth rates for many of these countries fell below import growth rates. Gambia, Mauritania, Chad, and Senegal experienced export growth rates which were negative compared to import growth rates for the years 1970-1982. For Mali, the export and import growth rates were even. Only Burkina Faso and Niger had export growth rates which exceeded their import growth rates.

To compensate for a deterioration in the balance of payments, countries had three options--increase exports, decrease imports, or some combination thereof. In the Sahel, increasing the volume of exports was not a viable solution. For the most part, Sahelian exports are primarily agricultural products which have never been in high demand. Reducing the import growth rate was a strategy option which several of the governments were unwilling or unable to take for a variety of reasons. In some cases these imports were vital to key productive sectors of the economy such as agriculture; cutting back would have undermined that sector. In other cases, reducing needed food imports would affect the health and welfare of the population (not to mention the stability of the governments). Many governments, motivated by the desire to industrialize and modernize on a grand scale, continued to import costly goods and services for projects of little productive value.

Thus the picture in the Sahel, as in many parts of Africa, was one of distorted priorities: countries were encouraging rather than diminishing dependencies. Even when export demand and commodity prices fell, governments were reluctant to curb spending to meet the shortage in export earnings. Despite grave balance of payments problems, most governments preferred to maintain consumption levels of goods and services (11). By the early 1980s, many African countries found themselves in a vicious economic cycle: adverse economic factors resulted in reduced export earnings; externally financed loans and grants were required if governments were to meet international economic

6

obligations; accumulated debts could not be ser-
viced due to falling government revenues, and additional loans were necessary.

Thus, external factors such as the declining
demand for exports, the decrease in the price
received for exports, world wide recession, inflation, and increased energy costs played a significant role in the deterioration of the Sahelian
economy in the 1970s and 1980s. The next section
examines the internal factors which contributed to
Sahelian regional stagnation.

INTERNAL FACTORS

In assessing the internal causes of the
decline in the Sahelian economy, several factors
stand out: the low standard of living, high population growth rates, inappropriate government
policies, and drought. The standard of living in
the Sahel, never high to begin with, continued to
stagnate and even decline in the 1970s. Four
states, Chad, Mali, Burkina Faso, and Niger rank
among the poorest in the world.

Per capita gross national product growth
rates proved to be lackluster after independence.
For Burkina Faso, Gambia, and Mali, average annual
growth rates for the years 1965-1983, were barely
over 1 percent, below the expectation of 3.5 percent, set by the United Nations Second Development
Decade (12). In addition, Chad, Niger, and Senegal experienced negative growth rates during this
period. No Sahel country had average annual
growth rates above 1.5 percent during those
eighteen years.

Stagnating and declining growth rates had
repercussions on the standard of living in the
region. The low level of financial resources
retarded efforts to improve the health and welfare
of the population as a whole. In 1985, in Burkina
Faso only 10 percent of the population could read
and write French which is the official language;
only 20 percent of the children of primary school
age were enrolled in school (13). Of course,
these aggregate figures mask the geographic
disparities in access to education. While over 50
percent of primary school age children residing in

7

TABLE 1.4
Basic Indicators of the Sahel

	Population in Thousands (1983)
Burkina Faso	6,500
Cape Verde	315
Chad	4,600
Gambia	697
Mali	7,200
Mauritania	1,600
Niger	6,100
Senegal	6,200

	GNP Per Capita	
	1983 $	average annual growth rate (%) 1965-1983
Burkina Faso	180	1.4
Cape Verde	320	-
Chad	80	-2.8
Gambia	290	1.4
Mali	160	1.2
Mauritania	480	0.3
Niger	240	-1.2
Senegal	440	-0.5

Source: World Bank, World Development Report 1985 (New York: Oxford University Press, 1985), p. 174.

the capital, Ouagadougou, were enrolled in school, in the rural town of Dori, primary school enrollment was only 5 percent (14). These conditions acted as a brake on raising the gross national product.

Population growth trends compound the low

standards of living. In 1959 there were 17.5 million Sahelians; by 1984 the population had risen
to 35 million, doubling in less than 20 years
(15). Estimates are that by the year 2010 the
population will reach 75 million (16). Rising
population growth rates are attributable to
advances in medical science which have reduced
childhood and adult mortality. While infant mortality rates are higher in the Sahel than in other
parts of the world, these rates have dropped because of better nutrition and immunization
against diseases and deadly illnesses such as
measles and cholera. Likewise, though life expec-
tancy in the Sahel remains lower than in other
regions of the world, it has still risen since
independence. Notwithstanding these scientific
advances, Sahelian women continue to have six or
more children on the average.

TABLE 1.5
Birth and Population Growth Rates

	Birth Rate per 1000 Live Births (1982)	Population Growth Rate (1970-1982)
Burkina Faso	48	2.0
Chad	42	2.0
Gambia	49	3.2
Mali	48	2.7
Mauritania	43	2.3
Niger	52	3.3
Senegal	30	2.7
All low-income countries	30	1.9

Source: Toward Sustained Development in Sub-
Saharan Africa, pp. 82 and 83.

In Table 1.5 the number of live births per 1000 is indicated for the year 1982. Birth rates in the Sahel are much higher than those for other low-income countries. Only Senegal, with the lowest birth rate of 30 per 1000 live births, is comparable to that of similarly placed low-income countries. High birth rates and population growth rates have a signficant impact on the region's ability to feed and care for its citizens.

Complicating the population growth rate are population pressures in the form of rural-urban migration, and the growth of urban areas. In 1959 only 1.2 million people lived in urban areas; by 1984 the numbers residing in urban areas had risen by 350 percent to 6.5 million (17). Before 1960, Senegal, Mali, and Gambia were the only countries with an urban population greater than 10 percent of their total population. In 1982, in all the Sahel states, with the exception of Burkina Faso, at least 1 out of 5 people lived in urban areas. Senegal had the highest rate of urbanizaion, 34 percent (18). For a variety of reasons, rural dwellers are abandoning their traditional ways of life for the cities and towns. The motives for this migration include: 1) increased economic opportunities, 2) relief from recurrent drought which has destroyed crops and livestock to a point beyond which a viable living can be earned, 3) improved sanitary conditions, 4) the attraction of cities, 5) a reduction in hardships, and 6) better educational facilities (19). Despite the migrant's unfamiliarity with city ways, the possibility of underemployment and unemployment, and the alienation and anomie that often accompany migration, this phenomenon continues unabated. The growth in population in urban areas where underemployment and unemployment are already critical adds to the burden upon governments to satisfy demands for social services. Left unattended, the rise in population and rural-urban imbalances could spell serious political and economic consequences.

As people abandon the villages for the towns, agriculture becomes a less attractive occupation. When fewer individuals value agriculture as a worthwhile enterprise, the desire to remain diminishes among those left behind. In the Sahel,

10

as in many parts of Africa, agriculture is no
longer viewed as a viable enterprise. Peasants
have begun to vote with their feet. The drought
has accentuated this migration process. The combination of drought and rural-urban migration has
negatively affected food production.

Before the 1960s, the Sahel was food self-
sufficient. After independence in the 1960s food
self-sufficiency declined. Food grain self-sufficiency is especially problematic for the coastal
countries: Gambia, Senegal, Cape Verde, and Mauritania. Burkina Faso, Chad, Niger, and Mali could
be food grain self-sufficient given the correct
mix of environmental variables and governmental
policies.

Between 1960 and 1980 annual food production
grew by 1.75 percent (20). Unfortunately, these
gains in food productivity were negated by the
region's population growth rate of 2.7 percent.
In comparing Tables 1.5 and 1.6, it can be seen
that the discrepancy between population growth
rates and food production rates varies from country to country. Gaps between food production and

TABLE 1.6
Average Annual Food Production Growth Rates
(1970-1982)

Country	Percentage
Burkina Faso	2.4
Chad	2.4
Gambia	-1.0
Mali	2.5
Mauritania	1.4
Niger	4.1
Senegal	1.5

Source: Toward Sustained Development in Sub-
Saharan Africa, p. 77.

11

population growth were serious for Gambia, Mali, Mauritania, and Senegal. Three of the inland countries, Burkina Faso, Chad, and Niger were able to produce enough food to supply demand. However, aggregate figures mask the fact that not every one had access or entitlement to this food (21).

While demographic factors tell part of the story of the region's inability to feed itself, other explanatory variables exist. Ninety-five percent of all agriculture is traditional drylands (or rainfed) cropping. A lack of technological inputs--improved seed varieties, fertilizers, and pesticides--and the use of draft animals have kept economic output low (22). In addition, low productive yields have been caused by below normal rainfall levels. Though some of the crops grown in the Sahel are drought resistant, not all crops are. The more susceptible a crop is to drought, the greater the chance it will fail in periods in which rainfall is late or nonexistent.

Government policies have systematically underdeveloped the agricultural sector. It has been taxed disproportionately and the funds extracted have tended to remain in the urban areas. Notwithstanding the fact that 75 percent of the population engages in agriculture for a living, government investment in this sector has never been a priority. The refusal to invest in improved technology, research, training, and extension services has left agriculture high and dry--in effect, feeding upon itself. What little revenue there is allocated to agriculture has gone primarily to cash crops (cotton and groundnuts) rather than to food crops (millet, sorghum, and corn). Twenty years after independence, peasants remain outside of the development process; those who produce food crops remain the most marginalized and the poorest of the poor (23).

It is also widely acknowledged that inappropriate government policies contributed to the decline in food production (24). By undertaking policies to provide food at a low cost to urban dwellers, real producer prices were held down. As a result, peasants had little incentive to improve and to expand agricultural output. Any increases in agricultural yields were the result of the expansion of the acreage under cultivation, and not related to increasing the productivity of the land through the use of technological inputs.

Finally, environmental factors played a role in the retrogradation of the Sahelian political economy. The 1968-1974 drought was a catastrophe for the region. Since then, rainfall has remained erratic throughout much of the Sahel. In 1981, just as the region was beginning to overcome this disaster another major drought hit. Again, agriculture yields declined precipitously and livestock herds were eliminated in some areas. As the economic situation worsened, other problems arose. Political conflicts, the growth in refugee populations, and major health and nutrition problems became more apparent.

The recurrence and intensity of famine is a manifestation of deep structural problems caused by the aforementioned internal and external factors. The legacy of colonialism, the impact of neo-colonialism and internal mismanagement have placed many at the edge of starvation and famine. In parts of the Sahel de-development has occured and this can be measured by the deterioration of infrastructure, the shrinking of health and welfare services, and the increasing gap between the rural and urban sectors (25). In short, some indicators of development have been reversed.

Recognizing the state of affairs, the local governments felt that only a concerted regional effort could reverse the situation. In 1973 these governments banded together to address the effects of drought and famine. The organization they formed, the Comité permanent Inter-états de Lutte contre la Sécheresse dans le Sahel (CILSS), follows a tradition of regional integration among African states (26). Unlike other regional integration schemes which tended to concern themselves with industrialization, CILSS has, from the outset, set as its target the improvement of the rural and least developed sectors. Thus, CILSS represents a departure from other regional schemes. By concentrating its activities in the rural sector, CILSS endorsed the conclusion of many scholars that agricultural development was the prerequisite for economic development.

Three years following the creation of CILSS, the donor community mobilized to form a parallel

group which would work closely with CILSS in executing rehabilitative programs. That organization,
the Club du Sahel, was organizaed along fluid
lines and it has sought to generate donor support
and donor resources for Sahelian development.

CILSS and the Club du Sahel fit into a
historical pattern of South-South and North-South
cooperative theory: at the same time they diverge
from that theory in several important respects.
For one thing, the formation of these two organizations resulted from a specific historic event,
the drought. The famine and the economic realities of the region suggested that new cooperative
efforts be tried. The needs of the Sahel states
(among the poorest of the poor) dictated that the
functions and operations of both organizations
concentrate on providing basic needs, rather than
on encouraging urban industrial development and
trade policies as most other African regional and
North-South organizations have done.

CILSS further departs from other regional
organizations in that it has taken into consideration Sahelian dependency in the world economy. In
light of this reality, CILSS has aligned itself
closely with the donor community and its organization, the Club du Sahel. Most regional organizations formed by developing countries have ignored
or attempted to eliminate the influence of the
more powerful Western economic forces and actors.
The result has been that external forces continue
to insert themselves into the development process,
thereby undermining the aims of the organzation.
Mytelka´s study of the Andean Group points out the
problems of external penetration in the integrative process in Latin America (27). The following
chapters examine these and other issues in relationship to drought and development in the Sahel.

NOTES

1. Michael Fleshman, "In Defense of Apartheid: South Africa and Its Neighbors," Socialist Review (1986), p. 114.

2. A series of articles by Clifford D. May on the issue of government priorities and corruption include: "Ancient Ethiopian Holy City Starves," The New York Times, December 27, 1984; "Aid Officials Say Ethiopia May Put Arms Before Food," The New York Times, February 1, 1985; "Relations Sour Between Ethiopia and Western Food Donors," The New York Times, February 18, 1985; and "In Ethiopia, Food Rots on the Docks," The New York Times, May 17, 1985.

3. While news coverage of the drought in the Sahel has continued, the photos accompanying articles on drought and famine in Africa are usually scenes of Ethiopia and not of the Sahel. Jonathan Derrick, "West Africa's Worst Year of Famine," African Affairs, Vol. 83 (1984), p. 283.

4. World Bank, Toward Sustained Development in Sub-Saharan Africa (Washington, D.C.: World Bank, 1984), p. 11.

5. Ibid, p. 80.

6. Ibid, p. 22.

7. World Bank, Accelerated Development in Sub-Saharan Africa: an agenda for action (Washington, D.C.: World Bank, 1981), p. 19.

8. Ibid.

9. Ibid, p. 18.

10. Toward Sustained Development in Sub-Saharan Africa, p. 62.

11. Ibid, p. 24.

12. United Nations, Everyone's United Nations, 9th ed. (New York: United Nations, 1979), p. 118.

13. USAID, Annual Budget Submission for FY 1987, Burkina Faso (Washington, D.C.: USAID, 1985), p. 1.

14. Ibid, p. 4.

15. Jacques Giri, Rétrospective De L'Economie Sahelienne (Paris: OECD, 1985), p. 6.

16. OECD, Aide Alimentaire Et Coopération Pour Le Développement: L'Expérience Du Sahel (Paris: OECD, 1984), p. 4.

17. Giri, p. 8.

15

18. Toward Sustained Development in Sub-Saharan Africa, p. 85.
19. Giri, p. 8.
20. Ibid, p. 18.
21. Amartya Sen, Poverty and Famines (Oxford: Clarendon Press, 1981).
22. OECD/CILSS/Club du Sahel, Development Of Rainfed Agriculture In The Sahel, Overview And Prospects (Paris: OECD, 1983), p. 14.
23. Giri, p.19.
24. Accelerated Development in Sub-Saharan Africa; Robert Bates, Markets and States in Tropical Africa (Berkeley: University of California Press, 1981); Richard Vengroff and Ali Farah, "State Intervention And Agricultural Development in Africa: a Cross-National Study," The Journal of Modern African Studies, 23, No. 1 (1985), pp. 75-85.
25. Toward Sustained Development in Sub-Saharan Africa, p. 1.
26. CILSS is the French acronym. The English translation is the Permanent Interstate Committee to Combat Drought in the Sahel.
27. Lynn K. Mytelka, Regional Development in a Global Economy (New Haven: Yale University Press, 1979).

2

Drought and
Drought Relief Efforts

DROUGHTS IN WEST AFRICAN HISTORY

Lovejoy and Baier and others have found the drought-recovery-drought cycle to be a historical and seemingly inevitable aspect of Sahelian life (1). Historians have chronicled the occurence of drought, in West Africa dating back to the six-teenth century but, with the exception of the 1968-1974 and 1982-1985 droughts, all appear to have been confined to small geographic locations. None was of a magnitude comparable to the recent droughts: the duration, destruction, and pervasiveness of these were, in many ways, unpre-cedented in modern African history (2).

A singular and particularly devastating characteristic of the most recent droughts is that so many nations were affected: 16 nations in 1968-1974 and 26 nations in 1982-1984. In addition, the duration and pervasiveness of these two droughts prevented the Sahelians from relying upon the traditional, fall-back desert economies.

Historically, Sahelians depended on a variety of economic alternatives when confronted with adverse environmental conditions. Migration, the initial response, entailed that herders move live-stock to more southern areas (outside of the nor-mal transhumance region). Division of the animal stock among males in the family was a secondary strategy. By dividing the stock and moving in different directions, herders were assured that at least part of the stock would survive. A third tactic employed was the tradition of lending ani-

17

mals to friends and family. Thus, if a herder encountered problems, he was assured that part of the loaned stock would be returned. Finally, species diversity protected the nomads during adverse times. Herders raised a variety of animals--goats, sheep, camels, and cattle--each with different alimentary needs. Some portion of a herder's stock could withstand the vagaries of the environment. If the cattle and the sheep succumbed during the lean years, the hardier species (camels and goats) could survive. In sum, centuries of confronting the vicissitudes of weather, vegetation, and water had taught nomadic groups how to avert economic ruin (3).

The dietary habits of nomads normally consisted mainly of meat and milk products. During the soudure (the period from late November to June when water and vegetation were critically low), the complement of grains, seeds and fruits in the herders' diet increased. In times of drought, additional relief was sought through increased contacts with neighboring groups. Herders could exchange their livestock with sedentary villagers for millet and other grains.

Another practice employed by some nomadic groups to stave off famine was to raid and plunder sedentary villages for grain. Depending on the needs of the herders and their relations with neighbors, contacts between nomads and farmers were characterized by both cooperation and conflict.

As was the case during other periods of drought and famine, all of these traditional desert survival tactics were utilized in the recent droughts; but, unlike previous occasions, the affected populations were circumscribed in several ways. Where they could carry out traditional coping practices, positive results were not successful. What changes had occured to militate against the effective outcome of traditional strategies?

COLONIAL AND POST-COLONIAL POLICIES

Some scientific experts view climatological or natural factors as a cause of drought (4).

18

Other authors place the blame with development policies (5). These authors are convinced that the roots of the drought and its resultant devastation are the political, social, and economic choices made by the French and continued by the African governments. This body of literature argues that, although the climatological reasons for the existence of drought are found in nature, "The magnitude of the impact of a climatological drought is dependent upon many regional, physical, social, and economic factors--emphasizing the relative rather than the absolute nature of drought" (6).

The conditions that led to widespread regional devastation originated in the implantation of French colonial rule. As the French exerted control over the Sahel, traditional methods of coping with drought could not be carried out or, if attempted, failed to minimize the destruction. The impact of French rule upon African life can be measured in three areas: geographical and poltical, economic, and cultural. It was in the first two areas that the desert economy of the nomads would undergo change under the French.

The first contact made between France and Africa was in the seventeenth century when the French established a colonial outpost at St. Louis in Senegal. Initially, the French were content to trade African products (gum arabic, skins, gold, ivory, and slaves) for French goods (paper, guns, gunpowder, and cloth). By the mid-1800s, with encouragement from the French government, Louis Faidherbe, the Governor of Senegal, expanded the French presence from the coastal administrative posts to the hinterland. To gain control over the territory, the French became entangled in a series of wars against African leaders which would last for about sixty years.

After the Franco-Prussian War in the 1870s, colonies took on an increased importance, not only for France, but for all of Europe (7). Economic and political power accrued to those European countries with colonies. Raw materials, market outlets, and cheap labor spurred the Industrial Revolution in the metropoles. The Revolution necessitated the pacification of Africa by the French, and set in motion the decline of the traditional way of life.

The caravan trade connecting Arab and black Africa, an important aspect of nomadic life and culture, was, by World War I, all but terminated. The trade routes gradually gave way as railways and ships replaced the need for camels to move goods in the region. For the first time, travel routes did not transport goods from north to south and from east to west, but rather from north to south to France. France became the intermediary and, in effect, the controller of inter-African and Arab-African trade and relations.

The elimination of the caravan trade contributed to the pauperization of the nomads. A change in the terms of trade was an inevitable result. At the turn of the century, a camel carrying a load of salt netted 15-20 sacks of millet; by 1950, the same load of salt equalled only 6-10 sacks of millet; and by 1975, a nomad could exchange the same load of salt for only two loads of millet. The value of a milk cow suffered the same declining terms of trade--a milk cow bought ten sacks of millet in 1955 and 4-5 sacks in 1975 (8). In effect, colonial policies altered the exchange environment and limited the purchasing power of the nomads with results that would be devastating during the drought years.

Economically, the Sahel was transformed by the French in another way. Two products produced in Africa--groundnuts and cotton--became very important to the French. Groundnuts were highly valued by the French in the manufacture of soap and cooking oil (9). Cotton, too, played a role in the satisfaction of European needs. The profits from these two products were important to French industrialists who manufactured finished goods from these African exports.

The expansion of the export sector in peanuts and cotton rapidly increased. Senegalese groundnut production grew from 45,000 tons in 1884-1885 to 600,000 tons in 1936-1937 to more than a million tons in 1965-1967 (10). In 1975 groundnut production peaked at 1.4 million tons (11). The same growth in peanut production occured in Niger: from 18,000 tons in 1929 to 182,000 tons in 1968 (12).

The growth in cotton production paralleled

the growth in groundnut production. Between 1960
and 1972, the amount of land in Mali devoted to
cotton production rose from 26,000 to 90,000 hectares (13). Cotton yields increased from 480
kilograms per hectare to 800 kilograms per hectare
(14). Thus, the economic transformation, begun by
French colonialism, continued after independence.

The increase in cash crop production was
achieved through various means. In regions where
the population density was low, peasants could
expand to what were previously uncultivated lands.
Another method practiced was the appropriation of
the most arable land for the production of cash
crops. A third tactic employed, if new lands
could not be exploited, was to reduce the time in
which the land was left to lie fallow. The traditional agricultural method used to prevent soil
degradation and erosion was to let land lie fallow
for 15-20 years. With the increased demand for
cash crops during colonialism and after
independence, fallow time was reduced to 1-5
years.

Other government policies were instituted to
augment cash crop production. Road systems were
established to facilitate the movement of products
from the hinterlands to the port towns and
marketing techniques were instituted to favor
export crops. Government credit policies geared
to cash crops worked against the production of
food crops. For example, in the case of Burkina
Faso, the government purchased 100 percent of its
estimated purchase of cotton. For cereals and
sesame, the government made only .007 percent and
.005 percent of the estimated purchases,
respectively (15). As a result of colonial and
post-colonial policies, the acreage under cultivation allocated to food crops declined (16).

The push to export more cotton and groundnuts
forced food crops to be cultivated on the more
marginal lands, and meant that traditional
agricultural methods for guaranteeing the ecological balance were abandoned. Deprived of long
fallow periods and crop diversification, the soil
grew less and less rich and, therefore, less and
less productive. The immediate effect on the
peasant was to reduce per capita food availability. According to Franke and Chasin, per capita

21

food availability in Senegal declined from 240 kilograms in 1920 to 145 kilograms in 1959 (17). The overproduction of cash and food crops on ever more depleted soil contributed to the intensity of the drought.

The spread of cash crop production also affected the amount of land available to herders. Lands that were traditionally free were now out of bounds to the pastoralists. Grazing lands, reduced in size, forced herders to overgraze on what territory was available to them.

An additional restriction was introduced with the erection of geographical and political limits which altered the social traditions and eroded the economic and poltical independence of the nomads. The shrinkage of land used for grazing came about when colonial policies established the artificial boundaries which would later delineate African nation-states. The division of land into separate nations imposed a legal limit on the land available for grazing. Now, customs duties, taxes or the threat of confiscation awaited herders who trespassed borders in search of water and vegetation.

The transformation of the Sahel by colonial and post-colonial governments brought an end to the cultural, social, and economic equilibrium between pastoral and agricultural peoples. Farmers moved north to expand food and export crop production, encroaching upon regions normally used by pastoralists. Likewise, the restricted freedom of movement forced pastoralists to move farther south in the search for water and vegetation. Cooperative herder-farmer interactions gave way to more conflictual relationships.

Finally, when planners instituted well-meaning aid projects to ameliorate the conditions under which people lived, beneficial results were sometimes accompanied by unintended and unwelcome developments. Traditionally, animal population growth rates were kept low by rinderpest and other diseases. Likewise, human populations were regulated by poor health and diseases such as measles, smallpox, and cholera. However, with the introduction of health improvement projects, this constraint on population growth was eliminated. Between 1930 and 1970, human and animal population

22

grew by 25 percent and 50 percent, respectively.
World Bank estimates showed that by 1970, animal
populations exceeded the optimal carrying size for
the Sahel by 9 million animals (18).

Development projects also expanded the number
of water sources. The boring of new watering
holes was a project carried out by several donors.
USAID built 1,400 wells in the Sahel (19). The
search for new watering points decreased and, as a
result, herders were no longer forced to move as
frequently. Human and animal populations clus-
tered around the bored water holes, placing great
pressure on the available vegetation.

These are examples of development projects
which enabled human and animal populations to
expand by removing natural checks on population
growth. But an increased population exerted undue
pressure on vegetation and soil ecology as larger
herds needed more shrubs and grasses upon which to
feed, and larger families required greater amounts
of firewood and plants.

The decline of the Sahelian ecology was pre-
cipitated by a combination of factors: the increase in human and animal populations with
greater needs for vegetation, the erosion of soil
due to the overproduction of crops, the institution of government policies which restricted the
mobility of groups, and the transformation of the
Sahel from a desert to cash crop economy.

Vegetation had begun to diminish even before
the drought appeared in 1968 (20). Though technology was introduced which created new water
sources and spurred population growth; little
technology was implemented to augment plant resources. Consequently, the balance of the Sahelian environment was destroyed. The lack of
integrated and coherent development policies and a
failure to take into account the response of the
inhabitants to change led to a regional catastrophe, the scope of which was never experienced
before. When the rains failed, the balance between population and resources no longer existed
(21). Once the balance was destroyed, the effects
of the drought were devastating.

Beginning in 1973, reports began to appear in
Western press of a little-known region in West
Africa, the Sahel, that was plagued by drought.
Although the drought began in 1968, it was not
until 1973 that people, other than the victims,
were made aware of the catastrophe. Located in a
200-300 mile wide belt between the Sahara Desert
and the tropical rain forest (north to south) and
extending from the Senegal River to near the Red
Sea coast (west to east), the drought touched the
lives of 30 million people (22). No aspect of
human life was left untouched: political, economic, social, or judicial. The 40 percent decline
in the levels of rainfall which occured from the
1950s to the 1970s set in motion the widespread
destruction and suffering (23).

That drought had occured was immediately
noticeable by the drop in the water table of the
familiar sources. The lack of rainfall decreased
the water levels of major water bodies and
completely dried up some small rivers. A UNDP
report documented the extent of the decline: the
Senegal River was reduced to 65 percent of normal
levels, and decreases of 35 percent for the Niger
River at Nioro; 54 percent for the Black Volta in
Burkina Faso; and 55 percent for the Chari River
in Chad were registered. By 1971 Lake Chad was
reduced to one-third of its normal size (24).

Naturally, with the lack of water came the
attendant problem of a reduction in vegetation.
The perennial grasses (with deep roots) disap-
peared first, followed by the coarse annual
grasses, and then finally by the leguminous plants
which, with their shallow roots, were unable to
hold much moisture. As the cycle of desertification intensified, the supply of shrubs and grasses
on which the animals could graze diminshed.

Without water or plants, animal mortality
rates began to climb. Livestock losses ranged
from 25 percent to 100 percent, depending upon the
region (25). In Mali, livestock losses approached
30 percent; in Chad and Niger losses averaged 33
percent; Mauritania's losses ranged between 25
percent and 40 percent, but some nomadic groups
suffered 100 percent losses; and Burkina Faso's

24

livestock diminished by 40 percent (26).

The drought also affected food crop yields. Between 1969 and 1971, corn production in Mali fell by more than one-third (27). According to Winstanley, the index of corn production for six of the nations plunged from 164 to 76 between 1967 and 1972 (1963=100). During the same period, indices for millet and sorghum also dropped from 111 to 84 (28).

Cereal production fell at the height of the drought in all of the Sahel countries except for Gambia, where it increased by 8 percent. The steepest declines in production occured in Mauritania and Niger where production fell by 68 and 50 percent, respectively. Cereal crop production was more seriously affected by drought conditions due to the fact that more marginal land had been utilized for the cultivation of subsistence crops.

Peanut production also declined during this same period. A fall in output of groundnuts occured in Burkina Faso (26 percent), Chad (57 percent), and Niger (41 percent). Production of groundnuts stagnated in the case of Cape Verde, Mali, and Mauritania. Senegal´s output of peanuts was 17 percent higher in 1973-1974 compared to levels in 1969-1970.

Cotton production in 1973-1974 was lower in Burkina Faso and Niger, 24 and 33 percent, respectively. Output of cotton in Senegal registered increases at the height of the drought. In 1969-1970, cotton production was 3,000 tons; in 1973-1974 it stood at 11,000 tons--an increase of 209 percent. Cotton production in Mali was 2 percent greater in 1973-1974 than in 1969-1970.

When comparing the production of cereals, peanuts, and cotton at the beginning and at the height of the drought, one notices that in most of these countries, cereals production fared much worse than that of peanut and cotton. There were greater declines in cereal output in Burkina Faso and Niger compared to the figures for cotton and groundnuts. Only in the case of Gambia were there declines in cotton production and gains in cereals production. Finally, Senegal was the only country in the region where food crop levels fell while cash crop levels increased. Overall, during the height of the drought, cereals production was much

25

TABLE 2.1
Average Production of Major Crops
(in 1,000 tons)

	1969-1970		
	Cereals	Peanuts	Cotton
Burkina Faso	945.0	78.0	11.5
Cape Verde	-	2.0	-
Chad	683.0	112.5	49.0
Gambia	37.0	137.5	-
Mali	756.0	111.0	17.0
Mauritania	95.0	1.0	-
Niger	1,311.0	254.0	3.0
Senegal	552.0	809.0	3.0

	1973-1974		
	Cereals	Peanuts	Cotton
Burkina Faso	677.0	64.0	11.5
Cape Verde	-	2.0	-
Chad	439.0	65.0	46.5
Gambia	40.0	126.0	-
Mali	562.0	110.0	20.0
Mauritania	30.0	1.0	-
Niger	662.0	130.0	2.0
Senegal	93.0	875.5	11.0

Source: United Nations, Yearbook of International
Trade Statistics 1970-71 (New York: United
Nations, 1973), p. 114 and United Nations. Statistical Yearbook 1975 (New York: United Nations,
1976), pp. 122 and 126.

more affected than were the cash crops--peanuts and cotton.

For many, the declines in food and/or cash crops posed severe hardships. Peasants were neither able to produce enough for their immediate needs, nor could they generate enough earnings from the sale of cash crops to purchase food imports. As a consequence, malnutrition increased dramatically, and it was acute among certain groups such as the Moors and the Tuaregs.

A 1973 Center for Disease Control (CDC) survey of 3,500 children conducted in Mauritania, Niger, Mali, and Burkina Faso found malnutrition occuring in 75 percent of the nomadic groups and in 10-25 percent of children in sedentary areas (29). Nomadic children were the first to feel the effects of the drought, a result of geographical and political factors. Nomads lived in more isolated regions and usually were not well-favored by those ethnic groups controlling the government.

One immediate result of the rise in malnutrition recorded by the CDC teams was the outbreak of illnesses such as measles, and cholera. The incidence of measles cases reported jumped 49 percent in Burkina Faso and 66 percent in Niger as can be seen in the table below.

TABLE 2.2
Average Number of Measles Cases Reported

	Before the Drought 1962-1967	During the Drought 1968-1973
Burkina Faso	14,623	21,896
Niger	10,559	17,589

Source: Hal Sheets and Roger Morris, Disaster in the Desert (Washington, D.C.: The Carnegie Endowment for International Peace, 1974), pp. 150 and 165.

In addition to measles, cholera affected the
populations already debilitated by malnutrition.
The World Health Organization documented an increase in the number of reported cases of cholera
between 1970 and 1973. Cholera was especially
rampant among the refugee populations where sanitary conditions were minimal at best. In the
World Health Organization´s annual of health
indicators, there were no known cases of cholera
in 1960 and in 1965. However, by 1971 the number
of reported cases jumped to 26,666. Once the
drought conditions diminished, so did the number
of reported cholera cases.

TABLE 2.3
Reported Cases of Cholera in the Sahel

Year	Number
1969	11
1970	2,919
1971	26,666
1972	592
1973	3,595
1974	1,689
1976	23
1977	219
1978	0
1979	316
1980	0
1981	435

Source: United Nations. World Health Organization,
World Health Statistics Annual 1983 (Geneva:
World Health Organization, 1983), p. 788.

Besides measles and cholera, health officials
reported increases in cerebral spinal meningitis,
whooping cough, viral hepatitis, tuberculosis, and
pertussis. Although many of these diseases are

28

endemic throughout the Sahel, one can probably
state that the drought and the resultant malnutrition increased the population's susceptibility to
the contraction of these diseases and contributed
to the increase in mortality due to such diseases
(30).

Estimates of the number of deaths attributable to the drought and its effects came to
about 66,000 though some argued that as many as
100,000 died (31). On the average, the Sahelian
mortality rate prior to the drought was 2.4 percent. Mortality rate figures rose during the
drought and reached as high as 7 percent for
Niger. While many died from starvation, most
succumbed to a combination of famine and illness.

The CDC health teams also found a higher
death rate among the nomads. Nigerien mortality
figures indicated that death as a result of
measles occured in 73 percent of the nomadic populations, but in only 32 percent of the sedentary
groups (32). Large discrepancies in the death
rates for nomadic and sedentary groups were also
found in Mauritania where nomadic death rates
climbed to 69 per 1,000 individuals; for other
groups the rate was 25 deaths per 1,000, a figure
equal to the pre-drought mortality rate (33).

To cope with the loss of water and pasturage,
nomads attempted to carry out their traditional
drought-coping responses. The difference in the
1968-74 drought was that entire families were
migrating south. The CDC found other unusual
migratory activities: migration to areas not
usually part of the territory covered by nomads,
migration to urban areas. Furthermore, the teams
discovered nomads migrating for reasons other than
to search for pasturage. Some groups were migrating solely for the purpose of reaching food distribution centers (34).

These unusual migration patterns caused both
international and national social and political
problems. Major Sahelian towns found that their
populations suddenly grew by 50 percent (Mopti,
Mali), 42 percent (Dakar, Senegal), and 66 percent
(Nouakchott, Mauritania). Rosso in Mauritania had
the largest increase in population as a result of
the drought, 94 percent. Domestically, urban
areas experienced dramatic swells in population;

internationally the border towns of neighboring countries found they were confronted with a sudden influx of refugees.

The exodus emptied between one-third and one-fourth of the Chadian rural population. Fifteen percent of the rural population of Senegal migrated to other ares. In northern Mauritania, because of the high cattle mortality rates, 80 percent of the inhabitants moved to the larger towns in the south (35).

This rapid influx into the larger towns and capital cities posed political and economic difficulties for the African governments which were ill-equipped to handle the situation. Relations between states were strained as affected populations moved to other countries. Migrants from Mali crossed into Niger, Benin, Nigeria, and Burkina Faso. The CDC survey reported 40,000 Malian Tuaregs crossing the border into Niger and 35,000 into Burkina Faso. Togo, Ghana, and the Ivory Coast received those fleeing Niger and Burkina Faso (36). Senegal and Mali, with their own problems, had to cope with Mauritanians (37).

As entire ethnic groups and families left the drought-affected regions, social customs and cultural values crumbled under the strain. Survival needs replaced traditional social values. Criminality increased, especially in the refugee camps. Evidence accumulated of family members too old or weak being killed or abandoned--an unnatural occurrence in normal times. Thefts of food and money were not uncommon. Where refugees congregated, prostitution flourished. Researchers also noticed a heightened pathological sense among surviving refugees because of the anguish and solitude they experienced as they attempted to cope with their conditions (38).

If the drought was a catastrophe for humans, it was a disaster for the economies of the region. Rosenthal, Walker, and Higgott and Fuglestad estimated revenue losses to be substantial (39). Livestock losses were estimated to be $400 million according to Temple and Thomas. This loss was particularly devastating to Burkina Faso and Mali where livestock accounted for a sizeable proportion of the GNPs. In the case of Mali, 52 to 64 percent of total exports were derived from the

30

sale of livestock between 1964 and 1972; for Burkina Faso, livestock accounted for half of its exports during the same period (40). Cattle tax revenues also declined, falling by over 40 percent in Niger and 20 percent in Mali (41).

The loss of livestock, fish, and locally-produced food stuffs fuelled the need for governments to import food products. Consequently, trade deficits grew for all the countries. Between 1968 and 1972 the trade deficit of the Sahel more than doubled--from 19 to 45 million CFA (42).

The deteriorating economic situation created political problems as well. To some extent, the drought played a role in the overthrow of the Diori regime in Niger when it was discovered that government officials were hoarding grain until prices rose. Peasant tax revolts took place in Chad, Mali, and Mauritania (43). Urban unrest in 1971 and 1973 in Senegal was attributable to the drought and its effects. In addition, the drought was conveniently used by some governments to settle old poltical scores with opposition groups. Mali and Chad used the drought to break the strength of nomadic groups opposed to their rule. By withholding aid, nomads were brought into submission.

Soon, it was evident that the effects of the drought could not be overcome by the Sahel governments. Nor could problems be remedied with aid from the French alone. Only a massive relief effort would turn conditions around.

AID RELIEF EFFORTS DURING THE 1968-1974 DROUGHT

Despite the fact that the drought began in 1968, it was not until 1973 that relief efforts commenced. Because the initial impact of the drought only touched the nomadic populations, the African governments ignored the problem. Only when sedentary groups began to be affected did the governments acknowledge the situation (44).

The African governments were hardly alone in their slowness to respond to the drought. For several years the major donors had been documenting conditions: poor harvests and larger

31

groups of Sahelians requiring assistance. The United States Department of Agriculture had reports, dating back to 1969, of the rising level of suffering (45). Field reports from the U.S. missions told of similar accounts of the mounting disaster. Unfortunately, the information documenting the drought and its effects was never organized systematically by the bureaucracies; nor did it ever serve as a foundation for coherent relief planning. By the time the major donors recognized the need for massive relief, many Sahelians had already succumbed to the famine or to famine related illnesses.

The tardiness with which documentation was organized prolonged relief efforts as each agency attempted to put together its own coherent plan of action (46). Once underway there were other factors which would plague the timely distribution of aid.

American relief was delayed because of the Soviet grain purchases that removed a substantial portion of the 1973 grain crop (47). In addition, bureaucratic jockeying between two USAID departments (the Africa Bureau and the Foreign Disaster Relief Coordination Office) over control of the entire relief operations impeded progress.

American deliveries of food were slow to arrive at their destinations. Of the 156,000 tons of food committed for the 1973 fiscal year, only 66,000 tons had reached the Sahel by July 1973.

Many delays resulted from conditions on the African side as the governments lacked the necessary administrative apparatuses to handle the emergency. The lack of trained personnel in the field made it difficult to accumulate the necessary documentation. Deliberate political choices made by the governments caused delays in the official acknowledgment of the drought. For example, Mali refused to admit to the drought because it initially only affected the nomads, long a force of political opposition (48). Some government leaders neglected to publicize the drought for fear of being ridiculed by the international community or domestic political groups.

By the end of 1972, the situation had deteriorated too much to be ignored. The accumulation of refugees in the larger towns and cities contributed to a politically explosive situation. On March 23-26, 1973, six Sahelian government ministers met to discuss the drought, to pronounce the region a disaster area, and to appeal for international relief. The six ministers represented Burkina Faso, Mali, Mauritania, Senegal, Niger, and Chad.

Until that March meeting, ambassadors of the donor countries, reluctant to declare emergencies where none had been declared officially, were constrained in their ability to request emergency aid (49). After the meeting, the donors proceeded to implement emergency relief plans. A large scale aid plan was put into motion, but the problems were far from over.

The lack of efficient transportation slowed the distribution of relief. There were not enough trucks, fuel, spare parts, and mechanics to facilitate a speedy delivery of food and supplies. Furthermore, the areas hardest hit by the drought were those most inaccessible by road. Roadways consisted of narrow, rugged tracks. Trucks broke down trying to reach the more remote areas. In one instance in Chad, foreign trucks and drivers, prevented from travelling outside of the capital without a permit from the Transportation minister, were delayed in Ndjamena for ten days during the minister´s absence (50). As a result of such bureaucratic inadequacies or transportation problems, food often sat on the wharves for weeks; what was not appropriated by urban dwellers was consumed by rats.

As the aid efforts intensified throughout 1973 and 1974, additional problems developed. One involved American shipments of coarse sorghum used in the United States for cattle feed but intended, in this case, for human consumption. Dietary habits of many nomads consisted of meat and milk products. Unaccustomed to the sorghum, many stricken refugees were further weakened and died. Again, this highlights the lack of useful information gathered on the Sahel. No one had inquired as to whether the inhabitants could digest food not normally found in their diet.

Corruption proved to be another problem affecting the relief program. Documentation of hoarding and speculation was commonplace in all of

33

the nations.   In Burkina Faso, the official price
for millet in May 1973 was approximately $12.42.
Nevertheless, a 100 kilogram sack fetched $27.10
in the marketplace.   In some villages, a sack of
millet sold for as high as $45.19 (51).   When the
government reminded the merchants of the official
price for millet, their response was to pull millet, corn, and rice from the market for three
days.   Needless to say, when these products reap-
peared, the selling price was that demanded by the
merchants (52).

Nowhere was the corruption more egregious
than in Niger.   Hoarding and corruption were conducted by Diori´s closest associates, including
his wife, who made a fortune during the drought.
In a Zinder warehouse, 3,000 tons of grain were
found stored by speculators who were waiting for
the price to rise before they distributed it.   In
the capital, Niamey, forty vehicles supplied by
relief agencies were being used as taxis (53).

Corruption in relief efforts was documented
by journalists and aid officials.   The Guardian
(London) reported that Chad and Burkina Faso refused to let planes carrying relief shipments land
and unload until import duties and landing fees
were paid in local currency (54).   Blatant
discrimination in the distribution of aid was
recorded by the CDC survey team who found nomadic
camps receiving less than their fair share of food
aid.

In sum, the inefficiency and waste which
characterized the relief efforts were attributable
to a number of factors: tardiness in responding to
the crisis, a lack of data, the inadequate audi-
ting of aid, corruption, hoarding, biases in the
distribution of aid, the dearth of trained African
personnel, and the poor quality of transportation
networks.   To donors and recipients alike, it was
apparent that the Sahel would need more than
short-term relief in order to recover.

THE 1982-1985 DROUGHT

By 1975 the rains returned again.   Through
the drought was considered to have ended (with the
exception of Cape Verde), rainfall levels

34

continued to be erratic. From 1974 to 1982 there
were more dry than normal years in the Sahel. By
1982 there was evidence of another major drought.
In Mauritania, rainfall in 1983 was 27 percent of
average annual rainfall levels for the years 1941-
1970 (55). For the region as a whole, rainfall
between the months of June through August 1984 was
40-60 percent below normal (56). As rainfall
declined, water levels of the major rivers fell.
Lake Chad which had never regained its original
volume after the 1968-74 drought, shrank even
more. In 1984 it was a mere one-quarter of its
normal size (57). One effect of this decrease in
river levels was to reduce the availability of
fish, a major source of protein. According to
Derrick, the failure of the annual overflow of the
Niger River affected fishing as well as irrigated
agriculture, trade, and the riverine transport of
relief materials (58).

TABLE 2.4
Sahel Food Self-Sufficiency Rates

Year	Percentage
1960	98
1973	65
1980	86
1984	55

Source: Le Soleil (Dakar) March 14, 1985

The drop in water levels also affected the
production of crops, especially food crops. Complete crop failures took place in Gambia, Mali,
Burkina Faso, and Niger, and in parts of Senegal.
The 1984 Nigerien cereals harvest was 50 percent
below normal (59). Cereals production in Mauritania plunged from 61,000 tons in 1981, to 20,000
tons in 1982, and then dropped to 15,000 tons in
1983 (60). The fact that Mauritania's annual

35

cereal needs total 255,000 tons meant that in 1983 only 6 percent of its estimated needs were produced locally. The remainder had to be imported. Throughout the Sahel cereal production fell as a consequence of the drought.

In general, food self-sufficiency has declined since independence when almost all of the region's food needs were produced locally. After 1974, the region improved its food production rate, though the figure was below that for 1960. By 1984, the Sahel was less capable of feeding itself than during the 1968-74 drought. Many analysts state that food shortages during this last drought were worse than the 1968-74 drought (61).

Not only did food production decline, but in some cases, export crop production was affected as well. Gambia's output of foodstuffs fell by 50 percent from 1982 to 1983. Its production of groundnuts, a cash crop, dropped by 25 percent, from 128,000 tons to 95,000 tons (62). Cape Verde's production of cereals as a percentage of total cereals consumption dropped from 20 percent before the drought to less than 5 percent afterwards (63). In other words, its structural deficit in cereals is now greater than 95 percent.

As in the previous drought, animal populations were affected by the adverse water and pasturage conditions. Major livestock losses were heavy for several of the countries: 50 percent for Niger, 40-50 percent for Mali, and 40 percent in Mauritania (64). United Nations estimates for Burkina Faso for 1985 indicated a livestock loss of 70-90 percent (65).

Needless to say, declines in food productivity and livestock deaths resulted in a rise of malnutrition among the affected populations. Again, children were some of the most debilitated victims of the drought. A health survey of Senegalese children in the hardest hit regions found that more than 50 percent were eighty percent below normal weight (66). Pockets of severe malnutrition were also discovered in Mali, Chad, Niger, and Mauritania. United Nations reports in November 1985 showed that malnutrition rates of children under 5 in the Fleuve region of Mauritania were between 52-65 percent (67). Another

survey in the Hodh region in southwestern Mauritania documented that 34 percent of all children
younger than the age of 5 suffered from malnutrition (68). The total number of Mauritanians
affected by malnutrition was 17 percent (69).
Severe malnutrition in Niger was most pronounced
in the areas where relief camps were located.
Here 27.6 percent suffered compared to 15.5 percent of the population living in rural areas (70).
    An attendant effect of drought and famine was
the increase in illness and disease. Human suffering from malnutrition led to a decline in the
health of the population groups most affected.
Outbreaks of measles, cholera, meningitis, and
tuberculosis were reported in Mali, Burkina Faso,
Senegal, and Niger (71). An outbreak of cholera
in Mali in June and July of 1984 resulted in
several deaths. Of the 1,195 cases of cholera
documented, 204 (17 percent) resulted in death.
    To escape drought and famine, many inhabi-
tants moved south into areas where food, water,
and other help was available. The percentage of
displaced persons ranged from 3 percent (Burkina
Faso and Mali) to 11 percent in Chad and 16 percent in Niger.
    As in the previous drought, unusual patterns
of migration were noted. Migration to areas
farther south than normal took place. In Dori, a
village in northern Burkina Faso, up to one-third
of its young people left (72). United Nations reports indicated that entire villages were abandoned as people migrated to more hospitable areas.
Migrations into neighboring countries were also
documented. Nigeriens fled to Burkina Faso,
Nigeria, Benin, and Mali; Malians moved into Burkina Faso; and Mauritanians crossed the borders
into Mali and Senegal.
    The level of suffering further eroded tradi-
tional social customs as people attempted to cope
with adversity. Mauritanian and donor officials
expressed concern that nomadic populations were
undergoing dramatic changes in their lifestyles
(73).

Table 2.5
Displaced Population as of September 1985

Country	Number of Displaced	Percentage
Burkina Faso	222,000	3
Chad	500,000	11
Mali	200,000	3
Mauritania	190,000	12
Niger	1,000,000	16

Source: United Nations. Office for Emergency Operations in Africa. Status Report On The Emergency Situation in Africa As of 1 September 1985, (New York: United Nations, 1985), p. 9-15.

The sedentarization of nomads reduced their percentage of the population from more than 50 percent to 25 percent (74). The traditional so- cial custom to aid the less fortunate also gave way: reports from Chad indicated that adults de- nied food to younger family members.

The economic costs of the drought escalated in 1983, 1984, and 1985. Livestock prices virtually crashed in Mali, Niger, and Senegal. Between 1983 and 1984 the price of one cow dropped from 100,000 CFA to 1,500 CFA; that of a camel from 118,000 CFA to 5,000 CFA; and that of sheep from 5,000 CFA to 50 CFA (75). Figures from Senegal showed that the purchase price of one cow fell by 60 percent as herders dumped their dying stocks on a surplus market (76). As the price for livestock plummeted, family purchasing power also fell. Prior to the drought the sale of one cow bought enough grain to last a year; after the onset of the the drought, it took 15 cows to purchase the same amount of grain. While livestock prices were falling, the price of food- stuffs, especially rice, millet, and sorghum, was climbing. Derrick notes that after the 1983 rainy season ended, prices for these three food products rose dramatically in Niger (77). Not everyone

38

suffered from the rise in the price of food and the fall in the price of livestock. Profiteering occured as cattle traders built up their stock with cattle purchased at bargain prices. Destitute herders and poorer farmers were dispossessed of their stock and their lands as traders and civil servants took over their assets (78).

For the many people affected by the drought, wages fell and prices rose throughout the Sahel. Washerwomen whose wages amounted to 100 Malian francs a day found themselves barely able to scrape together enough to pay for rice and beef which cost 350 MF per kilogram and 800 MF and per kilogram, respectively (79).

Falling wages and rising prices worried governments and donor nations alike. Countries such as Senegal and Mali, which had embarked on IMF and creditor policy reforms, found reform under such poor economic conditions difficult. It was possible that the economic downturn would lead to a situation in which continued structural adjustment efforts would be politically and economically suicidal. Moreover, the depressed economic conditions and the drop in purchasing power only compounded the balance of payments problems, and fuelled the demand by creditors for the continuation of adjustment and policy reforms.

Finally, political conflicts emerged within and between countries. Domestically, relations between pastoralists and agriculturalists, never without difficulties, continued to deteriorate. Chad and Mauritania experienced the most intense antagonisms between these two groups as drought and famine intensified. Internationally, relations between Mali and Mauritania and between Senegal and Mauritania suffered strains when large numbers of Mauritanian herders moved across these borders. The governments of Mali and Senegal, already stretched beyond their capabilities, were resentful of having to offer water and pasturage to Mauritanian herds. At one point, Malian officials refused to allow Mauritanian herds to migrate (80).

To summarize the situation, the serious lack of rainfall in the Sahel between 1982-1985 exacerbated social, political, and economic difficulties. In each Sahel country, a small proportion of the population faced starvation, especially nomadic and northern groups. However, an even greater percentage of the populations was affected in some way: 36 percent in Burkina Faso, 30 percent in Chad, 42 percent in Mauritania, 49 percent in Niger, and 98 percent in Cape Verde. At some level, everyone felt the drought's attendant effects. For some states, drought and famine conditions were more devastating in 1982-85 than in 1968-1974.

DROUGHT RELIEF EFFORTS IN THE 1982-1985 DROUGHT

Drought relief efforts in 1982-1985, though plagued by problems, showed a definite improvement over the 1973-1974 relief operations. One major improvement was observed in the timeliness of requests for help by the Sahel states. In the 1980s, the Sahel states appealed for help at the first sign of difficulty.

Another departure from the previous drought was the increase in information available to the donor countries and agencies. Since an increased number of donor nations had established on-going development projects after the 1968-1974 drought, there was more accurate knowledge of existing conditions. There was also a larger number of individuals able to monitor technical conditions such as the level of rainfall and vegetation.

International relief efforts began in the fall of 1984. Pledges of aid from private and public sources amounted to $2 billion for the entire continent by early 1985 (81). Aiding the relief efforts were the activities of the United Nations. As drought and famine intensified in 1984 and 1985, the United Nations organized a major conference to respond to the crisis. Held in March 1985, 125 countries and 30 non-governmental organizations responded to the United Nations' appeal for $1.5 billion. To help coordinate the mobilization and delivery of this aid, the United Nations created the Office for Emergency Operations in Africa (OEOA). The $1.5 billion was earmarked for emergency relief only and would pay for food aid, fertilizer, tools, seeds, shelter,

clothing, water, and logistical supplies (82). Of
this $1.5 billion dollars allocated for food and
non-food aid, the Sahel accounted for $396.8 mil-
lion or 26.1 percent of the total.

TABLE 2.6
Unmet Emergency Needs as of March 1985
(in million $)

	Food Aid	Non-Food Aid	Total
Burkina Faso	61.3	9.3	70.6
Cape Verde	4.1	11.3	15.4
Chad	39.8	14.1	53.9
Mali	76.9	16.7	93.6
Mauritania	22.8	27.4	50.2
Niger	70.1	10.8	80.9
Senegal	8.9	23.3	32.2
Grand Total	283.9	112.9	396.8

Source: United Nations. Status Report On The Emergency Situation in Africa (New York: United
Nations, 1985), p. 31.

        By November 1985, the response of the inter-
national community to Africa's food crisis was
overwhelming. Private contributions totalled almost $250 million. The United States alone con-
tributed $1.2 billion in food aid (83). When the
United Nations issued its Africa Emergency Report
in January 1986, food aid needs had declined to
zero in Burkina Faso, Cape Verde, and Mauritania.
For Chad, Mali, and Niger emergency food aid needs
did not surpass $5.5 million. Donor reponse re-
duced the need for food aid considerably (84).
        Still, the timeliness of response and the
quantity of aid did not mean that the mobilization
and delivery of relief were devoid of problems.
While donors were generous in their contributions
of food aid, critical breakdowns occured in

41

transporting the aid to the affected populations.

TABLE 2.7
Unmet Emergency Needs as of January 1986
(in million $)

	Food Aid	Non-Food Aid	Total
Burkina Faso	-	13.9	13.9
Cape Verde	-	10.7	10.7
Chad	5.0	17.0	22.0
Mali	5.1	14.0	19.1
Mauritania	-	10.8	10.8
Niger	5.4	9.3	14.7
Grand Total	15.5	75.7	91.2

Source: United Nations,Africa Emergency Report No.
6 (February-March 1986), p. 14.

The first problem arose in getting the food out of
the port cities. In the Cameroon, Ivory Coast,
Nigeria, and Senegal, aid could not be processed
fast enough. In the first two weeks of June 1985,
food aid backlogs rose to 155,150 tons.
   A second transportation breakdown occured in
the internal delivery system. The poor road conditions in the rural areas, the lack of a sufficient number of trucks to transport the aid, the
shortage of fuel, and the lack of spare parts
contributed to the delay of food and aid
deliveries. Old and inefficient railways and the
lack of roads--especially secondary roads--slowed
down deliveries to population groups already at
the edge of starvation. Though CILSS and the
donor countries had launched a number of road-
building and road-improvement projects after 1976,
the massive influx of aid proved too much for the
transportation networks to suppport. Where river
transportation was the sole means of getting aid
to isolated villages, boats could not traverse
areas where water levels were too low. Problems of

42

aid distribution were most acute in Niger, Chad, Burkina Faso, and Mauritania.

The previous drought relief program, poorly monitored by most donors, resulted in numerous instances of fraud and corruption. The 1982-1985 drought had far less egregious examples of corruption, though some food aid diversions occured. In Chad, the government proved reluctant to provide enough relief in the areas which it did not control politically. As in the last drought, war and conflict have provided governments the opportunity to punish groups and areas hostile to their authority.

A more serious problem during the 1982-1985 drought was the problem of the ill-timing of food deliveries with respect to successful harvests. Deliveries made just prior to harvest had detrimental effects for peasants. Food surpluses made it difficult for peasants to sell their crops. The price paid for locally-grown crops dropped as a result, and incentives to increase food production were reduced. In the end, donor shipments of foodstuffs undermined food self-sufficiency in the Sahel and made future needs for food aid a certainty (85).

Donor funding preferences define a final obstacle to the effectiveness of relief. Donors were willing to ship food but not agricultural inputs which were critical for a return to normal life after drought and famine. Without the full complement of resources, the transition from mendacity to productivity was impossible.

As the table above makes clear, donor pledges are substantial in the case of food but they are less so in the case of agricultural inputs. Donors have pledged to meet more than 100 percent of the estimates of food aid needs in Cape Verde, yet they have not offered to support the acquisition of seeds, tools, and other technical inputs. The implications of this oversight could be devastating: without the adequate inputs delivered in a timely fashion, peasants will be unable to plant and herders will be unable to build up their stocks. The prospects of another famine could loom once again.

To conclude, there were major differences in the effectiveness of relief operations during the

43

two droughts.   Delays and backlogs, though not as
serious as the 1968-1974 drought, did take place

Table 2.8
Donor Pledges for Food and Agricultural
Inputs as of September 1985
(in percentages)

	% of Food Aid Needs Met	% of Agricultural Input Needs Met
Burkina Faso	79	73
Cape Verde	107	0
Chad	72	52
Mali	71	64
Mauritania	93	68
Niger	83	0

Source: United Nations. Office for Emergency
Operations in Africa,Status Report On The Emergen-
cy Situation As Of 1 September 1985 (New York:
United Nations, 1985), pp. 95 and 96.

in 1982-1985 due to the lack of logistical supplies, poor transportation networks and unpre-
dictable weather conditions within the Sahel.   On
the whole, donors and Sahelians were better prepared to meet the challenge of famine the second
time   around.   There   was   better   information
gathered from the monitoring of the weather conditions, rainfall levels, and crop production. Response   time   of the donors to requests for help
also improved markedly.
    A critical reason for this difference in the
response   to   the two droughts was the   effort   of
Sahelians and donors to work together, a process
that   has been put into effect since the creation
of CILSS and the Club du Sahel.   The development
of this cooperation is the subject of the next
chapter.

44

NOTES

1.   P.E. Lovejoy and Baier, "The Desert Side
Economy of the Central Sudan," in _The Politics of_
Natural Disaster, ed. Michael Glantz (New York:
Praeger Publishers, 1976), p. 198 and Pascal James
Imperato, "Health Care Systems in the Sahel: Be-
fore and After the Drought," also in Glantz, p.
443.
2.   Finn Fuglestad, "La grande famine de 1931
dans l´ouest Nigérien," _Revue Francaise D´Histoire_
D´Outre-Mer, 61, No. 222 (1974), pp. 18-33; Jeremy
Swift, "Disaster and a Sahelian Nomad Economy," in
Report of the 1973 Symposium, Drought in Africa,
ed. David Dalby and R.J. Harrison Church (London:
University of London, 1973), pp. 71-78; Lovejoy and Baier, pp. 145-175; and Jonathan Derrick,
"West Africa´s Worst Year of Famine," _African_
Affairs,   83,   No.   332 (1984), pp. 281-299.
Historical   records   document droughts   having
occured in the 1540s, 1550s, 1650s, 1690s, 1700s,
1740s, 1847, 1855, 1890, 1912, 1931, 1968-74, and
1982-1985.
3. Swift, pp. 73-74.
4.   For discussion of the causes of drought
see: Glantz, particularly the articles by Imperato, Le Houerou, Mallock and Cockrum, Norton, Mac-
Leod, Winstanley, and Baker; Richard W. Franke and
Barbara H. Chasin, _Seeds of Famine_ (Montclair:
Allanheld , Osmun and Co., 1980); Michael Lofchie,
"Political and Economic Origins of African Hunger," _The Journal of Modern African Studies_, 13,
No. 4 (1975), pp. 551-567; Dalby and Church, especially the articles by Swift, Baker, and David;
the Comité information Sahel, _Qui se nourrit de la_
famine en afrique? (Paris: Librairie Francois
Maspero, 1974); and Lloyd Timberlake, _Africa in_
Crisis (London: Insitute for Environment and
Development/Earthscan, 1985).
5. _Ibid_.
6. Winstanley, p. 203.
7. Franke and Chasin, pp. 62-67.
8. _Ibid_, pp. 67-68.
9.   G. Wesley Johnson, Jr., _The Emergence of_
Black Politics in Senegal (Stanford: Stanford
University Press, 1971), p. 33.
10. Franke and Chasin, p. 76.

45

11. OECD/CILSS/Club du Sahel, Development Of Rainfed Agriculture In the Sahel, Overview And Prospects (Paris: OECD, 1983), p. 11.

12. Comité information Sahel, p. 222.

13. One hectare equals 10,000 square meters.

14. Comité information Sahel, p. 26

15. Ibid, pp. 105-109.

16. Lofchie, pp. 554-556 and Franke and Chasin, pp. 74-76.

17. Franke and Chasin, p. 74.

18. Nicholas Wade, "Sahelian Drought: No Victory for Western Aid," Science, 185, No. 4147(1974) p. 236.

19. Martin Walker, "Drought," The New York Times Magazine, June 9, 1974, p. 42.

20. While there is no doubt that the 1968-74 drought contributed to a reduction in vegetation and posed severe problems to some groups, there is no agreement as to the permanence or irreversibility of these phenomena. For a dissenting view, see: David W. Brokensha, Michael M. Horowitz, and Thayer Scudder, The Anthropology of Rural Development in the Sahel (Binghamton: Insitute for Developmental Anthropology, 1977), pp. 30-40 and Elliot Berg, The Recent Economic Evolution of the Sahel (Ann Arbor: Center for Research on Economic Development, 1975), pp. 26-38.

21. United Nations Development Program, Drought in Africa (New York: United Nations, N.D.), p. 15.

22. Franke and Chasin, p. 21.

23. Winstanley, p. 193.

24. United Nations Development Program, p. 17 and Hal Sheets and Roger Morris, Disaster in the Desert (Washington, D.C.: The Carnegie Endowment for International Peace, 1974), p. 11.

25. R.S. Temple and M.E.R. Thomas, "The Sahelian Drought-- a disaster for livestock populations," World Animal Review, No 8 (1973), p. 3.

26. Ibid; Jerry Rosenthal, "The Creeping Catastrophe," Africa Report, 18, No. 4 (1973), p. 8; Sheets and Morris, pp. 86, 93, and 145; and UNDP, pp. 19-20.

27. Lofchie, p. 555 and the UNDP, p. 22.

28. Winstanley, p. 194.

29. Sheets and Morris, p. 53.

30. Imperato, p. 295.

31. John C. Caldwell, The Sahelian Drought and its Demographic Implications, OLC Paper No. 8 (1975), p. 24.

32. Ibid, p. 133.

33. Ibid, p. 194.

34. Ibid, p. 134.

35. Ibid.

36. UNDP, p. 21.

37. Pascal James Imperato, "Nomads of the Sahel and the Delivery of Health Services to Them," Social Science and Medicine, 8, No. 8 (1974), p. 444.

38. Rosenthal, pp. 9-10; Richard Higgott and Finn Fuglestad, "The 1974 Coup d´Etat in Niger: Towards an Explanation," The Journal of Modern African Studies, 13, No. 3 (1975), pp. 383-388; and Walker, p. 45.

39. Rosenthal, p. 10; Higgott and Fuglestad, p. 390; and Walker, p. 45.

40. Comité information Sahel, pp. 135 and 140.

41. Winstanley, p. 199.

42. Brun, pp. 85-90.

43. Jean-Louis Ormières, "Les Conséquences Politiques De La Famine," in Copans, pp. 131-145.

44. Jean Mayer, "Coping with Famine," Foreign Affairs, 53, No. 1 (1974), p. 113.

45. Sheets and Morris, p. 16.

46. Ibid, p. 23.

47. Ibid.

48. Philippe Decraene, "Mali: La Sécheresse, arme politique," Revue Francaise d´Etudes Politiques Africaines, No. 98 (1974), p. 18.

49. Sheets and Morris, p. 25.

50. Mohamed El-Khawas, "A Reassessment of International Relief Programs," in Glantz, p. 87

51. Comité information Sahel, p. 201.

52. Ibid, p. 201.

53. Higgott and Fuglestad, p. 390.

54. Martin Walker, "The Sahara marches south," The Guardian, (London) June 30, 1973.

55. Derrick, p. 282.

56. United States embassy cables of 10 September 1984.

57. Henry Kamm, "Hungry Chad Children Sift the Dirt," The New York Times, January 2, 1985.

58. Derrick, p. 283.

59.   USAID, Niger Emergency Plan, mimeo, (Washington, D.C., 1985), p. 1.
60. Derrick, p. 283.
61. "Africa´s Shrinking Harvest: Food and Hunger 1985," Africa News, 24, No. 4 (1985), p. 9.
62. Derrick, p. 283.
63. United Nations. Office for Emergency Operations in Africa, Special Report On The Emergency Situation In Africa, Review Of 1985 and 1986 Emergency Needs, (New York: United Nations, 1986), p. 37
64.   USAID, p. 1; Richard Critchfield, "In Africa´s drought-stricken Sahel, ´even the vultures fled´," The Christian Science Monitor, April 9, 1984; and Derrick, p.283.
65.   United Nations. Office for Emergency Operations in Africa, Status Report On The Emergency Situation In Africa As Of 1 September 1985, (New York: United Nations, N.D.), p. 26.
66.   "Sahel on a knife-edge: 1," West Africa, April 16, 1984, p. 806.
67.   United Nations. Office for Emergency Operations in Africa, Status Report On The Emergency Situation In Africa As Of 1 November 1985 (New York: United Nations, 1985), p. 84.
68. Derrick, p. 296.
69.   Status Report On The Emergency Situation In Africa As Of 1 September 1985, p. 47.
70.   Ibid, p. 58.
71.   "The Struggle Against Drought," AfricAsia, No. 5 (1984), p.xix; "Sahel on a knife-edge: 3", West Africa (April 30, 1984), p. 916 and Status Report On The Emergency Situation In Africa As Of 1 September 1985, pp. 26, 44, 49, and 58.
72. Alan Cowell, "South of Sahara, The Intrusive Politics of Hunger," The New York Times, December 3, 1984.
73.   United Nations. Office for Emergency Operations in Africa, Status Report On The Emergency Situation In Africa, (New York: United Nations, May 1985), p. 17.
74. Derrick, p. 295.
75.   United States´ embassy cable for Niger, 19 July 1984.
76. "Sahel on a knife-edge:1", p. 806.
77. Derrick, p. 283.

48

78. Ibid, p. 295.

79. "Fighting in every possible way," Development Forum, May 1984.

80. Edward Schumacher, "Drought Turns Nomads' World Upside Down," The New York Times, March 2, 1985.

81. Elaine Sciolino, "70 Nations Meet Today in Geneva on Plea to Increase Famine Aid," The New York Times, March 11, 1985.

82. Ibid

83. "Famine Relief Shifts to Permanent Solutions," The New York Times, November 3, 1985.

84. Contributing to the decline in the need for emergency food aid was the fact that food production had improved by the Fall 1985 harvests.

85. "Improved African Food Outlook Seen at U.N.," The New York Times, December 18, 1985.

3

The Search for
Development Cooperation

Developing countries' efforts to lessen
their reliance upon the developed world have
taken many forms. The struggle for independence
entailed the dismantling of political control. In
the post-independence era, Africa turned its attention to the elimination of its economic and
psychological dependency. One significant strategy for the promotion of greater welfare and economic growth has been the organization of regional
integrative ventures such as the Council of the
Entente, the Cocoa Producers Alliance, and the
Economic Community of West African States, to name
a few. The goals and objectives of these organizations range from a narrow focus on agricultural
research (the West African Rice Development Association) to broad political and economic harmony
(the Organization of African Unity).
At the same time that African nations have
worked together, they have also negotiated new
political and economic arrangements with the
developed world. Efforts to unite developed and
developing nations date back to World War II: in
1942 the British and Americans formed the Caribbean Commission to coordinate military, social,
and economic activities in the British West In-
dies. France and the Netherlands joined the Commission in 1946, and activities expanded into the
areas of tourism, industrial production, and improved agricultural techniques.
After the collapse of the Commission in the
1960s, the World Bank was instrumental in
establishing another multilateral organization,

the CDCC (the Caribbean Development and Cooperation Committee). Formed in 1975, the CDCC brings
together the OECD and CARICOM states to work
cooperatively on projects. The program of the
CDCC included activities in the field of development and trade promotion. In addition, the group
made plans to channel aid resources into multilateral agencies working in the Caribbean. In sub-
scribing to the concept of North-South agreements,
CILSS and the CDCC are similarly structured. The
difference between them is that CILSS limits
itself to rural development. More recent attempts
at global and regional discussions between the
North and the South include the Lomé Convention
and the Cancun Conference.

African attempts to lessen their dependency
have been based primarily on emphasizing North-
South or South-South groupings. The promotion of
development through the twin strategies of South-
South and North-South cooperation make the
CILSS/Club du Sahel mechanism a unique institution
in Africa. In addition, CILSS and the Club du
Sahel, with their bureaurcratized secretariats,
differ from other African regional groups. The
CILSS model has been copied in Southern Africa.
Roy Stacey, involved with CILSS and the Club du
Sahel in the early years, also played a role in
the formation of the Southern African Development
Coordination Conference (SADCC). Formed in 1979,
after a multinational conference held in Tanzania,
SADCC unites Botswana, Lesotho, Swaziland, Zambia,
Tanzania, Angola, Malawi, Mozambique, and
Zimbabwe. The sole purpose of the organization is
to reduce links between the black-ruled states of
East and Southern Africa and white-ruled South
Africa. While SADCC works closely with individual
donors, as of yet, a parallel donor group,
corresponding to the Club du Sahel, has not been
established. The Southern African Development
Coordination Conference, has no Northern
bureaucratic link comparable to the Club. CADA,
the Concerted Action for Development in Africa,
is a donors consortium which works primarily at
the bilateral level and is not attached to any
African organization.

Another regional group, the Inter-Governmental Authority for Drought and Development (IGADD),

created by the East African states of Kenya, Somalia, Ethiopia, Sudan, Uganda, and Djibouti, has set goals similar to that of CILSS. Formed in February 1985, IGADD is to coordinate efforts against drought and desertification in East Africa. Again, it diverges from CILSS in that there is no consortium of donors working to help IGADD achieve its goals.

Thus, regional groups have been established which are similar to the CILSS and Club du Sahel models. Yet, for a number of reasons, none copy the CILSS/Club du Sahel model exactly. For this, CILSS and the Club du Sahel are a test case for North-South and South-South cooperation.

THE HISTORY OF SOUTH-SOUTH COOPERATION

Pan-Africanism

CILSS´ formation is part of a long, historical tradition in the direction of the unification of the African territories economically, culturally, and politically. The first modern attempt to create a multiethnic grouping in West Africa was begun by El Hadj Omar Tall in the mid-1800s (1). His efforts could not match the power of French colonialism and, thereafter, multiethnic regionalism was the result of colonial and not African desires.

At the turn of the century, Africans organized the first Pan-African Congress, held in London. Between 1900 and 1945, five additional Congresses took place (2). The Pan-African Congresses gave representatives of the African colonies the opportunity to meet and discuss problems encountered by all.

In Francophone Africa, the Pan-African movement was promoted through the educational system. The William Ponty School in Dakar and universities throughout France enabled African students to share with each other the common experiences of colonialism. Educational settings furnished opportunities for African students to unite and to work against colonialism.

In the post-World War II era, both Africans and Europeans sought to restructure the colonial

53

relationship. As a result of economic realities
following the war, the Europeans could no longer
maintain their colonies. For the Africans, political and moral factors contributed to their desire to restructure the metropole-satellite relationship. India's independence and the growing
will to be free of external control laid the seeds
for the decolonization struggle that emerged after
World War II within many African states--Kenya,
Guinea, Ghana, and Algeria, to name a few.
     With independence well on its way by the mid-
1960s, concern over economic issues began to dominate the discussions of African groups.   Independence had addressed the major political concerns
of the new African states, but it did not eradi-
cate the profound economic weaknesses facing them.
     As African governments searched for solutions
to their social and economic problems, they looked
to European models, models based upon regional
economic integration theory. Arguments based on
the rationality of regional integration were
thought to be applicable to Africa, and so Africans formed integrative groupings.

THE RATIONALE FOR REGIONAL COOPERATION

     Arguments for regional cooperation center on
the issue of the rationality of factor endowments.
By combining scarce resources and avoiding duplication of services, efficiency is promoted and
each member country achieves greater economic
rewards.   Actions carried out at a regional level
are expected to be cheaper than those attempted by
individual nations alone. For example, an agricultural research school for the entire Sahel region
would be a less expensive and more rational use of
scarce resources (financial, personnel, administrative and managerial) than such a project implemented by each of the nine individual states.
Through regional cooperation, the standard of
living of all could be raised.
     A second argument to support regional
integration schemes is the claim that they help to
breakdown existing disadvantageous trade patterns.
Like many developing nations, the Sahel countries
are extremely dependent upon the sale of a few

54

TABLE 3.1
Principle Commodities Exported

Country	Product	Percentage of Country's Total 1965
Burkina Faso	Animals	62.4
	Oil Seeds/Nuts	10.6
	Cotton	7.5
Chad	Cotton	77.5
	Meat	1.8
Mali	Cotton	16.9
	Oil Seeds/Nuts	16.0
	Animals	33.0
Mauritania	Iron ore	93.6
	Fish	4.1
Niger	Ores/Concentrates	–
	Animals	16.4
	Oil Seeds/Nuts	58.9
Senegal	Petro Products	0.0
	Vegetable Oils	41.4
	Fertilizer	8.4
	Animal Feed	8.9

TABLE 3.1 (Continued)
Principle Commodities Exported

Country	Product	Percentage of Country's Total 1970
Burkina Faso	Animals	31.2
	Oil Seeds/Nuts	25.6
	Cotton	25.7
Chad	Cotton	69.1
	Meat	19.8
Mali	Cotton	20.6
	Oil Seeds/Nuts	10.1
	Animals	34.3
Mauritania	Iron	87.1
	Fish	7.0
Niger	Ores/Concentrates	–
	Animals	15.8
	Oil Seeds/Nuts	56.9
Senegal	Petro Products	2.6
	Vegetable Oils	28.4
	Fertilizer	7.4
	Animal Feed	18.0

TABLE 3.1 (Continued)
Principle Commodities Exported

Country	Product	Percentage of Country's Total 1980
Burkina Faso	Animals	23.6
	Oil Seeds/Nuts	11.0
	Cotton	44.0
Chad	Cotton	35.6
	Meat	60.9
Mali	Cotton	40.2
	Oil Seeds/Nuts	7.2
	Animals	47.5
Mauritania	Iron ore	82.9
	Fish	11.0
Niger	Ores/Concentrates	82.9
	Animals	5.4
	Oil Seeds/Nuts	-
Senegal	Petro Products	18.7
	Vegetable Oils	12.8
	Fertilizer	16.3
	Animal Feed	-

Source: United Nations, 1978 Statistical Yearbook
(New York: United Nations, 1978) pp. 530, 531,
534, 535, and 537. United Nations, 1981 Statistical Yearbook (New York: United Nations, 1983), pp.
976, 978, 979, 980, and 982.

products to generate revenues (3).

With the exception of Senegal, all of the Sahel states have depended on the sale of two or three commodities to generate as much as three-quarters of their export earnings. Three countries, Chad, Mauritania, and Niger, sold at least one commodity which accounted for at least 60 percent of 1980 export earnings--meat in Chad, iron ore in Mauritania, and uranium in Niger. Between 1965 and 1980, Senegal and Upper Volta were able to reduce their concentrated export structure. On the other hand, Niger and Mali increased their concentration on one commodity for export receipts during this period.

While commodity concentration on one product has declined in several of the Sahel countries, it has sometimes simply been replaced by another product. For example, in 1965, Chad was heavily dependent upon cotton; by 1980 meat was the major product exported. Likewise, Niger in 1965 sold more oil seeds and nuts than any other commodity; by 1980, uranium, and not grounduts, was the principle commodity exported.

For a number of Sahel countries, the products upon which they depend are not drought resistant. Oil seeds and nuts, and cotton are products which are sensitive to unfavorable climatic conditions. Therefore, drought compounds the economic situation of these countries: it leads to a decline in export volumes which simultaneously reduces export earnings which could pay for food imports.

Another justification for the formation of regional organizational schemes in the Third World is to reduce their dependency upon the industrialized nations. In the building up of trade among members of a regional integration scheme, goods formerly obtained from a non-member country, would now be obtained locally. Through this method of trade diversion, member countries could expand their economic output, leading to improved economic growth.

Partner concentration (percentage of imports and exports from and to one´s trading partners) has always been a factor cited to justify the formation of regional integration schemes. For many African and Third World nations, dependency upon a few countries (mostly Western) has tended

Table 3.2
Major Import Partners
as Percentage of Country Total

	1965	1970	1980
Burkina Faso			
France	54.0	50.7	34.7
OECD	59.8	62.9	52.9
Chad			
France	46.4	39.0	
OECD	57.3	46.7	
Gambia			
United Kingdom	41.0	30.0	25.2
OECD	63.3	53.7	42.1
Mali			
France	24.1	38.4	37.5
OECD	25.5	41.2	51.9
Mauritania			
France	46.5	35.7	
OECD	83.8	52.8	
Niger			
France	53.1	45.8	43.2
OECD	63.2	60.3	56.4
Senegal			
France	54.5	51.3	34.1
OECD	69.1	68.2	40.6

Source: United Nations, 1978 Statistical Yearbook
(New York: United Nations, 1978), pp. 511, 512,
515, 516, 517 and 518 and United Nations, 1981
Statistical Yearbook (New York: United Nations,
1983), pp. 957, 959, 960, 961, and 963.

to be substantial. In the Sahel, concentration upon the imports from the former colonial power declined for Gambia, Niger, Senegal, and Burkina Faso from 1965-1980 (Table 3.2). Mali was the only country which increased its trade dependency upon France during these years. Dependency upon the OECD nations' imports also declined throughout the Sahel from 1965-1980. Here again, Mali was the only country in the region to increase its reliance upon its major OECD trading partners for imports throughout the 1960s and 1970s.

With regards to exports, dependency upon the former colonial power declined for Gambia, Niger, and Senegal between 1965 and 1980 (Table 3.3). The percentage of exports to France as a percentage of total exports actually increased for Mali and Burkina Faso from 1965-1980. Exports to the major OECD trading partners dropped in the case of Senegal and Gambia (though the decline was statistically insignificant for Gambia). For Mali, Niger, and Burkina Faso, exports to the major OECD trade partners increased during this period.

In sum, the reliance upon imports from the major OECD trading partners declined substantially during the 1960s and 1970s. Partner concentration of exports has been less significant. For some Sahel nations there has been a growth in their exports to the West. The decline in dependency upon the OECD nations for trading purposes does not necessarily indicate that inter-Sahelian trade has grown to replace the declines in Sahel-OECD trading links.

Underdevelopment is the state of affairs for the CILSS nations, in part due to a commodity and partner concentration which has changed little since independence. One way out of this poverty and low economic performance is through the formation of regional organizations. Inter-Sahelian cooperation would be an important way to overcome drought, dependency and underdevelopment. The questions remains--what type of cooperative venture is best suited to the needs of the Sahel. nations?

TABLE 3.3
Major Export Partners
as Percentage of Country Total

	1965	1970	1980
Burkina Faso			
France	8.0	12.3	18.2
OECD	12.5	24.4	28.1
Chad			
France	45.2	70.3	
OECD	–	–	
Gambia			
United Kingdom	49.7	47.9	28.4
OECD	84.7	93.4	84.0
Mali			
France	5.9	17.1	28.8
OECD	5.9	18.3	49.3
Mauritania			
France	20.5	19.8	
OECD	61.8	64.1	
Niger			
France	56.2	46.7	53.9
OECD	56.9	46.9	73.0
Senegal			
France	80.7	57.0	32.0
OECD	82.6	64.5	38.0

Source: United Nations, 1978 Statistical Yearbook
(New York: United Nations, 1978), pp. 521, 522,
525, 526, 527, and 528. United Nations, 1981 Statistical Yearbook (New York:United Nations,
1983), pp. 966, 968, 969, 970 and 971.

Third World attempts to establish regional cooperative groups led to a proliferation of literature which analyzed the potential benefits, the probability of success, and the problems encountered by regional integrative schemes (4). Writings on integration theory involved debates among the contending schools of thought--federalism, functionalism, and neo-functionalism. Federalist concepts of integration focused on power arrangements. The federalists believed that governments could be coaxed into handing their authoritiy over to a supranational organization. Unlike the functionalists and neo-functionalists, the federalists preferred to work in the political, rather than social or economic arenas (5).

Functionalism, on the other hand, did not argue for a frontal attack on nation-states. Functionalists reasoned that a growth in technology and the desire for welfare benefits would be demanded by the populations of nations. The nation-state would then become virutually obsolete since only international bureaucrats (or technocrats) would be capable of providing welfare benefits to the populations (6). The underlying assumption of functionalism is that technocrats, unlike politicians, are not motivated by diplomatic or political gains. Unlike federalism, functionalism does not see a suprastate as the final goal, but it seeks to bring about a sense of community as nations suppress provincial national concerns in the process of building integration.

Neo-functionalism went a step further. Neo-functionalists argued that functionalism would never lead to any kind of political integration since no effort to transcend the boundaries between non-controversial to controversial issues would be made. Neo-functionalists posited that debates should arise over potentially political and contentious issues. In this way, the settlement of immediate issues would force nations to resolve other issues until actors were more deeply commited to the process of integration. Neo-functionalists reasoned that once integration began it would be like a genie out of the bottle which nations would find hard to put back in. Unfortunately, l'engrenage, as it is called, did not work in the European Community or in Third

World regional organizations as nicely and as neatly as it did on paper. Quite often the process of integration stalled or died out.

AFRICAN MODELS OF COOPERATON

In Africa, the rationale for and the form of integration reflected local realities. African commitment to economic integration was deeply influenced by the process of decolonization in the 1950s and 1960s. As a result, integrative schemes reflected the desire to improve material benefits as well as the intention to consolidate and strengthen political power (7). At the time of independence, African states, weak and unstable, viewed political integration as a way to strengthen national political power. In addition, African regional groups also resembled other Third World attempts in that they tended to organize around the concepts of economic integration, reminiscent of Viner´s notions and involving free trade areas, common tariffs or quotas, customs unions, common markets, economic unions and total economic integration (8). Reliance was placed upon trade and industrialization; little preoccupation with agriculture or rural issues surfaced.

One of the first attempts was the Mali Federation, joining Senegal and Mali in political union. Formed in January 1959, the Federation collapsed less than two years later in August 1960 when Senghor realized that success of the Federation could jeopardize his domestic political power (9).

After the break-up of the Federation, Mali joined Guinea and Ghana to form the Ghana-Guinea-Mali Union in 1960. The Union brought together three African states considered to be the most radical and most desirous of pan-African unity. They planned to follow a common ideological orientation based upon the pan-African theme. To carry out this goal, the Union set out to coordinate the internal mass organizations of member states such as labor, students, women, and political parties (10). For three states that did not speak a common language and which were not geographically contiguous, this was no small endeavor. The characteristics that divided the three nations more than outweighed those that brought them together. By 1963, the Ghana-Guinea-Mali Union disintegrated.

One of the earliest attempts to establish economic coordination, the Council of the Entente, brought together the Ivory Coast, Togo, Benin, and two CILSS nations, Burkina Faso and Niger (11). The original purpose of the Entente was to strengthen the political base of member states through economic means, rather than to develop comprehensive plans for economic integration. To this end, a Solidarity Fund was created to guarantee the loans that member countries contracted with external sources. Plans elaborated by the Council's creator, President Houphouet Boigny of Ivory Coast, also called for the creation of a customs union, the elimination of barriers to labor migration, joint industrial planning, and other economic activities. To date, little has been accomplished (12).

Throughout the 1960s, African leaders continued to be concerned about problems of development and economic growth. These concerns were also taken up within regional groupings. A common practice in regional organizations was to create customs unions or common markets to spur economic development. The West African Customs Union (UDEAO), formed in 1959, joined the Ivory Coast, Benin, Senegal, Mali, Niger, Burkina Faso, and Mauritania. The UDEAO yielded modest trade growth among its members. After some time Mali felt shortchanged by the organization. It argued that the coastal and larger states (the Ivory Coast and Senegal) were reaping the lion's share of the benefits. In 1966, the UDEAO was reorganized to take Mali's complaints into account. The reorganization, essentially, changed nothing. The UDEAO lacked the institutional machinery to implement the agreement regarding the distribution of import duties under the refund system. Even with the modified structure, the inland states failed to gain as much as the coastal ones. Having been unsuccessful in effecting any meaninful changes, the UDEAO languished for several years. In 1970, the members met to take stock of the situation. The meeting culminated in the decision to form a new economic organization, the Economic Community of West Africa (CEAO).

The CEAO, begun officially in 1973, is primarily a customs union. In addition, the CEAO planned to formulate joint development projects within the region (in communication and transportation), to set up regional research programs in solar energy and cereals, and to implement projects in the areas of meat production, agriculture, fishing, trade, and water resources. For all of its ambitious plans, more has been accomplished in the areas that do not address conventional economic integation issues such as trade and tariffs. For example, considerable progress has been achieved in financing development projects and studies on solar energy.

From the discussion so far, the pattern of African regionalism that emerges involves integration-disintegration-integration. As a result, progress in building regional integration in Africa has been slow. What accounts for this tendency of African regional groups to disintegrate?

WEAKNESSES OF AFRICAN REGIONAL COOPERATION THEORY

Proponents of regional economic integration were correct in their analysis: economic integration has the potential to exert a positive influence on African development. It encourages a rational division of labor among African countries, each of which is too small to benefit alone. Integration allows coordinated planning. Moreover, regional integration affords states the opportunity to lessen their vulnerability to external influences through the development of inter-regional trade.

Finally, integration can accelerate development through the establishment of more efficient and larger industries (13). Yet, time and time again, the alleged benefits of integration have failed to develop in Africa.

Upon critical analysis it becomes clear that the models employed for the development of African cooperative groups were not entirely suited to

65

African conditions. For example, the function-
alist approach assumes that welfare issues can be
separated from political ones, but in Africa,
welfare issues quickly became politicized. Secondly, the extent to which African countries were
affected and shaped by the external environment
was never given adequate treatment in the theory.
In his study of Central American integration,
Schmitter found that integration had the effect of
encouraging external penetration as private interests and public authorities attempted to take
advantage of growing market and investment opportunities (14). Schmitter´s findings are also
supported by Mytelka´s study of UDEAC (15).

Integration theories presuppose an existing
advanced level of trade among members. Yet, this
is not true for most African states, especially
the Sahel. Inter-Sahelian trade has always been,
for the most part, lower than the level of trade
between it and the West. Trade in imports averaged about 3.18 percent from 1968 to 1981, while
trade in exports averaged 4.58 percent for those
same years (16). Imports from the other Sahelian
nations to Cape Verde and Senegal have registered
levels of less than .01 percent (17). Burkina
Faso´s purchase of products from the other CILSS
states declined from 7.3 percent in 1968 to 1.2
percent in 1981. On the export side, only Sene-
gal´s exports to its neighbors increased from 1968
to 1971 (rising from 6.8 to 17.2 percent). For
Niger and Mali, exports to the other CILSS member
countries dropped during this period. Inter-Sahel
trade in exports for Cape Verde, Chad, and Gambia,
low to begin with, remained at less than .01
percent (18).

Integration also requires a developed
transportation and communication network to
facilitate the increased movement of goods among
the member states. In West Africa, road transportation, built by the colonial administration,
reinforced hinterland-coastal connections.

For the CILSS nations, rail and road
transportation systems connect Senegal and Mali,
Mali and Burkina Faso, and Senegal and Mauritania.
Cape Verdean and Gambian links are only to one
other member country, Senegal. Road connections
between Chad and the other CILSS nations are ex-

tremely poor. Besides the dearth of good roads joining the Sahel states, there are practically no railway connections. What rail system that does exist was built by the French to facilitate the movement of goods from the hinterlands to the coastal ports. Thus, there are rail connections between Mali and Senegal and between Burkina Faso and the Ivory Coast. Mauritania´s railroad is located in the northeast corner of the country, and was constructed to move iron ore to the coast for transport to Europe. Furthermore, it does not extend beyond Mauritania´s borders. For decades, discussion of a trans-Sahelian railroad has been on the drawing board, but no funding has been made available to begin construction. The lack of a strong transportation network connecting the member states undermines the concept of integration and is a force working against successful regional cooperation in Africa and within the CILSS countries.

Furthermore, there are factors related neither to economics nor to logistics which make integration a difficult objective to achieve in Africa. Two concepts--pan-Africanism and nationalism--are co-existing and sometimes competing desires. Nationalism is a tool commonly used by African leaders to build and to maintain political power. Concurrently, the desire for cooperation with other African states propels governments to form regional alliances. Yet nationalism in its most extreme forms can be antithetical to regional cooperation. Often, African leaders view integration as a means to enhance national poltical and economic objectives rather than as a way to achieve future regional economic or political union. The weakness of integration theory, as applied to Africa, is that it often abscribed goals to African leaders which they did not have. In the case of the Mali Federation, when integration came at the expense of Senghor´s domestic political power, he quickly abandoned any notion of regional cooperation with Mali.

An evaluation of the evolution of integration in the African context has led its proponents to question conventional schemes based upon European realities. In the European context, a major goal of integration was to expand trade and industrialization. Whether this goal is relevant to Africa is debatable. While the majority of European economies are oriented towards industrial and manufacturing activities, the same is not true in Africa where agriculture is the primary economic activity. Therefore, integration schemes placing heavy reliance upon industrialization and manufacturing are likely to fail in Africa. The industrial base upon which economic growth would take place is too small in scale to make integration workable, and integration based upon industrialization becomes too costly and inefficient to benefit the majority of the population.

In Africa only a small percentage of exports is derived from the manufacturing sector; agriculture and primary products represent the bulk of African exports. Within the CILSS states, the primary products accounted for at least 96 percent of their total exports in 1965 and 90 percent in 1980 (19). Manufacturing, on the other hand, only accounted for a small portion of total exports, 3 percent in 1965 and 8 percent in 1980 (20). This is not to suggest that cooperation, based upon the industrial and manufacturing sectors, is unimportant, but perhaps scarce resources in African would be better utilized if integration efforts involved those sectors more relevant to the African environment.

In sum, the historical experience of African cooperation, narrowly constructed along European lines, has not been positive. Those attempts to reproduce European structures and copy goals, ignoring the economic and political realities in Africa, have dissolved or are close to dissolution. The CEAO has achieved success in some areas reflecting African needs--agriculture, energy, and transportation. Virtually, no progress has been made by the CEAO in establishing a common market. The failure of African regional integration as a strategy points out the gap between the theory and reality of integration.

The disappointing record of Third World integrative efforts and the inability of the theories to accomodate variables critical to the local realities, caused many to question the validity of the models (21). The shift from a focus on integration theory, conventionally defined, to a broader conception of cooperation occured at a time when economists, themselves, began to question traditional development theory.

The emphasis on trade and industrial policies between 1950-1965 reflected academic and economic development policy thinking. Regional organizations subscribed to the theories enunciated by W. Arthur Lewis, Raul Prebisch, and others who espoused development strategies based upon import substitution and industrialization. Traditional academic thinking relegated agriculture to an unimportant role in economic development. The agriculture sector was to support industrial expansion by providing inexpensive foodstuffs. The weakness in the performance of the industrial sector in Africa led to a new development perspective. Development economics moved from a position stressing industrialization and manufacturing to one emphasizing the agricultural and rural sectors as the sine qua non of development.

By the late 1960s, a new school of thought emerged, armed with the evidence of a "Development Decade" that had not proved very successful, the discovery of miracle seeds (the Green Revolution), and the critiques of the dependency school that looked to external factors to explain the lack of development within the Third World. The new school of thought argued that, without agricultural and rural development, industrial growth would either be limited or would cause internal imbalances, exacerbating problems of unemployment, inequality, and poverty (22).

The changing notions of the shape that development should take, the cooperative organizations needed to generate economic growth, and the inadequacy of the older theories of cooperation opened the door for new theories on South-South cooperation. By the same token, changing African realities demanded cooperation, but not cooperation aimed at total economic or political integation. Moreover, the needs of the Sahel pointed to the importance of developing the rural areas. Cooperation, if it was to help the majority and promote economic development, would have to direct itself to the rural sector.

In the end, the drought and the pressing needs of the Sahel states paved the way for a new type of cooperation. In the context of African regional organizational history, CILSS represents the evolution of thinking on regional cooperation: away from a primary focus on manufacturing and trade, to one concerned with meeting basic human needs. The establishment of CILSS formalized the argument for the development of the primary and rural sectors as the sine qua non of the development of the industrial sectors.

CILSS IN THE CONTEXT OF SOUTH-SOUTH COOPERATION

Unlike many other West African regional organizations, CILSS is an effort to build a comprehensive program for rural development (23). No sector touching upon rural development has been left out of the CILSS strategy. Nine sectors-- Dryland and Irrigated Agriculture, Hydraulics, Livestock, Fisheries, Ecology and Forestry, Crop Protection, Transportation and Infrastructure, Price-Marketing-Storage, and Human Resources--fall within CILSS´ domain of interest. Other organizations might include one or a few of these sectors in their activities, but only CILSS has established activities in such a vast number of sectors affecting the rural population.

CILSS differs from other regional organizations in that its creation resulted from a single cataclysmic event--the drought. The problems engendered by the ecological destruction served to galvanize actions to ameliorate the most affected areas.

Thirdly, compared to other regional organizations, CILSS states comprise the poorest of the poor. The overwhelming commonality is the poverty and weakness within the Sahel community. Unlike other regional groupings, the CILSS states are not dominated by a wealthy state (the Ivory Coast in the CEAO and the Council of the Entente; Nigeria in ECOWAS). The CILSS countries, because of their shared poverty, and common ethnic and colonial backgrounds (with the exception of Cape Verde and Gambia), are relatively homogeneous.

70

TABLE 3.4
Membership of CILSS States in African IGOs

Organization	Country							
	BF	CV	CHAD	GAMB	MALI	MAUR	NIGER	SENE
CILSS	X	X	X	X	X	X	X	X
OAU	X	X	X	X	X	X	X	X
LCBC			X				X	
OMVS				X	X	X		X
CEAO	X				X	X		X
ECOWAS	X	X		X	X	X	X	X
CE	X						X	
OICMA	X		X	X	X	X	X	X
OCLALAV	X		X		X	X	X	X
CIEH	X		X		X	X	X	X
OCAM	X		X				X	X
WARDA	X			X	X	X	X	X
OCCGE	X				X	X	X	X

Key:

CILSS   = Permanent Inter-State Committee to
          Combat Drought in the Sahel
OAU   = Organization of African Unity
LCBC   = Lake Chad Basin Commission
OMVS   = Senegal River Basin Development
          Authority
CEAO   = Economic Community of West Africa
ECOWAS = Economic Community of West African States
CE   = Council of the Entente
OICMA   = International Organization for African
          Migratory Locust Control
OCLALAV = Joint Organization for Bird and Locust
          Control
CIEH   = Inter-African Committee for Hydraulic
          Research
OCAM   = Afro-Malagasy Common Organization
WARDA   = West African Rice Development
          Association
OCCGE   = Organization for Coordination and
          Cooperation in Combating Major Endemic
          Diseases

Finally, CILSS´ uniqueness derives from its close association with the donors. CILSS has taken into account its vulnerability to external forces and actors, not by ignoring them but by acknowledging and uniting with them. No other regional organization in Africa has attempted to do this to such an extent.

All of these factors have given CILSS a place in the annals of African regionalism. Its emergence at a particular historic juncture gives it a form unlike that found in other groupings. A comparison of CILSS with other regional groupings highlights the differences.

CILSS stands apart from other regional groupings. Unlike the OAU, CILSS is not a general purpose organization and, therefore, does not concern itself with political matters. In contrast to the Council of the Entente, OCAM, ECOWAS, and the CEAO, CILSS´ goal is not the promotion of economic benefits through trade and industrial policies. Furthermore, CILSS´ broader approach to rural development differs from the narrow perspectives addressed by the OMVS, the CIEH, OCLALAV, OICMA, the OCCGE, and WARDA. Its domain encompasses the problems faced by the Sahel: the extreme poverty within the region, the degradation of the environment through desertification and drought, the reliance upon agriculture which increasingly fails to satisfy regional food consumption needs, the absence of a decent transportation network, and the dependence upon the donor community.

THE HISTORY OF NORTH-SOUTH COOPERATION

The efforts of Third World states to improve their economic lot and overcome the disappointments of the past twenty years included increasingly sharpened demands addressed to the developed world, and culminated in the call for a New International Economc Order (NIEO) at the U.N. Sixth Special Session held in 1975. At the Session, two resolutions were endorsed by member states--the Declaration On The Establishment Of A New International Economic Order and the Programme Of Action.

The resolutions of the U.N. Sixth Special Session were incorporated in the Charter of Economic Rights and Duties of States. The New International Economic Order, adopted by a majority of developing states, can be categorized by six broad objective or issue areas: 1) aid and assistance, 2) trade, 3) finance, 4) industrialization, technology transfer, and business practices, 5) social, and 6) political and institutional matters (24). In brief, the NIEO is an outline for change designed to improve economic and social conditions within the Third World and to make the international system a more just one. However the NIEO was defined, one certainty was that it emerged as a controversial program that split the developed and developing states over four basic proposals--national sovereignty over natural resources and the right to nationalization, improved terms of trade for raw materials through the linkage of the price of commodities to the price of manufactured goods (indexation), regulation of multinational corporations, and the right to establish producer commodity cartels (25).

Arguments over the NIEO concerned the depth of change, the agents of change, and the beneficiaries of change. Some NIEO proponents believed that the international system only required some fine tuning to make it work more equitably (26). Others called for radical structural transformation, arguing that the existing system was inherently linked to the pauperization of poor states (27).

Disagreements over the locus of change revolved around those who (like many in the Third World) felt that change in the system was incumbent upon the developed states since they were the ones responsible for the inequalities (28). Still others maintained that steps to make the system more just should come from both developed and developing states since conditions within the latter arise from both external and internal conditions (29). Finally, the debate over a NIEO surrounded the issue of the beneficiary. Leff posits that no one will emerge as a beneficiary, least of all the Third World (30). Hansen's essay in which he discussed the embourgoisement of the

OPEC states supported the conclusion that the better-off developing countries would gain the most from the main NIEO proposals (31). Other analyses of the effects of a NIEO ranged from those which posited that both developed and developing would gain equally (32). Another body of literature predicted that the developed states would be the sole winners from a new international economic order (33).

To observers of the new international system, the call for a NIEO was neither sudden nor unexpected; it was the culmination of various political, historical, and economic events. Four circumstances stand out as contributors to the NIEO drama. They include the political independence attained by the majority of the Third World after 1960, the lack of progress achieved by many developing states during two "Development Decades", the economic disorder that beset the world during the 1970s, and the success of the OPEC cartel.

Following World War II, reconstruction sapped Europe of the poltical and economic will to rule its colonies. As the former German and Japanese colonial possessions fell under the aegis of the United Nations, the colonies began to acquire some autonomy. Simultaneously, colonial possessions of Great Britain and France exerted increased demands for self-rule or some form of limited self-rule. The United Nations system with its myriad social, political, and economic entities encouraged a global agreement on the issue of self-determination and the right of peoples everywhere to free themselves of external domination.

With the political control removed, developing nations and the United Nations began to address global economic problems. The growing percentage of developing states within the United Nations contributed to a change in the issues taken up by this global body. In 1945, the Third World made up 58 percent of the U.N. membership. By 1976, it accounted for 75 percent of the membership. The numerical dominance of developing states in the United Nations increased the attention devoted to the economic problems confronted by them.

Targets for economic growth, set by the

United Nations, were held up as the goals for
which the developing states would strive. Statistics gathered by the various international agencies cogently demonstrated the widening gap
between rich and poor. The share of world exports
from developing states declined from almost 33
percent in 1950 to slightly over 20 percent in
1962 (34). By 1970, developing nations´ share of
world exports dipped below 20 percent (35). The
lack of economic progress was also evident by per
capita income growth rates. The table below shows
the fall in per capita income growth rates to
levels below those set by the United Nations Development Decade.

TABLE 3.5
Per Capita Income Growth Rates   (In percent)

	Averaged Annual Growth Rate (1965-1983)
Low-income Developing Countries	2.7
Sub-Saharan Africa	-0.2
Sahel	.7
Middle-income Developing Countries	3.4
Sub-Saharan Africa	1.9
Sahel	-0.1
Developed Market Countries	2.5

Source: World Bank. World Development Report 1985,
(New York: Oxford University Press, 1985) p. 174.

For the poorest developing countries per
capita income growth rates steadily declined
between 1950 and 1983. The higher per capita
income growth rates for the middle-income countries were most likely attributable to the
favorable economic positions of the oil-producing

75

nations and to the inclusion of several nations that were able to take advantage of economic activities which resulted in their strong economic growth. Countries such as Singapore, South Korea, Taiwan, Argentina, and Brazil benefited from industrialization, trade, and banking operations in their countries. However, many other Third World countries experienced a lack of economic growth coupled with high population growth. The combination of these two factors resulted in low or negative GNP growth rates. Of all low-income countries, African states had the most dismal economic growth, -0.2 percent from 1965-1983.

For the low-income Sahel states, average annual per capita GNP growth rates amounted to .7 percent, a figure that was higher than that of all low-income Sub-Saharan states. During the years indicated in the table above, growth rates were 1.2 percent for Mali, 1.4 percent for Burkina Faso and Gambia, and -1.2 percent for Niger. The two middle-income Sahel states actually averaged lower per capita GNP growth rates. Senegal´s per capita GNP was -0.5 percent and that of Mauritania stag-nated at 0.3 percent. The composite per capita growth rate for the Sahel averaged annually .43 percent between 1965 and 1983. The Sahel economic performance was well below United Nations´ Development Decade targets.

The perceived lack of economic growth in most of the Third World was one of the factors which contributed to the call for a New International Economic Order. There were other factors as well. The demand for a NIEO was prompted by the break-down of the international economic system (the Bretton Woods Agreement). Begun in 1945 at the close of the war, the Agreement provided for a system of fixed exchange rates. The system, es-tablished to reduce economic instability and to guarantee free trade, was based upon the dollar standard. To ensure that the Agreement operated effectively, unilateral management was maintained by the Americans until the 1960s (36).

By 1968, the solutions to international mone-tary management were no longer effective due to a number of emerging trends and forces: increasing global interdependence, detente, the end of U.S. hegemony, as well as the system´s inability to

76

cope with the large American balance of payments deficit. Confidence in the dollar, the linchpin of the system, declined and, in turn, jeopardized the agreements that had been worked out (37). Ad hoc crisis management enabled the monetary system to continue for a few years longer. But, by 1971 short-term arrangements could not keep the economic system functioning. In August of 1971, President Nixon unilaterally declared that the dollar would no longer be convertible into gold (38).

The collapse of the Bretton Woods Agreement left no new global economic arrangement in its place. The lack of stability was felt sharply by the developing nations, dependent upon the exports of a few commodities to generate large revenues. The lack of any satisfactory global trade and monetary policies has been one of the complaints they registered during the NIEO debate.

Finally, the issue of oil and energy is a component of the call for a NIEO. The five-fold increase in the price of oil between 1973 and 1979 was an unprecedented shock to many states--both developing and developed. Oil producer cartelization injected a countervailing bargaining force into the global political equation by introducing, for the first time, a mechanism for resource transference. Instead of large capital flows going primarily to the developed world, a number of developing states were receiving massive amounts of petrodollars. The industrialized West, along with other oil-consuming nations from the developing world, witnessed a decline in their international reserves, or worse, experienced severe balance of payments deficits.

The growing importance of the Third World as a producer of raw materials and as a potential market for the developing countries´ products introduced a new variable in global economic and political relations. Declining Western hegemony and growing world interdependence, backed up by the threat of expropriation and cartelization, made the demand for a NIEO a serious issue.

The threat posed by the Third World motivated the advanced industrial societies to at least begin a dialogue on matters of concern to the former. As such, the CILSS/Club du Sahel arrangement represented an attempt to work cooperatively on a number of issues deemed important to the Sahelians. Other examples of the North-South dialogue during the 1970s include the Conference on International Economic Cooperation (CIEC) and the Lomé Convention.

NORTH-SOUTH NEGOTIATIONS

The impetus for the CIEC resulted from the West's alarm over rapidly rising energy prices. Initially, the North planned a conference to concentrate on questions of oil production and export. At the request of France's President, Giscard d´Estaing, a preparatory meeting convened in April, 1975. The outcome of this first meeting was considerably less than successful.

Accord between the North (the EEC, the United States, and Japan) and the South (Algeria, Iran, Brazil, Saudia Arabia, India, Venezuela, and Zaire) could not be reached over the name of the conference, the agenda, or the list of participants (39). Furthermore, divergent opinions on the objectives of the conference reduced the initial meeting to a series of attacks and counterattacks between the two sides. Disagreement arose over the issue of linkage of oil and raw materials. The North pushed to concentrate the discussion on the issue of guaranteed access to supply; the South preferred to focus on the price of raw materials.

After that April meeting, France worked behind the scenes to revive the idea for a conference. At the second preparatory meeting, held in October 1975, agreement was reached to expand the number of representatives. The North grew to include eight (40). In addition to the seven members on the South's side, twelve other countries joined (41). The two sides came to be known as the "Group of Eight" (G-8) and the "Group of Nineteen" (G-19). In December 1975 the CIEC opened officially.

The major issues of the Conference concerned energy, finance, raw materials, and development. The demands advanced by the Group of Nineteen mirrored those made in other international fora.

On raw materials, the South requested the establishment of a commodity fund, the elimination of barriers to trade, and an end of volatile price fluctuations in raw materials (42). Northern interest concerned the issue of compensation in the event of nationalization of foreign property. Splitting the two sides was the question of energy--the South's desire to protect the purchasing power of its export earnings and the North's interest in stable access to energy sources at reasonable prices.

On the question of development, the South requested increased aid levels from the North, help in expanding their technological capabilities, an increase in the production of manufactured goods in the South, and the development of infrastructure within Africa.

Financial matters encompassed the problems of debt relief, expansion of the World Bank's Third Window, and the establishment of new financial institutions more favorable to the needs of the developing states.

The Conference lasted two years with a brief adjournment after the December 1976 session. The outcome of the Conference proved to be a disappointment to most of its participants. While agreement was reached on twenty items, differences remained on twenty-one other points. Building a consensus on the problematic items of restructuring the global economy was beyond the ability of the Conference participants. Disagreement remained over defining what a commodity entailed, compensation for the nationalization of foreign properties, the creation of new international lending institutions, and the use of indexation in reducing drastic price fluctuations of raw materials.

Despite these problems, the CIEC still merits an evaluation. What is important here is an evaluation in the context of CILSS and the Club du Sahel. First of all, it should be noted that none of the G-19 were among the poorest of the poor, least of all the CILSS nations. In fact, the majority of the nineteen were major suppliers of essential raw materials--bauxite, copper, and petroleum. For these nations, issues of trade and price policy were more critical; the CILSS states,

79

on the other hand, were and are interested in increased aid flows. Although the Group of Eight promised to augment aid to the least developing nations, there were no guidelines or timetables established. In the final analysis, the CIEC was less beneficial to the Sahel countries.

The identification of the beneficiary of the NIEO was a subject taken up in a study by Weintraub. He analyzed the principle items of the NIEO (debt rescheduling, removal of trade barriers, and commodity agreements), issues discussed at the CIEC. In the main, Weintraub finds that the beneficiaries of such agreements will be the higher-income countries (43).

On the subject of commodity agreements, Weintraub's data revealed that the poor nations would not be helped substantially because the products on which they depend have a tendency to fare poorly in the market place. On debt rescheduling, Weintraub reached the same conclusion. Because the wealthier developing countries would receive most of the loans provided by international lending institutions, they would benefit in greater proportion from cancellations of their debts. Finally, Weintraub estimated that the elimination of trade barriers would increase revenues in the poorest developing nations by $4 million and $29 million for middle-income countries (44).

Efforts to recast relations between developed and developing nations may not fundamentally alter the current situation of the low-income developing countries. If Weintraub's thesis bears out, then only a few Sahelian countries stand to gain from the changes proposed by the NIEO.

Any benefits accruing from the NIEO proposals will favor Mauritania and Senegal, the two wealthier states. Because the majority of the Sahel states are in the low-income category, their gains from the removal of trade barriers, debt relief, commodity agréments, and increased investment strategies, while helpful, will not provide the type of assistance needed to eliminate the impediments to growth. For the Sahel, other remedies must be included in any North-South agreement.

TABLE 3.6
Sahel Per Capita Income (1983)

GNP Less Than $300	GNP Between $300-$500
Burkina Faso--$180	Cape Verde--$320
Gambia-- 290	Mauritania-- 480
Mali-- 160	Senegal-- 440
Niger-- 240	

Source: World Bank, World Development Report 1985, p. 174.

        One effort at North-South negotiation which
has provided benefits to developing nations (and
the CILSS states) has been the Lomé Conventions;
Lomé I (signed in 1975), Lomé II (signed in 1979),
and Lomé III (signed in 1984). The idea of the
Lomé Convention evolved from the formation of the
European Economic Community and French and Belgian
desires to maintain their special relationship
with their former colonies. Both countries pushed
for the incorporation of their former colonies in
the EEC structure.
        Negotiations for some type of "associated"
relationship between the African countries and the
original 6 members of the EEC culminated in the
signing of the Treaty of Rome in 1957. African
dissatisfaction with the Treaty led to its
replacement by Yaoundé I and Yaoundé II.
        Beginning in 1969, talks began on the
enlargement of the Yaoundé membership in view of
the fact that Britain's admission into the Community appeared imminent. The need for an arrangement with the Commonwealth countries, coupled with
the inadequacies of Yaoundé II, set the stage for
new EEC and African negotiations. In 1973, African ministers, representing the Yaoundé states,
and the Commonwealth partners met to begin the
first steps in the formulation of a new EEC/Afri-
can relationship. Among the Africans consensus
was attained on a number of principles (45). By

the time the African members sat down to negotiate with the European Community, agreement on eight principles had been reached.

Negotiations began in July 1973 between the nine European members and an expanded Third World group--46 countries (46). The talks resulted in the Lomé Convention which has been hailed as a breakthrough in North-South relations. The accord signed between the EEC and the ACP (African, Caribbean, and Pacific) states covered issues of trade (cooperation and promotion), export earnings (stabilization), industrial cooperation, financial and technical cooperation, and institutional mechanisms charged with implementing the articles of agreement (47). Certain provisions of the agreement stand out as improvements from previous EEC/ACP negotiated settlements.

Lomé I attacked the problem of unstable export earnings by agreeing to the stabilization of the earnings for a number of products: groundnuts, cocoa, coffee, cotton, coconut, palm oil, palm nuts and kernels, hides, skins and leathers, wood, bananas, tea, sisal, and iron ore. The accord provides for stabilization of the ACP countries' export earnings when they, "...fall by at least 6.5 percent below a reference level established by calculating an average of the export earnings for that product in the EEC markets, for the previous four years...For the least-developed, land-locked, and island states the shortfall must be at least 2.5 percent of the reference level." (48)

STABEX coverage of the Sahelian countries' exports is listed in the table below. Coverage ranges from 24 percent of total exports (Niger) to 94 percent of total exports (Gambia). Under Lomé I, products which received the most coverage were groundnuts, groundnut oil, iron ore, and cotton. This would explain the high percentage of coverage for Gambia and Mauritania; the former exports primarily groundnuts and groundnut oils and the latter exports iron ore. Although Lome II expanded the number of products covered to include 44 items, by and large, the additonal products did not substantially affect the export earnings of the CILSS nations.

TABLE 3.7
Percentage of Exports Covered
by STABEX under Lomé I

Country	Percentage of Total Exports Covered
Burkina Faso	30
Chad	69
Gambia	94
Mali	46
Mauritania	73
Niger	24
Senegal	35

Source: Ravenhill, "What is to be done for Third World commodity exporters? An evaluation of the STABEX scheme?" International Organization, 38, No. 3 (1984), pp. 52-53.

Several authors have questioned the benefits of the Lomé Convention agreements to developing countries. Galtung, Mytelka, and Langdon argue that the scheme fails to stabilize the market for raw material exports since it touches upon export earnings and not export prices (49). Furthermore, the accord does not provide a mechanism to tackle the root cause of the problem--the declining terms of trade for Third World countries. Galtung and Ravenhill believe that the scheme only serves to freeze the current international division of labor because the developing countries will only be encouraged to concentrate on exporting raw materials and not to shift to higher levels of processing for export earnings (50). The impact on the CILSS states could be a growing emphasis on the cultivation of export crops which are covered by STABEX) rather than on improvements in the production of subsistence crops.

Another criticism of STABEX is that the transfer payments are not made automatically when the reference level of export earnings drops.

Under the terms of the accord the evidence must be examined by the Commission empowered by the agreement to approve payments based upon the availablity of resources (51). In light of the economic situation of the CILSS nations, the need to receive the transfer payments in a timely fashion is critical.

As signatories to Lomé, the Sahel nations stand to gain somewhat from STABEX and the promise of increased aid. On the other hand, Lomé is only a partial solution to the region's problems. Lomé concentrates on exports and trade, and, essentially, does not attack other economic difficulties facing these countries. It does not encourage the promotion of subsistence crops (cowpeas, millet, and sorghum), but promotes the expansion of export crops favored by the European Community. Lomé does not confront the pressing issue of food self-sufficiency in the region, and it does not respond directly to the challenge of meeting basic human needs such as the expansion of educational opportunities and health care. Nor does Lomé address environmental issues such as desertification and ecological destruction. Finally, Lomé does not promote infrastructural development (transportation and communication) which would contribute to economic development throughout the Sahel by facilitating inter-Sahelian transport of goods and services.

In the end, Lomé is a remedy for meeting short-term emergencies, but does not provide the resources or the strategy to overcome the legacy of poverty and famine. Multilateral agreements such as Lomé are only a partial answer. Meaningful development cannot rest solely on a concept for trade promotion. From the Sahel's perspective, the promotion of export crops has come at the expense of subsistence crops.

CILSS, at least on first inspection, stands apart from other North-South accords. It relies on: 1) aid rather than trade, 2) rural rather than urban development, and 3) agricultural rather than industrial production. Although the CILSS/Club du Sahel framework departs from other North-South agreements, it remains to be seen whether the outcome will be more beneficial to the CILSS states than Lomé or the CIEC proposals. It remains to be seen whether results achieved will serve to alter the relationship between the Sahel and donor communities? The next section examines the theories of North-South cooperation.

THEORIES OF NORTH-SOUTH COOPERATION

Theories about North-South cooperation have been developed using a variety of analytical constructs. Among the most frequently cited are: decolonization, dependency, and counterdependency.

Researchers such as Gruhn and Zartman are proponents of the decolonization framework. Decolonization theory posits that through compromise, aggressive negotiations, a willingness to understand the value system of the other side, and a desire to reduce global inequalities, reductions in North-South tensions are possible.

Decolonization theorists acknowledge the tendency of the international system to ignore the problems of the poor, but they affirm the ability of the system to make adjustments. Central to this approach is the premise that some fine tuning of the instruments of international relations is all that is needed. Proponents reject the Marxist solution which espouses the overthrow of the existing international economic regime.

One of the main adherents to this school of thought, I. William Zartman, has outlined his thesis in a number of works. Zartman's initial work, a study of the EEC and ACP negotiations leading to the Treaty of Rome, concluded that weak states are not necessarily disadvantaged when bargaining with powerful ones. In another article, he used the Lomé Convention as a case study of North-South relations (52). Zartman concluded that decolonization and not dependency theory was a more accurate model of North-South relations. Zartman asserted that changes in monetary zone arrangements and new agreements on capital flows and control proved that the ACP states could reduced their dependency upon their former colonial metropoles.

Bilateralization, which Zartman equated with dependency was in the process of being replaced by multilateralization (decolonization). Additional refinements of this thesis were expressed in a subsequent article (53). According to the author, multilateralization refers to the "...relations between groups of countries, more specifically to arrangements in which the direct link from non-African to African and other Third World states is mediated by the need for prior collective agreements within each of the two groupings" (54). Multilateralism increases the power of individual African states to promote their common interests as they bargain with the North.

Another concept discussed by Zartman is the notion of diversified relations, the process by which relations between a single African state and another non-African (industrialized) state are modified. "As a successor to bilateralism, diversification replaces one source of relations with several, dependency with alternatives, and the promise of fidelity with the threat of going elsewhere as the major source of power; it enhances national autonomy by extending the freedom to maneuver" (55).

There are several problems with decolonization in its applicability to the CILSS states. First of all, partner concentration has not declined for all of these states. Between 1966 and 1976, Burkina Faso and Mali increased their share of French imports (56). Similarly, exports to France increased for Mali, Burkina Faso, and Niger during this period (57). The percentage of exports to France did, however, decrease for the other Francophone CILSS nations. In sum, bilateral trade links did not drop for all of the Sahel countries. In some cases, dependency upon France declined only slightly; in other cases, dependency upon the former metropole has actually increased. (See Tables 3.2 and 3.3 for evidence of multilateralized dependency.)

Secondly, the link between multilateralism and diversified relations, on the one hand, and decolonization, on the other, is not convincingly articulated. The fact that Third World states may now enter into relations with several developed nations does not necessarily prove that dependency has diminished. An equally cogent argument can be made that dependency´s form has been altered. Challenor argues that the post-independence era in

Africa has led to the multilateralization or the collectivization of bilateral interests (58). Now, the developing nations are dependent on a small group of countries--the former metropole and its allies. Multilateralism and diversification in trade means that the Sahel's primary trade partners are the OECD nations. Between 1965 and 1983, the percentage of merchandise exports to the OECD increased for Mali (from 7 to 72 percent); Burkina Faso (from 17 to 48 percent); Niger (from 74 to 76 percent); and Chad (from 64 to 72 percent) (59). Only Mauritania and Senegal reduced the percentage of their total exports to the industrialized market economies, from 96 to 94 percent for the former and from 92 to 54 for the latter (60).

While Zartman finds evidence of multilateralism among the developing nations in their dealings with the developed world; he fails to acknowledge the reverse--the occurence of coordination among the developed countries in their negotiations with the South. CILSS has enabled the Sahel states to collectivize and harmonize their demands; the same holds true for the donors.

Finally, decolonization theory is more applicable to nations with resources vital to the West. This is not the situation in the Sahel states. They have very few resources with which to bring the donors to their "economic knees". The principle commodities exported--cotton, meat, and groundnuts--are products for which the price elasticities of demand are low and substitutes are readily available. The few minerals in the Sahel vital to the West have made the Sahel nations more dependent upon external forces and actors than ever. Mauritania and Niger, by expanding their export of iron ore and uranium to a small group of consuming nations, have become more vulnerable to the economic fortunes and needs of the West.

The focus of the decolonization approach is on the gains that can be won by the South. Little attention is paid to the interdependency of developed and developing nations. Mazrui has looked at the inter-connectedness of North and South which can be used to the latter's advantage. He has labelled this approach the counterdependency model. One of the strategies the Third World may employ is to penetrate the centers of Northern power in order to "...increase the share of the Third World in the economies of the developed nations themselves" (61). According to the author, counterdependency can be used in favor of the South. The industrialized world's reliance upon developing countries' raw materials and markets offers a point of departure for making demands to reduce global inequality.

What implications does a strategy of vertical counterpenetration have for the CILSS states? Like decolonization theory, counterdependency necessitates that the Sahel countries produce a commodity deemed critical to the donors. So far, the Sahel does not possess materials which could make such a strategy effective. The donors are not dependent on Sahelian exports of uranium, iron ore, or manganese. Therefore, unlike Zaire, South Africa, or Nigeria, the CILSS states hold no economic leverage.

Secondly, counterpenetration is a less than feasible strategy because the Sahel's primary concern is aid, rather than trade. The impoverishment of the region and its need for substantial amounts of official development assistance places it in a more vulnerable position, economically speaking, vis-à-vis the donors.

Perhaps, the model could be applied to aid sources. Here again, the Sahel is at a disadvantage. Diversification does not automatically reduce dependency. Although aid flows from France have declined, aid relations are confined to a few OECD countries. The Sahel receives approximately 55 percent of its ODA from Western bilateral and multilateral sources. The percentage of aid coming from OPEC, the United Nations, and other organizations is quite small.

The discussion so far has been limited to approaches to North-South relations which acknowledge the gains to be won by developing states. On the other side, dependency offers a more pessimistic view of the South's bargaining power.

Dependency theory originated from critiques of neo-classical development theory. One of the earliest dependency proponents, Andre Gunder Frank, began his investigation of the causes of underdevelopment within Latin America as a result of dissatisfaction with ECLA´s promotion of import substitution development models (62).

Dependency theory challenges modernization and development theory in several ways. Modernization theory placed the blame for underdevelopment on internal factors--a lack of modern entrepreneurial classes, a reliance upon traditional methods of problem solving, a shortage of modern political structures, to name a few. Dependency theory, on the other hand, looked at the external factors which inhibited development in Third World countries. Dependency theory chose to examine the interplay between the internal and international structures, using the tools of class analysis to explain why development did not occur.

Early criticisms of dependency centered on its simplistic analysis of events in the Third World. Since then, the works of Cardoso and Faletto and others have contributed a more dynamic interpretation of North-South interactions (63).

While dependency has made an important contribution to understanding Third World realities by interjecting the concepts of hegemony, class, and core-periphery relations, the theory is not without its shortcomings. For one thing, dependency theory is sometimes guilty of simple determinism in that it does not acknowledge the potential gains that Third World states can achieve from cooperation with the North. Events since 1974 support Zartman and those who posit that the South holds some economic leverage over the North (64).

In essence, the weakness of the dependency analysis rests upon its failure to grant a degree of autonomy within developing nations. The Third World is viewed as a supine force in North-South relations, unable to reject or mold Western influences to suit its own needs.

The contending approaches to poverty and underdevelopment in Africa were characterized by disputes over ways in which to solve those problems. The World Bank´s Accelerated Development in Sub-Saharan Africa, known as the Berg Report, and the Organization of African Unity´s, Lagos Plan of Action for the Economic Development of Africa exemplify the dispute over the methods needed to stimulate economic growth in Africa.

Alarmed at the economic deterioration within the continent, a group of African finance ministers requested that the World Bank undertake a report to identify and to suggest solutions to Africa´s crisis (65). The World Bank´s analysis placed the responsibility squarely on the African states themselves. In brief, the Bank argued that improper policies led to conditions such as an overextended public sector, the reliance on biases against exports, the lack of incentives to encourage peasants to produce, the weak private sector, import controls, and distorted industrial development which were at the root of the economic crisis in Africa (66). To meet this crisis, the Bank´s suggestions for policy reforms included: an outward-looking (export-oriented) development strategy, a greater reliance on the private sec-tor, the dismantling of the massive public sector, greater attention paid to agriculture (especially export crops), and the reduction of export biases and import controls (67).

A different response to Africa´s crisis was offered by the Lagos Plan of Action. The Plan originated from a series of meetings bringing together African Ministers of Planning, techni-cians, development experts, and representatives of other ministries (68). An initial document, the Monrovia Declaration, was issued in July 1979, and offered a skeletal analysis. Building upon this work, the OAU issued a second document in 1980 which described in greater detail a strategy to achieve the goals of the Monrovia Declaration (69). In its analysis of the origins of the problems and the solutions to resolve them, the Lagos Plan of Action departed in every way from the Berg Report. Unlike the Berg Report, the Plan placed the major blame for Africa´s stagnation upon external forces: dependency, declining terms of trade, commodity price fluctuations, high interest rates and inflation within developed countries. Naturally, the policy prescriptions of the Lagos Plan of Action were quite unlike those proposed by the Berg Report. Rather than pursue an export-oriented development strategy, the Lagos Plan of Action called for some disengagement from the world economy through regional and continental collective self-reliance schemes. Furthermore, the Plan advocated that increased attention be paid to the production of food crops, the development of industry linked to Africa´s resource base, and increased aid (70).

In two recent articles, Shaw argued that approaches to the solution of Africa´s problems can be divided into two theoretical camps, the nationalist camp and the internationalist camp (71). The nationalists tend to be the more radical states which favor a strategy of self-reliance and African collectivism. This nationalist group, exemplified by Tanzania, Angola, Ethiopia, and Mozambique, leans more toward the development strategy outlined in the Lagos Plan of Action (72). On the other side, the internationalists adhere to policies which promote the linkage of African economies to the world economy. Countries such as Kenya, Nigeria, Ivory Coast, and Egypt favor the policy proposals of the Berg Report (73). The weakness of this argument is reflected in the fact that the CILSS countries have not chosen between the Berg Report or the Lagos Plan of Action, but are pursuing both strategies simultaneously. In sum, the CILSS/Club du Sahel framework works at internationalist and nationalist policies.

THE FORMATION OF CILSS AND THE CLUB DU SAHEL

CILSS in the Early Years

At the March 1973 meeting attended by Senegal, Burkina Faso, Mali, Mauritania, and Niger, the Ministers of Rural Development formed a committee to coordinate the actions to be taken against the drought (74). They proposed that the Heads of State adopt a common emergency program to confront the effects of the drought, including action in the areas of livestock, agriculture, pastoral hydraulics, food security stocks, transportation, and reforestation. The ministers also suggested that studies on tropical climate, drought, and rainfall be conducted. The March gathering was the organizational meeting of CILSS. In a following meeting in September 1973, the Heads of State officially created the Comité per-

manent Inter-états de Lutte contre la Sécheresse
dans le Sahel.

Thus, CILSS was launched. In addition to the
five signatories, Chad is considered a founding
member, though it was not present at the March
meeting. In addition to the six original members,
two nations subsequently joined--Gambia in December 1973 and Cape Verde in March 1976. The ninth
member, Guinea-Bissau, joined in January 1986.

The Heads of State expanded CILSS´ role by
endorsing the idea that the organization would
coordinate short-term relief efforts as well as
formulate medium- and long-term development. A
list of 123 priority projects was agreed upon.
The Ouagadougou Programme, as it was called, comprised a variety of national and regional projects
in agriculture, livestock, forestry, and water
resources, and carried a price tag estimated at $3
billion. During the September meeting, the estimate was lowered to $1 billion when representa-
tives of the donor community suggested that CILSS
should determine aid levels which the donors could
consider feasible (75).

The emergence of CILSS was heralded as a
unique concept in regionalism. For the first
time, donors seemed willing to participate in an
aid program aimed at food self-sufficiency and
drought control, rather than aid programs geared
towards the industrial sector. Previously, donor
aid committees concentrated in the areas of infrastructural investments in order to exploit and
export natural resources and cash crops (76).

From the African perspective, CILSS was unlike other African regional economic organizations
in that it put aside such issues as trade and
investment in the industrial areas to tackle the
gnawing and stubborn problems of basic human needs
in the rural areas. The uniqueness of CILSS was
due, on the one hand, to the fact that it was
created to grapple with the consequences of a
single historic event--the drought. On the other
hand, CILSS´ uniqueness was a result of its inception at a particular juncture which was
characterized by changing African perceptions of
forms regionalism should take.

The initial burst of interest for the Sahel
did not elicit massive contributions from the

92

donors. Two years after its creation, CILSS, unable to achieve much in the way of funding for the Ouagadougou Programme, was floundering and on the brink of collapse. At the second conference of the Heads of State, held in Dakar in December 1975, it was noted that only 28 projects (22 percent) had been funded.

While sympathetic to the plight of the Sahelians, the donor community had not translated their sympathy or concern into resources for CILSS. Although donors within the advanced Western nations supported CILSS´ efforts, they did not, on the whole, believe CILSS was in a position "...to offer the expected framework for coopera- tion and implementation of actions between donors and recipients." (77). The major Western donors agreed that a lack of political will and political difficulties among the members would brake CILSS´ effectiveness.

Despite these reservations, consultations among high level American and French officials (Samuel Adams and David Shear both of USAID and Jean Audibert, the French Minsiter of Overseas Cooperation) resulted in the agreement that aid to the region should not fall below the pre-drought levels (78). Moreover, these officials believed that some type of global arrangement, uniting donors and recipients, was the key to solving the Sahel´s problems, problems which required sus- tained, costly and unified action. From these talks, the concept of a donor-Sahelian organiza- tion emerged.

The Creation of the Club du Sahel

In March 1975, Maurice Williams, who, at the time, was chairman of the Development Assistance Committee (DAC) of the OECD, presented the idea of a Club des Amis du Sahel at the CILSS Third Coun- cil of Ministers meeting. Williams stressed the notion of the Club as an informal, loosely-struc- tured organization, uniting donors and Sahelians to support CILSS´ goals.

Initially, the Council of Ministers and CILSS were less than enthusiastic about the creation of a parallel donor group. Resistance to the idea of a Club des Amis du Sahel arose from fears that it would usurp CILSS´ activities. At the Third Council of Ministers meeting, the Rural Development ministers, expressing the sentiments of their governments and CILSS, declared that donors should endow CILSS with sufficient means to carry out its tasks, rather than create an overlapping and competing organization.

To win support for the idea, the OECD, in the fall of 1975, organized a series of missions to brief the Sahel governments. During these missions to the Sahel capitals, OECD officials emphasized that the formation of the Club would increase donor participation and contributions (79).

At the Fifth Council of Ministers meeting in March 1976, the Club des Amis du Sahel was officially endorsed by the Rural Development ministers. To assuage CILSS´ fears, it was agreed that the Club

> ...would be informal, flexible, and would act to facilitate exchange and cooperation on a broad front at the request and initiation of the Sahel governments...Concerning its functions, the Club was not intended as a means to develop strategies nor to set policies or priorities...The Club would not act to determine needs. Rather it would be the instrument in bringing to fruition a fuller donor response to those needs as identified by the Sahel governments and their designated governmental agent, the CILSS (80).

Consultations between OECD officials, CILSS, and the Sahel governments led to agreement on the Club´s functions: 1) to suppport the work of the CILSS Executive Secretariat by informing the international community of Sahelian needs, 2) to help maintain a dialogue on priorities for medium- and long-term development, 3) to facilitate the mobilization of financial resources to carry out the dialogue, and finally, 4) to foster cooperation among donors for the implementation of actions requested by CILSS and the Sahel governments (81).

The Club du Sahel (the "des Amis" was soon

dropped) held its constitutive meeting in Dakar in
March 1976. Since the Club´s mandate decreed that
donors and Sahelians participate on an equal
basis, the first meeting was co-chaired by the
Presidents of Senegal, Leopold Senghor, and Mauritania, Mouktar Ould Daddah and the chairman of the
DAC, Maurice Williams.

Membership in the Club was opened to all the
Sahel states and any government or institution
having an interest in the development of the Sahel. Regular participants in the Club´s activities are the CILSS states, CILSS, twelve bilateral
and eight multilateral donor groups. Involvement
in the periodic Club du Sahel conferences is
greater--at the Fourth Club du Sahel Conference
held in November 1980, seventeen bilateral and
twenty-eight multilateral organizations attended.

One of the first tasks assigned to the Club
was the organization of the working groups necessary to ascertain the problems of rural development and to propose a strategy and program through
which to overcome those problems. Ten working
groups were created: four in the production areas
(livestock, irrigated agriculture, dryland
agriculture, and fisheries) and five in the
supporting services areas (human resources,
transport, marketing-price-storage, ecology, and
technology). The tenth, the Synthesis Group, was
given the task of assuring coherence between projects in the production and supporting services in
order to avoid the situation whereby the activities of one group impacted negatively on the
activities of another.

The document for a Sahel development program,
put together by the working groups working closely
with the CILSS governments, was approved of and
adopted by donors and Sahelians. The strategy
comprised three generations covering development
in the short-, medium-, and long-terms.

The short-term program, known as the First
Generation, spanned a five-year period (1977-
1982), and comprised 612 national and regional
projects. Within a few years, the list grew to
714 projects, raising the estimated cost of the
FGP from $3.1 to over $4.2 billion. Since its
creation, the Club du Sahel has devoted most of
its efforts to securing donor funding for the

projects of the First Generation Program.

The Club du Sahel is housed within the OECD in Paris. The small secretariat is run by four staff members (from France, the United States, the Netherlands and Canada) who collaborate with the donors in carrying out CILSS´ activities and goals. In addition to the time spent looking for donor funding for projects, the Club holds periodic conferences, donors meetings, and sectoral meetings which are chaired jointly by Sahelians and non-Sahelians.

The Club du Sahel depicts itself as a model of North-South cooperation. To emphasize this point, the Club Secretariat readily compares the animosity between North and South found in other international arenas (for example, UNCTAD and the CIEC) with the cooperation said to exist between Sahelians and donors.

But to what extent does cooperation exist within the CILSS/Club du Sahel framework? Certainly the formation of the Club was not a cooperative venture as Sahelian reluctance to accept the idea attests. In reality, the creation of the Club had less to do with the donors´ assessment of Sahelian capabilities and more to do with the national interests of the donors, particularly the Americans. Any analysis of the Club´s formation must be placed in the context of global economic and political realities at the time of its creation.

CONSOLIDATION OF DONOR INTERESTS

The creation of the Club du Sahel united donor interests at a time when North-South relations were strained. The disappointing results of two Development Decades, the emerging power of OPEC, and the South´s dissatisfaction with the global economic system led to the call for a restructing of the world economy. Furthermore, the growing dependence of the North on the South for raw materials and markets added fuel to the NIEO fire. The South´s economic challenge threatened to undermine the policies and the economic order erected by the United States and its allies after World War II.

The United Nations became the locus of bitter economic debates. No longer could Northern interests take precedence in bodies dominated by Third World voting blocs.

Thus, it was not by accident that the idea of the Club originated within the bosom of the OECD. As Western hegemony seemed to decline in the United Nations, other international fora took on increased roles as the focal points of Western decision-making. Examples of this included the Trilateral Commission and the resurgence of activity within the OECD. Both organizations enabled the United States and its allies to harmonize policies in order to face rising Third World demands for economic reform. The Club, housed within the OECD, provided the donors with a vehicle in which discussions of economic reform and Sahelian development could be carried out in a Western-dominated setting (82).

Proponents of the NIEO accused the West of being indifferent to the plight of the Third World. The creation of the Club enabled the donors to refute these charges of indifference, and served a second donor interest. Through the Club mechanism, the donors could join with the most affected nations and demonstrate, therefore, their concern for the developing world (83).

For the Americans, other considerations made the formation of the Club attractive. Traditionally, most of the Sahel, under French influence, had long been inaccessible to the United States. French domination had effectively locked out American commercial and political interests. The drought opened the door for American penetration and the Club ensured Americans of a continued role in the development of the region.

American geopolitical concerns could also be advanced through the Club. In the fall of 1975, Soviet and Cuban activity in Angola raised the specter of Communism throughout Africa. A convergence of opinion among governmental and congressional officials held that increasing American aid to Africa would help to counter Soviet and Cuban gains and prevent the establishement of revolutionary African regimes (84). In light of Soviet gains in Southern Africa, other regions of the continent assumed a more important place in

97

American geopolitical and military strategy. Political instability in the Sahel, the result of
the drought, could be exploited by the Soviets or
Cubans. The Ford Administration was determined to
foreclose any Soviet incursions in this region,
too.

In a related manner, the United States departure from Vietnam in the spring of 1975 left
hundreds of officials and development personnel
without employment. The creation of the Club and
growing American involvement in Africa opened the
door for these displaced USAID personnel. As the
USAID offices were being closed in Vietnam, the
opening of consulates in several Sahelian capitals
provided continued employment for many (85).

American's growing need for strategic resources and potential markets placed the Sahel in
a more favorable position. Studies showed that
the region contained important quantities of uranium, phosphate, petroleum, manganese, iron ore,
and other vital resources. It is also believed
that the Sahel contains unknown, but important,
quantities of many other strategic and vital resources. The exploration for much of the Sahel's
wealth has only recently begun. Geopolitical and
economic concerns dictated that Americans involve
themselves in the development of the Sahel in
order to benefit from its resources.

Another factor which encouraged U.S. participation in the Club du Sahel was the importance it
would have for Black Americans. Several influen-
tial Black leaders (former Congressman Charles
Diggs; development expert C. Payne Lucas; and
USAID official, Dr. Samuel Adams) were instrumental in urging the Nixon and Ford Adminstrations to
address the concerns of Black Americans in formulating American foreign policy toward Africa. The
Congressional Black Caucus pushed these
administrations to do more for the Sahel than
drought relief; it favored a long-term commitment
to the region. By increasing U.S. involvement in
the Sahel, these administrations could appeal to
the Black voters and Black opinion makers.

Finally, humanitarian concerns played a role
in growing American involvement in the Sahel and
in the creation of the Club du Sahel. American
officials felt that the Sahel needed a long-term

international effort to help these countries
develop in order to avoid future droughts (86).
Secretary of State Kissinger believed it was
better to provide funding which would help to
stabilize the Sahel rather than to face future
drought and related problems ten years in the
future (87).

In sum, a convergence of issues and interests
led to the formation of the Club du Sahel. American and European donors saw an opportunity to
advance their own interests within the CILSS/Club
du Sahel framework. Through partnership the major
Western donors could portray themselves as willing
to compromise on issues important to developing
countries, and at the same time influence those
very issues more successfully.

It would be erroneous to think that the donors were the only ones to gain from the creation
of the Club. The Sahelian governments could
advance their own interests, although this was not
immediately apparent to them.

CONSOLIDATION OF SAHELIAN INTERESTS

The drought and the subsequent international
attention given to the area put the Sahel on the
map. Aid levels to the Sahel rose substantially.
Assistance to the Sahel (bilateral and
multilateral) totalled $800 million between 1952
and 1972 (88). Between 1974 and 1979, total official development assistance (ODA) to the Sahel
jumped to $6,053 billion (89).

The drought touched off political problems
for all of the Sahel governments, even to the
extent of contributing to the overthrow of the
Diori regime in Niger. Increased donor aid provided the governments with a measure of economic
stability and political legitimacy. Aid--and food
aid in particular--helped to minimize the political and social tensions which resulted from food
deficits and low food and livestock prices. Aid
could be used by the governments to diffuse the
serious threats to their stability.

In addition to addressing the interests of
the governments in maintaining legitimacy, there
was a second need which the Club fulfilled. The

strategy and program for drought control
concentrated efforts on rural development, a
sector neglected by many African states. Even
though agriculture comprises the largest
proportion of the GNP and employs the largest
segment of the population, the extracted surplus
is not reinvested in the rural areas, but is
siphoned off to pay the burgeoning costs of
government bureaucracies and services in the urban
areas (90).

Rural investment accounts for the majority of
investment expenditures, but per capita expenditures favor those who reside in urban areas. Riha
in his study of Francophone Africa found a strong
positive relationship between urban population
size and government expenditure such that the
distribtuion of expenditures is skewed to favor
"...the urban and a few privileged rural areas,
while vast areas of the country, where the majority of population resides were...completely ignored" (91).

In addition, the tendency to favor the urban
sector exacerbates the rural-town migration. As
more individuals pour into the urban areas, the
demand for greater government expenditures in the
urban areas also rises (92). The creation of
CILSS and the Club du Sahel highlighted the importance of increasing the resources granted to the
rural sectors in order to expand output. While
governments have traditionally paid lip service to
the development of the rural sectors, they have
failed to follow through with resources.
Increasingly, domestic financing of rural
investment projects, especially of food crops, has
declined. One study of domestic financing of the
agricultural sector in Gambia revealed that the
government devoted fewer of its own resources to
this sector, preferring to rely on external aid
(93). In a 1981 USDA report of agricultural prospects in Africa, it was noted that Mali and Niger
expected that 80 percent and 60 percent of their
agricultural plans would be paid for out of
foreign asssistance (94). To sum up, the Club du
Sahel has facilitated increased aid to the rural
sectors, enabling the governments to put their own
resources into other sectors.

CONCLUSION

The creation of CILSS and the Club du Sahel occured at a specific historical juncture which dictated the acknowledgment of certain needs and objectives. The drought, the catalyzing agent, motivated donors and Sahelians to form these two international organizations to confront the changing political and economic realities. Through the Club and CILSS, both donors and Sahelians could pursue their own national interests. Gains could be maximized with a minimum of sacrifice: the donors could pursue geopolitical, economic, and humanitarian goals; the Sahelians could realize rural development without the costs.

The goal of the Club and CILSS is to foster cooperation in order to help the region overcome problems of drought and underdevelopment. Both parties readily stress the cooperation existing between North and South within this framework. Thus, CILSS and the Club offer the researcher the opportunity to examine North-South and South-South cooperation simultaneously. How much cooperation has been achieved? Who benefits from this cooperation?

In the following three chapters I will examine cooperation as measured by donor and Sahelian support for staffing, functions and operations, contributions, and project investment. How much money do Sahelians and donors place at CILSS' and the Club's disposal? How much are CILSS' policies and procedures supported (in terms of resources) by both sides? Which types of projects are more willingly funded by donors and Sahelians? What can be said about aid levels to the Sahel before and after the droughts?

In measuring the cooperation achieved, what theories of North-South cooperation are supported or rejected? What can be said about the three models using CILSS as a case study? Is interest convergence or divergence the norm between donors and Sahelians? Finally, what are the limits to North-South cooperation using this framework?

By the same token, what level of cooperation has been achieved among the governments of the region? Has there been more willingness to support regional rather than national interests. In what areas have the Sahel states grown more supportive of CILSS?

NOTES

1. William J. Foltz, From French West Africa to the Mali Federation (New Haven: Yale University Press, 1979), p. 8.

2. Chimelu Chime, Integration and Politics Among African States (Uppsala: Scandanavian Insitute of African Studies, 1977), pp. 122-126.

3. Johan Galtung, "A Structural Theory of Imperialism," The African Review, 1, No. 4 (1972), pp. 93-138.

4. For works on integration theory, see Ernst Haas, The Uniting of Europe, 2nd ed. (Stanford: Stanford University Press, 1968); Karl W. Deutsch, Political Community and the North Atlantic Area, (Princeton, 1957); Adebayo Adediji, "Prospects of Regional Economic Cooperation in West Africa," The Journal of Modern African Studies, 8, No. 2 (1980), pp. 213-232; Abdul Jalloh, Political Integration in French Speaking Africa (Berkeley: University of California Press, 1973); Joseph S. Nye, ed., International Regionalism (Boston: Little Brown, 1968); Philippe C. Schmitter, Autonomy or Dependence as Regional Outcomes: Central America (Berkeley: University of California Press, 1972); and Phillip Taylor, Nonstate Actors in International Politics: From Transregional to Substate Organizations (Boulder: Westview, 1984), Chapter 3.

5. Chime, pp. 35 and 49.

6. Harold K. Jacobson, Networks of Interdependence (New York: Alfred A. Knopf, 1979), pp. 67-68.

7. B.W.T. Mutharika, Toward Multinational Economic Cooperation in Africa (New York: Praeger Publishers, 1972), p. 13.

8. Networks of Interdependence, p. 226.

9. Foltz, p. 178.

10. Chime, p. 150.

11. Togo joined in 1966; the other four in

1959.
    12. Virginia Thompson, West Africa´s Council
of the Entente (Ithaca: Cornell University Press,
1972), p. 266 and Mutharika, pp. 286-289.
    13. Mutharika, p. 26 and Michael P. Todaro,
Economic Development in the Third World (London:
Longman Group, 1977), pp. 315-316.
    14. Schmitter, previously cited. See also
Michael Teubal, "The Failure of Latin America´s
Economic Integration," Latin America: Reform or
Revolution?, ed. James Petras and Maurice Zeitlin
(Greenwich: Fawcett Publications, 1968), pp. 120-
144.
    15. Lynn K. Mytelka, "Foreign Aid and Regional
Integration: The UDEAC Case," Journal of Common
Market Studies, Vol. 12 (1973), pp. 138-158.
    16.   The figures are derived from United
Nations trade data found in various years of the
United Nations publication, Yearbook of Interna-
tional Trade Statistics (New York: United
Nations).
    17. Data for Cape Verde are for the years
1969-1975 and for Senegal from 1969-1980. Again,
the source is the United Nations, Yearbook of
International Trade Statistics, various years.
    18. The data for Chad are from the years 1969-
1975, for Cape Verde from 1969-1975, and for Gam-
bia from 1969-1977. The source is the same as the
above.
    19. World Bank, World Development Report 1985
(Washington, D.C., 1985), p. 192.
    20. Ibid.
    21.   Constantine V. Vaitsos, "Crisis in
Regional Economic Cooperation (Integration) Among
Developing Countries: A Survey," World Develop-
ment, Vol. 6 (1978), pp. 719-769; W. Andrew Axline
and Lynn K. Mytelka, "Sociétés Multinationales Et
Intégration Régionale Dans Le Group Andin Et Dans
La Communauté des Caraibes," Etudes Interna-
tionales, Vol. 7 (1976), pp. 163-192; and Arthur
Hazelwood, "The End of the East African Community:
What are the Lessons for Regional Integration
Schemes?" Journal of Common Market Studies, Vol.
18, (1979), pp. 40-58.
    22. Todaro, p. 205.
    23. At the 1985 Council of the Entente´s
summit meeting, it was decided that the group

103

would now devote its activities to improving rural populations.

24. Ervin Laszlo, Robert Baker, Jr., Elliot Eisenberg, and Venkata Ramon, The Objectives of the New International Economic Order (New York: Pergamon Press, 1978).

25. Jahangir Amuegar, "The North-South Dialogue: From Conflict to Compromise," Foreign Affairs, 54, No. 3 (1976), p. 550 and Branislav Gosovic and John Ruggie, "On the Creation of a New International Economic Order : Issue Linkage and the Seventh Special Session of the U.N. General Assembly," International Organization, 30, No. 2 (1976), p. 514.

26. C. Fred Bergsten, "The Threat From the Third World," Foreign Policy, No. 22 (1973), pp. 102-124. See also the work by Anthony J. Dolman, ed., Reshaping the International Order, A Report to the Club of Rome (New York: E.P. Dutton and Company, 1976).

27. Samir Amin, "Self-Reliance and the New International Economic Order," Monthly Review, 29, No. 3 (1977), pp. 1-21 and Immanuel Wallerstein, "An Historical Perspective on the Emergence of the New Interntional Order: Economic, Political, Cultural Aspects," The Capitalist World-Economy, essays by Immanuel Wallerstein (Cambridge: Cambridge University Press, 1979), pp. 269-282.

28. Robert L. Rothstein, "The North-South Dialogue: The Political Economy of Immobility," Journal of International Affairs, 34, No. 1 (1980), pp. 1-17.

29. Daniel P. Moynihan vigorously argued that the Third World has only itself to blame for its poor economic condition. See his article, "The United States in Opposition," in At Issue: Politics in the World Arena, second edition, ed., Steven L. Spiegel (New York: St. Martin's Press, 1977), pp. 87-111.

30. Nathanial Leff, "The New Economic Order--Bad Economics, Worse Politics," Foreign Policy, No. 24 (1976), pp. 202-217.

31. Sidney Weintraub, "The New International Economic Order: The Beneficiaries," World Development, 7, No. 3 (1979), pp. 247-258 and Roger D. Hansen, "The Political Economy of North-South Relations: How Much Change?," International

Organization, 29, No. 4 (1975), pp. 921-948.

32. Bergsten, pp. 120-124 and Richard N. Cooper, "A New International Order for Mutual Gain," Foreign Policy, No. 26 (1977), pp. 117-120.
33. Samir Amin, previously cited and Johan Galtung, "The Lomé Convention and Neo-Colonialism," The African Review, 6, No. 1 (1976), pp. 32-42.
34. Branislav Gosovic, UNCTAD: Conflict and Compromise (Leiden: A.W. Sijthoff International Publishing, 1972), p. 7.
35. Jacobson, P. 297.
36. Joan Edelman Spero, The Politics of International Economic Relations (New York: St. Martin's Press, 1977), p. 35.
37. Ibid, p. 37.
38. Ibid, pp. 47-50.
39. S.D. Muni, "The Paris-Dialogue on International Economic Cooperation: The North's Strategy and the Outcome," Foreign Affair Reports, 26, No. 10 (1977), p. 209.
40. Joining the EEC, Japan, and the United States were Canada, Spain, Sweden, Australia, and Switzerland.
41. The twelve new participants included: Indonesia, Iraq, Nigeria, Peru, Yugoslavia, Mexico, Egypt, Cameroon, Argentina, Jamaica, Zambia, and Pakistan.
42. The CIEC agenda is discussed in Muni, pp. 205-223; Gerard Tardy, "Development," Europe and the North-South Dialogue, ed. Wolfgang Wessels (Paris: The Atlantic Institute for International Affairs, 1978), pp. 63--73; and Amuzegar, pp. 547-562.
43. High-income countries are defined by Weintraub as those with annual per capita incomes greater than $500.
44. Poor developing nations were those with per capita incomes of less than $200; middle-income developing countries were defined as those in the range of $200-$500.
45. C. Dodoo and R. Kuster, "The Road to Lomé," The Lomé Convention and a New International Economic Order, ed. Frans A.M. Alting von Geusau (Leyden: A. W. Sijthoff International Publishing, 1977), p. 30.
46. The original 18 African members were :

Benin, Burkina Faso, Burundi, Cameroon, the Congo, Central African Republic, Chad, Gabon, Guinea, Ivory Coast, Madagascar, Mali, Mauritania, Niger, Rwanda, Senegal, Togo, and Zaire. In 1972, Mauritius joined to become the nineteenth member. Lomé I added the following nations: the Bahamas, Barbados, Botswana, Ethiopia, Equatorial Guinea, Fiji, Gambia, Ghana, Grenada, Guyana, Guinea Bissau, Kenya, Lesotho, Liberia, Malawi, Nigeria, Sierre Leone, Somalia, Sudan, Swaziland, Tanzania, Tonga, Trinidad and Tobago, Uganda, Western Samoa, and Zambia. Lomé II, signed in 1979, added eleven other states: Cape Verde, Comoro Islands, Djibouti, Dominique, Papua New Guinea, Sao Tome and Principe, Seychelles, Saint Lucia, Solomon Islands, Surinam, and Tuvalu.

47. A copy of the Convention's articles of agreement can be found in von Geusau, pp. 197-224.

48. Isebill V. Gruhn, "The Lomé Convention: inching towards independence," International Organization, 30, No. 2 (1976), p. 255.

49. Galtung, p. 40 and Lynn K. Mytelka and Steven Langdon, "Africa in the Changing World Economy," African in the 1980s, eds. Colin Legum, I. William Zartman, Lynn K. Mytelka, and Steven Langdon, (New York: McGraw-Hill Book Company, 1979), p. 197.

50. John Ravenhill, "What is to be done for Third World commodity exporters? An evaluation of the STABEX scheme," International Organization, 38, No. 3 (1984), pp. 537-574.

51. Chapter 2, Article 19 of the Convention.

52. See Zartman's article in Foreign Affairs.

53. See Zartman's article in Africa in the 1980s.

54. Ibid, pp. 100-101.

55. Ibid, p. 101.

56. United Nations, 1977 Yearbook of International Trade Statistics, Volume I (New York: United Nations, 1978), pp. 629 and 975.

57. Ibid, pp. 629, 705, and 975.

58. Quoted in Pearl T. Robinson, "The Political Context of Regional Development in the Sahel," The Journal of Modern African Studies, 18, No. 4 (1978), p. 592.

59. World Development Report 1985, p. 196 and World Bank, Toward Sustained Development in Sub-

Saharan Africa (Washington, D.C.: World Bank, 1984), p. 66.

60. Ibid.

61. Ali A. Mazrui, The African Condition (London: Heineman, Ltd., 1980), p. 84.

62. David Booth, "Andre Gunder Frank: An Introduction and Appreciation," Beyond the Sociology of Development, eds. Ivar Oxaal, Tony Barnett, and David Booth (London: Routledge and Kegan Paul Ltd., 1975), pp. 61-69.

63. Later works sought to explain this process using a variety of theoretical constructs: exchange theory--Arghiri Emmanuel, Unequal Exchange: A Study of the Imperialism of Trade (London: New Left Books, 1972); the world-system approach--Immanuel Wallerstein, The Capitalist World-Economy (Cambridge: Cambridge University Press, 1979); modes of production analysis-- Mahmood Mamdani, Politics and Class Formation in Uganda (New York: Monthly Review Press, 1976) and Aidan Foster-Carter, "Can We Articulate 'Articulation'?" The New Economic Anthropology, ed. John Clammer (New York: St. Martin's Press, 1978), pp. 212-242; peripheral capitalism--Samir Amin, Imperialism and Unequal Development (New York: Monthly Review Press, 1976); and neo-dependency-- F.H. Cardoso, and E. Falletto, Dependency and Development in Latin America (Berkeley: University of California Press, 1979).

64. For a critique of dependency theory, see: Timothy M. Shaw and Malcolm J. Grieve, "Dependence as an Approach to Understanding Continuing Inequalities in Africa," The Journal of Developing Areas, 13, No. 3 (1979), pp. 229-246.

65. Robert S. Browne and Robert J. Cummings, The Lagos Plan of Action vs. The Berg Report (Washington, D.C.: African Studies and Research Program, Howard University, 1984), p. 21.

66. World Bank, Accelerated Development in Sub-Saharan Africa (Washington, D.C.: World Bank, 1981), Chapters 4 and 5.

67. Browne and Cummings, pp. 39-47.

68. Ibid, p. 20.

69. Ibid, p. 12.

70. Ibid, pp. 39-47.

71. See the articles by Timothy M. Shaw, "The African Crisis: Alternative Development Strategies

for the Continent," Alternatives, No. 9 (1983), pp. 111-27 and "Debates About Africa´s Future: the Brandt, World Bank and Lagos Plan Blueprints," Third World Quarterly, 5, No. 2 (1983), pp. 330-44.

72. Shaw, "The African Crisis: Alternative Development Strategies for the Continent," p. 116.

73. Ibid.

74. In English the translation of CILSS is the Permanent Inter-state Committee for Drought Control in the Sahel.

75. Richard W. Franke and Barbara H. Chasin, Seeds of Famine (Montclair: Allanheld, Osmun, and Company, 1980), p. 135.

76. Robinson, p. 583.

77. OECD memorandum, February 4, 1975.

78. Robinson, p. 588.

79. OECD memorandum, October 25, 1975.

80. OECD, The Club des Amis du Sahel, Proposal of Purpose and Function (Paris: OECD, N.D.), p. 2. Also underlined in the original text.

81. USAID, Sahel Development Program, Annual Report to the Congress (Washington, D.C.: USAID, 1980), p. 10.

82. Robinson, pp. 589-90.

83. Ibid, pp. 590-92.

84. Franke and Chasin, p. 137 and Noel V. Lateef, Crisis in the Sahel: A Case Study in Development Cooperation (Boulder: Westview Press, Inc., 1980), p. 14.

85. From personal observations made in Ouagadougou, I noticed several USAID officials had tours in Vietnam.

86. Anne de Lattre and Arthur M. Fell, The Club Du Sahel: An Experiment in International Co-Operation (Paris: OECD, 1984), p. 41.

87. As told to me in a personal conversation with James M. Anderson, Assistant Director of USAID in Mali in June 1985.

88. Hal Sheets and Roger Morris, Disaster in the Desert (Washington, D.C.: The Carnegie Endowment for International Peace, 1974), p. 9.

89. CILSS/Club du Sahel, Official Development Assistance to CILSS Member Countries from 1975 to 1979, Volume I (Paris: OECD, 1980), p. 171.

90. Rita Cruise O´Brien, "Introduction," The Political Economy of Underdevelopment, ed. Rita

108

Cruise O´Brien (Beverly Hills: Sage Publications, 1979), p. 30.

91.   Thomas J. F. Riha, "Determinants of Government Expenditure: French-Speaking Countries of Africa South of the Sahara," The Philippine Review of Business and Economics, 11, No. 1 (1974), p. 47.

92. Riha, p. 49.

93.   OECD/CILSS/Club du Sahel, Development of Rainfed Agriculture in The Gambia (Paris: OECD, 1983), p. 79.

94.   USDA, Food Problems and Prospects in Sub-Saharan Africa (Washington, D.C.: USDA, 1981), p. 130.

4

The Structure of CILSS:
Administration and Operation

THE CILSS STRUCTURE

At the first meeting convened by the Sahelian
Heads of State in March 1973, the concept of CILSS
was approved. The five ministers, in declaring
the region a disaster area and in resolving to
promote all drought control efforts, felt that the
formation of a regional organization would aid in
the appeal for donor support. At the next
meeting, held in September 1973, the
organizational structure was established and Ouagadougou, Burkina Faso, was made the permanent
headquarters of CILSS. Admission criteria were
established: Any African nation could become a
member of CILSS if its agricultural and pastoral
economy were dominated by the ecological conditions of the Sudano-Sahelian zone, if it had been
declared a disaster zone, and if it were officially recognized as such. Apart from the six original members, eight nations--Guinea, Cape Verde,
Guinea-Bissau, Nigeria, Cameroon, Benin, Gambia,
and the Central African Republic--applied for
admission. Cape Verde, Gambia, and Guinea Bissau
were admitted: Gambia in 1973, Cape Verde in 1976,
and Guinea-Bissau in 1986.

At the September 1973 meeting CILSS was
charged with the following mandate: 1) the
coordination of regional activities to counter the
drought and its effects, 2) the sensitization of
the international community to the problems of the
drought, 3) the mobilization of resources to carry
out the drought control program defined by member

111

states, 4) the preparation of project proposals and the execution of certain activities of regional interest and cooperation, and 5) the provision of assistance to member states and existing agencies in the Sahel zone in looking for funding for their own programs (1).

To carry out the tasks assigned, the Sahelian presidents created an organizational structure comprised of the Conference of the Heads of State, the Council of Ministers, and the Executive Secretariat. The activities of each of these, as they were mandated at the time of CILSS´ inception, will be described in the following sections.

The Conference of the Heads of State

At the apex of CILSS is the Conference of the Heads of State, comprised of the nine Sahelian presidents. Initially, the statutes stipulated that it would meet periodically, but this was later modified and the Conference of the Heads of State meetings are convened biennially. The presidency has a two-year term and rotates among the nine members.

The duties of the Conference of the Heads of State are to set the broad lines and define the policies for drought control. At the meetings, the presidents review and determine policy and

Table 4.1
Presidents of the Conference of the Heads of State

Year	President	Nationality
1973-75	Aboubacar Sangoule Lamizana	Burkina Faso
1976-77	Mokhtar Ould Daddah	Mauritania
1978-79	Dawda Kairaba Jawara	Gambia
1980-81	Moussa Traore	Mali
1982-83	Aristides Maria Pereira	Cape Verde
1984-85	Seyni Kountche	Niger
1986-87	Abdou Diouf	Senegal

resolve special problems. Decisions for admission into the organization are granted by the Conference of the Heads of State.

Sangoule Lamizana, the former President of Burkina Faso, was selected as the first President of CILSS. After Lamizana's tenure ended, the Presidency devolved to six other Heads of State.

Council of Ministers

Beneath the Conference of the Heads of State is the Council of Ministers, made up of the Ministers of Rural Development from each member country. In December 1973, the Council of Ministers met to elaborate the tasks which had first been approved by the Conference of the Heads of State at the September 1973 meeting. The Council of Ministers laid the foundation which would direct CILSS' operations for the next four years. But as CILSS took on more activities, necessitated by the goals it had set for itself and the sheer volume of work to be accomplished, the existing organizational structure appeared inadequate. Therefore, at the Seventh Council of Ministers meeting held in April 1977, the Ministers approved of a new organizational structure.

After the reorganization several changes were made. Council meetings were regularized and the Council of Ministers was to convene twice a year. Later this was dropped to once a year. One minister is charged with the task of heading the Council of Ministers. Antoine Dakoure, Burkina Faso's Minister of Rural Development, was first selected for the position of Regional Coordinator. Following the reorganization, the title was changed to Minister Coordinator.

The Council has the primary task of determining the actions to be undertaken by CILSS. The Council's other tasks include: 1) reporting on the annual activities conducted by CILSS, 2) establishing the program required to realize project implementation, 3) assessing the progress made in executing the projects and programs selected for development, 4) reviewing the budget status and the audit report, and 5) approving the budget for the coming year (2).

113

TABLE 4.2
Minister Coordinators of the Council of Ministers

Year	Minister Coordinator	Nationality
1973-75	Antoine Dakoure	Burkina Faso
1976-77	Boulama Manga	Niger
	Moussa Bayere (a)	Niger
1978-79	Adrien Senghor	Senegal
	Djibril Sene (b)	Senegal
1980-81	Joao Pereira Silva	Cape Verde
1982-83	N´Fagnanama Kone	Mali
1984-85	Saihou Sabally	Gambia
1986-87	Messoud Ould Belkheir	Mauritania

(a)The coup d´etat that brought down the Diori regime led to Manga´s replacement by Moussa Bayere.

(b)In June 1979, Djibril Sene became the new Rural Development Minister of Senegal and consequently took over the role as the CILSS Minister Coordinator.

As the Chief Executive Officer of CILSS, the Minister Coordinator supervises the execution of the Council´s duties. The Minister Coordinator also represents CILSS at all national or international gatherings, and signs agreements on CILSS´ behalf. Although the Minister Coordinator is entitled by mandate to carry out the duties and operations of CILSS, in practice, such responsibilities are passed on to the Executive Secretary of CILSS, the chief operating officer of the organization.

The Executive Secretariat

The primary responsibility of the Executive Secretariat is to develop a coherent development strategy and program from the policies and decisions established by the Conference of the Heads of State and the Council of Ministers. Heading the Executive Secretariat is the Executive Secretary, selected by the Council of Ministers for a three-year term. The first Executive Secretary (originally called the Regional Advisor of the Technical Secretariat) was Ibrahima Konate who served until 1977. In 1977, Aly Cisse of Mali became the Executive Secretary until July 1980 when Seck Mane N´Diack of Mauritania took over. His term was followed by that of Mahamane Brah of Niger.

The Executive Secretary has a staff of technical advisors and experts to help execute the policy decisions of the Council of Ministers. These tasks are:

1) To prepare and carry out the resolutions of the Council of Ministers;

2) To prepare the projects and programs for drought control and development in the Sahel in collaboration with the national services;

3) To review and report on the status of the projects and programs adopted for implementation;

4) To prepare the preinvestment dossiers required to rehabilitate the drought affected areas in collaboration with the national services;

5) To seek and coordinate the bilateral and multilateral aid and assistance necessary to finance the projects and programs;

6) To formulate proposals for establishing a development policy and strategy which would re-establish ecological equilibrium between the natural resources of the Sahel and its human and animal populations;

7) To contribute to the enhanced operations of institutions created by CILSS for the attainment of the common objective within a regional framework, and also, to coordinate their activities; and,

8) To assure the close and constant coordination of the actions of CILSS with those of regional or sub-regional groups concerned with the Sahel, or to which CILSS member states are or shall become members (3).

After the Club du Sahel Secretariat was created in 1976, it joined with the CILSS Secretariat, the CILSS member countries, and the donors to develop short-, medium-, and long-term program for action. Donors and Sahelians spoke of a "contract for a generation". To work together for the development of the Sahel, the Club du Sahel and CILSS set up a Working Group, comprised of Sahelians and non-Sahelians, and coordinated by the CILSS Minister Coordinator (4). Meeting for the first time in June 1976, the Working Group created four teams to identify development programs in the four productive sectors--dryland agriculture, irrigated agriculture, fisheries, and livestock. The Working Group also organized experts to appraise the situation within the areas of human resources, technology transfer, transportation and infrastructure, ecology, and macro-agricultural policy (5). After conducting their investigations, the teams and experts were asked to present their findings to the CILSS Council of Ministers. From this undertaking, the experts were "...expected to progress towards a drought control strategy and to identify the approaches in different sectors which would lead to the objectives set by CILSS countries" (6). Their blueprint for a Sahelian development strategy, jointly approved by the CILSS Council of Ministers at its Seventh Meeting (in April 1977) and the Club du Sahel´s Second Conference (in June 1977), is known as the Strategy and Program for Drought Control and Development in the Sahel (7).

Linked to the strategy and program is a list of 714 national and regional projects to be

116

implemented.   This list of projects was developed
by   the   Sahelians who wanted some guarantee   that
donors would not withhold aid until a strategy for
drought control more to their liking was developed
(8).   The   First Generation Program, as this list
came   to   be called,   was to ensure that   Sahelian
efforts to develop and modify their policies would
not   go unfunded as the Ouagadougou Programme   had
been.   To expedite the realization of these   projects, donors and Sahelians initially granted them
a priority status. In addition to the implementation of the projects, other actions were to be put
into effect in the short-term. For example, CILSS
and the Club du Sahel constantly worked to improve
the   quality of data on the Sahel.   To this   end,
seminars,   colloquia, and meetings on the economic
and   social   conditions were conducted in   all   of
the strategy sectors.
    In   addition,   the   CILSS   Secretariat   was
authorized   to develop a strategy for the   medium-
term.   Plans   for   the   medium-term   development
effort entailed:

1) The inventory of existing or proposed projects
   in   the   region with recommendations for   their
   coordination   and development within   an   integrated   strategy   which would   optimize   investment;

2) The collection of data and facts required for
   the   further   study of action plans,   and also,
   for   the identification and formulation of   new
   projects;

3) The   establishment of a regional plan for the
   mobilization and coordination of assistance   in
   the event of another drought;

4) The proposal of a storage network of "security
   stocks"--food and seed to be strategically
   stored at the national level of each country as
   a reserve against future calamity;

5) The   design of a production and distribution
   policy for selected high yield seeds which are
   well adapted to the local soil and climatological conditions;

117

6) The study of the impact of the drought on the animal and forage resources in order to establish a regional program for the restoration of herds and the reclamation of pasture lands;

7) The definition of a policy that would assure an adequate supply of water on a permanent basis for both the human and animal populations of the Sahel (9).

Programs and activities which required either a long germination period or exhorbitant costs were included in the long-term development strategy:

1) Sponsorship of further studies on climatology, including the use of satellite imagery and remote sensing;

2) Assistance in the establishment of studies leading to an effective and ecologically sound use of pasture lands, especially in the Sahelian zone;

3) Coordination of the development of appropriate hydro-agriculture projects, including village and pastoral hydraulics, as well as river basin control and irrigation schemes;

4) Continuation of anti-desertification measures by coordinating activities in reforestation, environmental protection, land management and the eduction of the rural inhabitants (10).

In total, the tasks which CILSS and the Club selected to carry out were to span three periods. The short-term extended from 1977-1982. The medium-term strategy was to cover the period from 1983-1990 and was to build upon the work of the First Generation Program. In the final phase, from 1990-2000, it was hoped that the machinery for food self-sufficiency and a self-sustaining economic development would be in place.

To fulfill the tasks required of the three development strategies, four divisions were created within the Executive Secretariat. Technical experts (Sahelian and non-Sahelian) were

to oversee the implementation of the drought
control strategy. The divisions of the Executive
Secretariat are: the Division of Administrative
and Financial Affairs (DAF), the Division of Docu-
mentation and Information (DDI), the Division of
Relations with Non-Governmental Organizations
(ONG), and the Division of Projects and Programs
(DPP).

Division of Administrative and Financial Affairs

The Division of Administrative and Financial
Affairs is charged with the following duties:

1) To assist the Executive Secretary in the preparation and execution of the budget;

2) To administer and manage the personnel and the
   implementation of the regulations relative to
   the personnel;

3) To study the wide range of administrative and
   financial questions faced by CILSS; and

4) To manage the durable goods of CILSS (11).

To accomplish these tasks, the head of the
DAF was assisted by the CILSS auditor, who, by
statute, could not be of the same nationality as
the DAF Division Chief or the Executive Secretary.
In addition to the management of the regular
budget, the DAF is also responsible for the operations of three special funds: the Sahel Special
Fund, the Reserve Fund, and the CILSS Building
Construction Fund, all created by resolutions of
the CILSS Council of Ministers.
The Sahel Special Fund provides money for: 1)
emergency help in case of new calamities; 2) emergency operations for the fight against crop and
harvest pests in case of massive invasions; 3)
CILSS project studies; and 4) the financing of
projects of a regional interest. The resources
for the fund come from exceptional contributions
of the member states, gifts, subsidies, loans, and
diverse receipts.
The Reserve Fund was created for the payment

119

of expenses decided upon by the CILSS Council of Ministers. The resources of the Reserve Fund come from budgetary surpluses of preceding fiscal years.

The CILSS Building Construction Fund was created to finance the construction of a central headquarters to house all of the CILSS Secretariat staff who were located in four separate buildings. This spatial separation necessitated an inordinate amount of travel time to and from the various buildings.

Division of Documentation and Information

In addition to the Division of Administrative and Financial Affairs there is the Division of Documentation and Information. Assisting the chief of the DDI are four staff persons who worked as archivists, translators, and documentation-alists. The tasks assigned to this unit are: 1) the collection, classification, and the diffusion of all documentation relative to the problems of the Sahelian and Sudano-Sahelian zones; 2) the classification and the conservation of the ar-chives of the Executive Secretariat; 3) publicity and information aimed at reinforcing understanding and cooperation between CILSS governmental ser-vices, non-governmental agencies, and interna-tional agencies interested in the problems of the Sahel; and 4) public relations (12).

Division of Relations with Non-Governmental Organizations

The third division, the Division of Relations with Non-Governmental Organizations (ONG), dis-charges the following functions: 1) sensitizing the non-governmental organizations to the problems of the fight against drought and its consequences; 2) establishing personal and professional contacts between non-governmental organizations and the member states with a view to assuring the coor-dination of the activities of non-governmental organizations, and the insertion of these activi-ties in national development plans; 3) encouraging exchanges of experience between non-governmental organizations with the aim of increasing the effectiveness of their actions (13).

Finally, the Division of Projects and Programs, responsible for carrying out the CILSS projects and programs, is staffed by a Division Chief and seventeen Sahelian and non-Sahelian technical experts. The work of the DPP consists of the following: 1) to collaborate with the national services and external aid sources, initiate investigations and studies, and prepare the projects and program dossiers; 2) to coordinate and finalize the state of advancement of programs and projects approved of by CILSS; and 3) to coordinate the actions of CILSS with those of regional and sub-regional agencies (14).

TABLE 4.3
Division Chiefs of the CILSS Secretariat

Division Name	Division Chief
Administrative and Financial Affairs (DAF)	Salomon Abba
Documentation and Information (DDI)	James Grey Johnson
Relations with Non-Governmental Organizations (ONG)	Issoufou Abba Moussa
Projects and Programs (DPP)	Boubakar Yobi Hama

CILSS SPECIALIZED INSTITUTES

In addition to the Executive Secretariat, CILSS operates two specialized institutes, the Agrhymet Center and the Sahel Institute. The former is located in Niger; the latter in Mali.

The Agrhymet Center

The idea for Agrhymet originated from a resolution adopted at the First Council of Minister's meeting which called for the strengthening and development of the national meteorological and hydrological services in the CILSS countries and the establishment of a regional center for the training of personnel in agrometeorology and hydrology. This would serve to increase agriculture and livestock production and the rational use of the available water resources. The First Council of Ministers meeting also approved of a resolution calling for the creation of the Sahel Institute, charged with applied research and training and the coordination of all research and training activities in the Sahel countries. At the Sixth Council of Ministers meeting both institutions were formally created.

Chapter II, Article 2 of the Convention creating the Agrhymet Center established the Center's duties:

1) To function as a place for training and application in operational agrometeorology and hydrology;

2) To train meteorological, hydrological, and agricultural personnel for their mastery in climatology, hydrology and operational agrometeorology;

3) To train specialists in the use of instruments required for agrometeorology and hydrology;

4) To gather and process data of the entire region and evaluate forecasts and agrometeorological and hydrological warnings;

122

5) To undertake the applied research of common problems affecting all the countries of the area;

6) To develop new technologies capable of contributing to the development of rural farming production; and,

7) To help to adjust and repair meteorological and hydrologic instruments of the member countries´ services (15).

In essence, the work of the Agrhymet Center is to train personnel in the areas of agrometeorology and hydrology, and to collect and disseminate agrometeorological and hydrological information deemed important to the national services. To carry out these tasks, the program was directed by the Board of Administration, comprised of a minister from each of the Sahel countries, the Director of the Agrhymet Center, and a CILSS representative. The Board of Administration, responsible for the smooth running of the Agrhymet Program, meets once a year.

Control of the pedagogic and scientific matters is in the hands of the Board of Pedagogic and Scientific Perfection. The Board is comprised of two representatives from each member country, two representatives from the CILSS Secretariat, and the Coordinator of the Agrhymet Program (selected by the World Meteorological Organization). The Board of Pedagogic and Scientific Perfection meets once a year.

The training program conducted at the Center lasted from twelve months for instrument technicians to twenty-four months for agrometeorology and hydrology technicians. In 1982, the Center could only accomodate about fifty students due to housing constraints. The majority of the student body come from the CILSS member countries, but because the statutes allow for the matriculation of students from non-CILSS states, a few non-member states (Benin, Togo, and the Ivory Coast) send their nationals for training.

The cost of the Agrhymet program and training center is born principally by donors´ contributions, by the fixed assessments of the member states, and by the fees paid by other African countries who elect to send their students to the Center for training.

To ensure the smooth running of the Agrhymet Center, a Director is chosen for a three-year term. Chapter IV, Article 7 of the Agrhymet Center´s statutes established that the Director of the Center is reponsible for the pedagogical, administrative, and financial affairs of the Center (16).

In May 1974, a UNDP/WMO/FAO mission conducted a study to define in broad terms an agrometeorology and hydrology program that would meet CILSS´ objectives. The mission resulted in a WMO/CILSS agreement in which CILSS contracted the WMO to carry out the Agrhymet Program. The CILSS/WMO agreement (Article 6) stipulated that the "WMO will recruit the Coordinator of the Agrhymet Program who will be responsible for the Program under the guidance of the WMO and who will exercise control over the experts and other WMO staff members. This Coordinator will also be responsible for the equipment provided to the Program by the UNDP or the donors" (17).

Thus, Article 6 of the CILSS/WMO agreement and Article 7 of the Center statutes, drawn up by the CILSS Council of Ministers, were in conflict. After 1978, when the Sahelian Director of the Center took up his duties, disagreements occured between the CILSS-appointed Director of the Center and the WMO-selected Coordinator of the Agrhymet Program. Both the Director and the Coordinator interpreted the articles in question to give them jurisdiction over the teaching staff. The Director of the Center interpreted Article 7 to mean that the Coordinator was responsible to the Director of the Center, while the Coordinator felt he was responsible solely to the WMO, and not to the Center´s Director. These opposing interpretations over duties and responsibilities severely affected the efficiency of the entire Agrhymet Program.

Once the problem of the interpretation of the cooperation agreement surfaced, missions and meetings were convened in an effort to resolve the disagreement. These meetings began in 1979. As a first step towards resolving the conflict, both CILSS and the WMO agreed to remove both the Center

124

Director and the Coordinator of the Program.
Nevertheless, by August 1980 reconciliation of the
articles had not been achieved and negotiations
continued through the fall of 1980. Finally, in
March 1981, CILSS and the WMO signed a new accord
which ended the dispute over the conflicting statutes.

The Sahel Institute

The other specialized institute, the Sahel
Institute, has the objective of contributing to
the resolution of the basic problems of overall
and integrated development in the region through
research and training (Chapter II, Article 4).
The statutes of the Institute (Chapter I, Article
II) specified that the "...Institute is a tool of
regional cooperation which shall coordinate, harmonize, and promote research and training activities of the CILSS member states" (18). The
Sahel Institute was not to conduct applied research and training, but to serve as a
clearinghouse for research and training activities
in other Sahelian institutes and agencies
concerned with these two tasks.

To achieve its objectives, the Institute
carries out the tasks listed below:

1) The collection, analysis, and dissemination of
   the results of scientific and technical research;

2) The transfer and adaptation of technologies;

3) The promotion, harmonization, and coordination
   of scientific and technical research;

4) The training of researchers and technicians in
   the field of scientific and technical research;

5) The disposition of technical assistance given
   to participating states in the form of missions, consultations, and studies;

6) The establishment of a liaison with research
   insitutions, intervention agencies, African

125

and foreign universities, and African, international, or interstate organizations (19).

The management of the Institute is
controlled by the Board of Directors (Chapter III,
Article 6). The members of the Board of Directors
include: the Minister Coordinator of CILSS, two
ministers from each member state who represented
research or training departments, and the ex-
officio members--the CILSS Executive Secretary or
his representative, the Agrhymet Center Director,
and the Director General of the Institute. To
ensure the proper management and good functioning
of the Sahel Institute, the Board of Directors
meet biannually. In general, the Board of Directors functions:

1) To propose to the governments of member states
   possible modifications to the statutes of the
   Sahel Institute;

2) To appoint the Director General of the Institute;

3) To approve the working schedules of the Institute and the corresponding budgets and determine the corresponding contributions to be
   paid by member states;

4) To draw up the general principles and the
   policies governing the Institute's activities;

5) To examine and adopt the report of activities
   of the Institute and the execution of the
   budget of the preceding year;

6) To sign contracts with various universities,
   professional, African, interstate, or international organizations;

7) To determine the conditions under which the
   Institute would intervene in the form of
   technical assistance to the various CILSS
   member states; and,

8) To approve the rules of procedure of the
   Institute (20).

The day-to-day operations of the Sahel Institute which concern scientific and technical matters are placed in the hands of the Scientific and Technical Council. The Council was responsible for the policies, programs, and the professional personnel of the member states, and for the coordination of scientific and technical research between them (21).

Membership on the Council is reserved for scientists of an international repute, a representative from the CILSS Executive Secretariat, the Director of the Scientific and Technical Research Division, and the Director of the Training Division. The Council meet once a year to discuss business.

Another organ is the Consultative Council, formed to sensitize contributors to the work of the Institute and the needs of the region. Furthermore, the Consultative Council evaluates projects in conjunction with the financing institutions and drafts recommendations on the Institute's programs. The Council meets once a year and is comprised of the representatives of CILSS' member states and the representatives of the donors and cooperating bodies.

The Sahel Institute is divided into a number of departments which executed regional goals. The principle departments are: Research, Training, Communications, and USED (Unité Socio-Economique et Demographique). The Department of Research engages in a number of projects designed to study and improve food and cash crop production, conditions in the agro-sylvo-pastoral zones, and small animal husbandry. In its work, the Research Department worked closely with the Unité de Gestion Régionale (UGR). The Department of Training concentrates on the training of researchers, specialists, and high level technicians in order to provide the member countries with qualified technical and scientific personnel and to reinforce their national training institutions in the areas of scientific and technical knowledge.

The Socio-Economic and Demography Unit (USED) was concerned with research and training pertaining to socio-economics and demography. After its creation in 1978, USED worked to define regional research themes and Sahelian training

127

priorities in three broad areas: 1) demography; 2) health, water, and nutrition; and 3) ecology and forestry. By providing baseline data and research studies, USED is able to help Sahelians formulate better national development plans.

Finally, the Department of Communications disseminates information gathered by the Sahel Institute to promote the exchange of knowledge between the various departments and programs of the Institute, on the one hand, and between the member countries and the international community, on the other.

STRATEGY AND PROGRAM TO COMBAT DROUGHT

Of all the departments and organs of CILSS, the Division of Projects and Programs is the most important due to the role it plays in implementation of the First, Second, and Third Generation Programs. The work of this unit evolved from the strategy and program begun by the Working Groups. After the formation of the Club du Sahel, one of the first joint CILSS/Club du Sahel tasks was the formation of ten sectoral working groups. In June 1976, these Working Groups were given the responsibility of formulating a strategy and program for the development of the region from 1977-2000. Ten Working Groups were organized into four vertical teams in charge of production--rainfed crops, irrigated crops, livestock, and fisheries--and five horizontal teams in charge of supporting services--transportation, marketing-price-storage, ecology, technology, and human resources. The tenth Working Group, the synthesis group, was to ensure a coherence between vertical and horizontal programs so that the work of one sector would not create unintended and negative consequences for another.

To emphasize the multilateral spirit, the Working Groups were headed by a Sahelian and a non-Sahelian, who acted as animateur and rapporteur, respectively. Furthermore, strong efforts were made to balance the compositions of the Groups with Sahelian, American, and European experts.

128

The experts of these Working Groups were given the role of defining a development strategy suitable for the Sahel, one which would lead to regional food self-sufficiency and make the Sahel less vulnerable to drought. To formulate a development strategy suitable to the Sahel, missions were sent to each of the Sahel nations to initiate a dialogue with governmental officials. The missions de dialogue took place amid general confusion as to CILSS' role in the elaboration of programs. CILSS viewed the missions as a way to understand the nature of the projects and programs needed if the Sahel states were to achieve regional goals. This viewpoint suggested that CILSS would formulate the projects and programs with the assistance of the governments. The governments, however, took sovereignty of the states as a postulate and some members of the missions subscribed to the notion that the local government officials were best placed to know the needs of their countries and the nature of the programs which would guarantee development consistent with the broad strategy outlines agreed upon by the participants.

Because of these opposing ideas over the role and the purpose of the missions, some Working Groups held less than successful dialogues with their counterparts in the governments. In many of the countries, the Working Groups were limited to recording the demands of government officials. The outcome of the missions de dialogue were colored by the form of the dialogues; determined, for the most part, by the Sahelian governments. In the end, many of the programs and projects requested by the governments were those that, heretofore, had failed to generate any donor support.

The work of the Groups lasted from eight to ten months. By the Second Club du Sahel Conference in June 1977, the Groups had put together a detailed and extensive report for a strategy and drought control program for the Sahel. At the Conference, CILSS, the donor community, the Club du Sahel Secretariat, and the national governments adopted the document of the Working Groups. In adopting the Strategy and Programme for Drought Control and Development in tne Sanei, donors ana Sahelians agreed to make the document the sole platform of action for CILSS and the Club du Sahel.

One of the first objectives of the strategy was to bring about an increase in food production. The Working Groups accepted FAO estimates of Sahelian staple crop needs. From these estimates, the Groups decided upon certain programs deemed essential for improving Sahelian food production.

TABLE 4.4
Sahelian Production Targets--1974-2000
(in thousand tons)

	1974-76	1990	2000
Millet and sorghum	4,250	6,300	8,150
Wheat	210	500	900
Paddy rice	895	1,540	2,200
Maize	310	625	1,000
Sugar	220	400	660
Meat (cattle, sheep,goats)	350	500	980
Fish	400	570	820

Source: Club du Sahel/CILSS, Strategy for Drought Control and Development in the Sahel (Paris: OECD, 1980), p. 19.

As the figures in Table 4.4 indicate, Sahelian demand for millet and sorghum will almost double between 1976 and 1990; the demand for rice, fish, and meat will more than double. By the year 2000, the demand for maize and sugar will triple and that of wheat will more than quadruple. Because of the population trends, the production targets, if attained, will provide an additional daily increase of only 100 calories per capita between 1975 and 1990. As in most Third World countries, high population growth rates outpace the gains made in food production.

To meet production targets, the Working Groups created three teams within the CILSS Secretariat, pertinent to food production: Dryland Agriculture, Irrigated Agriculture, and Village and Pastoral Hydraulics.

Dryland Agriculture Sector

Rainfed crops (millet, sorghum, and other cereals) play a major role in agriculture production in the Sahel and account for 95 percent of all grain production. The objectives for this sector, established by the Working Group, include:

1) Production--doubling dryland crop production by the year 2000;

2) Food Security--making rainfed crops less vulnerable to drought;

3) Employment--increasing employment opportunities in the rural sector;

4) Quality of life--improving the living conditions for rural people (22).

To attain these four objectives, three actions were agreed upon. First, the Working Group declared that new lands must be brought into production. The cultivation of underexploited lands, the clearing of disease-infested areas (such as the black fly areas), and the encouragement of migration to less densely populated areas are the tactics being used. Secondly, the intensification of lands already in use is to be pursued. Actions conducted in this domain call for the use of modern agricultural techniques (intensified use of fertilizer, crop rotation, draft animals, and mechanical and motorized farm implements). Finally, the dryland crop sector plans to introduce improved seed varieties--more resistant to drought and requiring shorter growth periods and low rainfall.

The original estimated cost of the First Generation Program in Dryland Agriculture amounted

131

to $640 million. Factoring in inflation, the cost
grew to exceed $730 million.

Irrigated Agriculture Sector

Crops which required irrigated production
methods such as sugar, wheat, rice, and cotton
were included under the work of the second food
production team, the Irrigated Agriculture sector.
Irrigated agriculture was afforded detailed attention by the Working Group due to the growing
Sahelian consumption of rice and wheat and the
expectation that exports of irrigated crops would
increase tremendously in the years ahead. In
1985, only 4 percent of all crops cultivated in
the Sahel were produced by this method. The plan
for this sector was to make the production of all
rice, wheat, and sugar based on irrigated agriculture by the year 2000.

Two actions were envisioned to meet this
objective: 1) to increase the efficiency of existing irrigation operations and 2) to introduce new
irrigated perimeters, starting with the most eco-
nomical ones (23). The operations proposed
involve a major shift to irrigated agriculture
from 80,000 hectares (1976 figures) to 600,000
hectares by the year 2000. However promising the
benefits from irrigated farming techniques may
have seemed this sector was faced with major constraints.

Irrigated agriculture demands adequate water
and soil resources, trained manpower, the
construction of needed infrastructure, and vast
financial resources, none of which the Sahel pos-
sessed in abundance. The need for over 2,000
trained cadres by the year 2000 and the amounts
required for the first phase study projects alone
made this an expensive enterprise. The cost of
the FGP in Irrigated Agriculture was originally
set at $563 million for investments. The figure
was revised in 1977 and in 1981 the cost of projects in this sector amounted to $981 million.

Village and Pastoral Hydraulics Sector

132

Working closely with the two food production teams is the Village and Pastoral Hydraulics unit. Based upon the Working Group's estimate of water needs (25 liters per day for each inhabitant and 30 liters per day for animals), the central objective of the Hydraulics sector was to increase water resources and the awareness of water availability in the region (24). To this end, four action areas were designed by the working group which would:

1) Increase knowledge of the groundwater tables;

2) Strengthen or create national hydro-geological services which would make inventories of resources;

3) Strengthen and create properly equipped maintenance services for the water points and water extraction systems;

4) Improve training for hydraulics technicians at all levels (25).

The Working Group estimated the cost of the FGP projects in this sector to be $227 million. The revised 1977 estimate lowered the cost of projects to $83 million.

In addition to dryland agriculture and irrigated agriculture, the Working Groups formulated development strategies for two other areas within the production sector--livestock and fisheries.

Livestock Sector

The intensification of agricultural production has often conflicted with livestock production. Where herders and farmers encroached upon each other's territories, the result was sometimes violent. Like farming, livestock constitutes a major food source and a principle means of economic activity for many Sahelians. Sahelian annual per capita consumption of meat in 1970 was between 15 and 17 kilograms, and it is increasing.

133

One of the main objectives of the Livestock sector was to ensure a continuing supply of animals to meet this growing need. The sector proposed to: 1) increase animal production; 2) maintain the Sahelian position in meat exportation; 3) make work animals available to the farmer; and 4) improve the quality of life and income levels of the herders while avoiding overgrazing (26).

Attainment of these objectives required doubling herd size. The action program of the Livestock sector was organized in five categories. The first action entailed the evaluation of range management and natural resources in order to develop better planning strategies. The second category was the implementation of pastoral management projects. Plans were to implement integrated projects involving research on rangelands, sanitation services, water resources, and comprehensive pastoral-agro-sylvo projects.

To overcome the conflicts which occur between pastoralists and agriculturalists, the Working Group proposed, as the third program, projects which would entail the cooperation between these two groups. Associations between farmers and herders would promote the use of animals in agricultural production and the utilization of forage and fodder crops, as well as agro-industrial by-products, to feed cattle.

The development of animal health actions made up the fourth component of the Livestock action program. Activities in this area were geared to the dissemination of animal health services and the improvement of animal health delivery systems.

The Working Group also acknowledged the need for increased training and communications in livestock management. Therefore, training programs for herders and government officials were instituted as the fifth component. In addition, activities to improve relations between training institutes and government agencies involved in the assembly and dissemination of knowledge concerning livestock were developed. Finally, improvements in livestock marketing were envisioned. The goals were to increase herder and export earnings and to strengthen the governmental institutions that supervised livestock marketing.

The Working Groups's figure for the cost of

134

the FGP in livestock activities was estimated at $330 million. The revised 1977 calculation was reduced to $269 million.

Fisheries Sector

Sahelian and donor attention in the production areas was also turned to the the fisheries sector. Although regional per capita consumption of fish was high in 1973 (15 kilograms compared to 15.3 kilograms for meat), few governments devoted much attention to this sector. By 1980, consumption of fish declined to 13 kilograms per capita. Still, fish is a potentially important food source in the region. Furthermore, fish are relatively immune to the vagaries of climate, unlike meat or cereals. With this fact in mind, the Working Group established the Fisheries unit and entrusted it with the following objectives:

1) To improve the knowledge of the region's potential and to conduct research needed to obtain more precise information on fish resources;

2) To reinforce the fisheries services with more qualified and appropriate personnel;

3) To improve fishing and fish processing techniques;

4) To develop fish marketing systems;

5) To train senior management staff (27).

The work of the Fisheries sector for the First Generation Program concentrated on continental (inland) and maritime (coastal) fishing and the construction of training and research centers. The cost of projects of the FGP was initially calculated at $69 million. Revised estimates raised the cost of projects to $72 million.

In formulating production projects, each sector touched upon environmental constraints which impeded the progress of the First Generation Program. Irrigation projects needed trained personnel. Projects to increase food production in

the rural areas necessitated an adequate transportation system to get these products to the market.
To overcome impediments to the success of projects
in the four production areas, the Working Groups
also envisioned projects and programs in the five
supporting services areas. Thus, the supporting
services work closely with the four production
teams. In addition to the Village and Pastoral
Hydraulics mentioned previously, the other
supporting services areas include: 1) Human
Resources, 2) Ecology and Forestry, 3) Price-
Marketing-Storage, and 4) Transportation and
Infrastructure.

Human Resources Sector

Foremost among the horizontal teams was the
Human Resources unit. Concerns of this team--the
problem of employment, the lack of trained personnel, the weakness and inappropriateness of
existing educational institutions and health care,
and the lack of rural communciations--were inti-
mately linked to the problems facing the production teams.
The strategy of Human Resources Working Group
revolved around the resolution of four critical
deficiencies in the Sahel: 1) the transformation
of education and training systems; 2) the promotion of employment; 3) the development of information and communications networks; and 4) the
establishment of village based health care
systems (28).
To overcome these four deficiencies, the
Human Resources Working Group outlined a number of
actions to be undertaken: staff training, farmer
training, education for rural development, increasing jobs in the rural sector, and increasing
labor-intensive activities. In addition, measures
were taken to develop rural radio capacity, promote the use of traditional medicine, improve
sanitation systems, and provide rural health care
systems. Initial costs for these projects were
set at $267 million, but revisions escalated the
cost to $365 million.

136

Ecology and Forestry Sector

In addition to human resources activities, the strategy and program for drought control elaborated plans to combat the problem of desertification caused by human and animal consumption of vegetation. Firewood is used for many purposes-- to preserve fish, to cook food, and to meet heating needs. Animals consume vast amounts of plant cover to satisfy their daily food requirements. As Sahelian populations increased, the demand for firewood, accounting for 60-90 percent of regional energy use in 1980, also increased. The growing consumption of vegetation caused soil fertility to decline. A vicious cycle ensued: as soil fertility declined, food production yields decreased. This forced peasants to farm more intensively on already marginally productive lands, further contributing to poor soil quality.

To break the cycle of degradation, the Working Group created the Ecology and Forestry team within the CILSS Secretariat. The essential task of this unit was to safeguard the Sahelian resource base. Four sub-programs, designed to cope with environmental problems, were agreed upon: 1) wood production; 2) agro-sylvo-pastoral management; 3) wildlife conservation and exploitation; and 4) education and training (29).

Actions in the sub-program of wood production included: planting trees, utilizing improved cook stoves, and improving the management of the existing forests. Pastoral management, biotope control, and the use of windbreaks and plant exclosures, were some of the activities incorporated into this component. In the area of wildlife conservation and exploitation, the Ecology and Forestry team planned to restore wildlife species.

Finally, the education and training subprogram was to train over 6,000 cadres at all levels in ecology, forestry, and energy. In addition to these actions, the Ecology and Forestry unit planned to alter energy consumption by encouraging the use of solar energy, wind power, fossil fuel, biogas, and the pyrolysis of vegetable waste.

The cost of the projects in Ecology and

137

Forestry was initially set at $363 million. The revised 1977 figures scaled down the cost to $173 million.

Price-Marketing-Storage

The Working Group felt that the proposed production projects would need accompanying action in the areas of pricing policies, efficient marketing structures, and storage facilities. It is of little value to improve agricultural or livestock production if there exists no place to store the grain or no market structure to move the cattle from producer to consumer. Without an equitable and fair price policy for the producer, no amount of improved farming techniques will induce the farmer to plant more.

The objective of this unit was to formulate policies and projects to support the activities of the production sectors in the areas of price, marketing, and storage. Regarding price policy, the Working Group, mindful of the repercussions felt in urban centers after sudden increases in producer prices, suggested steps to improve price policies--guarantee the purchase of supply, publish price scales before sowing time, and subsidize improved farming techniques. The Working Group decided that these actions were necessary in order to ensure that farmers would increase their production of cereals.

In the area of marketing, the Working Group suggested that state support of the private trading structure and improved marketing cooperatives be established. In addition, this unit proposed to implement projects related to grain storage: the increase in storage capacities, the maintenance of security and emergency stocks, and the development of regional storage systems were some of the projects suggested.

Another objective of this unit was to increase baseline data on the cereals situtation. The total estimated cost, originally $18 million, was revised to $35.8 million.

138

Transportation and Infrastructure Sector

Marketing and storage projects necessitate an adequate transportation network to move the goods. Improvements in the road networks are vital to the functioning of other sectors. Getting fish and livestock from producer to consumer cannot occur in the absence of an effective transportation network. In the short-term, the Working Group's Transportation and Infrastructure team proposed that projects concentrate on the construction of new access roads and tracks. For already existing roads, the Transportation and Infrastructure team worked on road maintenance and renovation projects.

An additional component of the Transportation and Infrastructure unit's work was the design of a disenclavement project to improve the mobility of labor, goods, and services in the region. These efforts would facilitate the distribution of emergency aid in drought-stricken areas, as well as speed up the circulation of grains and other products in non-crisis periods.

The Transportation and Infrastructure unit planned medium- and long-term transportation projects as well. One of these, the heavy duty east-west road axis, would link more closely the land-locked and coastal countries. In addition, the completion of the Dakar-Niamey railway connection was forseen. The current railway system connects Dakar to Bamako, and Bobo-Dioulasso to Ouagadougou and Abidjan. For these projects, CILSS planned to conduct feasibility studies and to find donors to finance their completion.

The financing of the FGP transportation projects was estimated at $651 million. In 1977, after an evaluation of the program, the cost was reduced to $296 million.

As was mentioned before, the totality of the Working Group's efforts was compiled in the CILSS strategy document, Strategy and Programme for Drought Control and Development in the Sahel, and was accepted by both donors and Sahelians at the Second Club du Sahel Conference. After the Conference, the work of the Working Groups continued. In the first year of the Club's existence, the groups convened many meetings and organized mis-

139

sions in Africa and Europe. The donors and Sahelians realized this was a costly and inefficient
manner in which to conduct business.

At the Third Club du Sahel Conference it was
decided to incorporate the Working Groups´ activities directly into CILSS´ structure. As a result,
CILSS´ operations and staff expanded. The
reorganization increased the Division of Projects
and Program to the nine production and supporting
services teams. The task of formulating the projects of the First Generation Program rested with
the DPP. To carry out these tasks, the nine units
continued to maintain close contact and to convene
yearly meetings with their experts in non-Sahelian
countries.

The DPP is not the only unit which is mandated to formulate and implement projects. Two
special programs within CILSS are the Food Crop
project and the Regional Management unit (Crop
Protection Program).

SPECIAL PROJECTS

The Food Corps Program

At the 1977 FAO Conference, former U.S.
Ambassador Andrew Young suggested the formation of
a Food Corps to promote rural self-help development, food self-sufficiency, and integrated
development. Following the Conference, interested
nations formed the Comité Internationale de Liaison du Corps pour l´Alimentation (CILCA), or the
Food Corps Program. CILCA contacted the CILSS
Minister Coordinator, Adrien Senghor, in order to
interest CILSS in the implementation of an experimental project in the Sahel. A number of missions
conducted between CILSS and CILCA led, finally, to
the Council of Ministers approving the idea of a
Food Corp project as part of CILSS´ work.

Fundamental to the Food Corps Program was the
idea that the best way to achieve food self-sufficiency and improve living standards was to establish "...a program of both participation and productivity which closely integrates the production
plan, vulgarization and credit; it also hinges on
the reinforcement and the attribution of responsi-

140

bilities to existing socio-professional structures" (30). The Food Corps project was based on
the participation of villagers in the decision-
making process, the minimal use of outside technicians, the use of appropriate technology in the
development package, and the <u>encadrement</u>
(training) of peasants.

While experimental projects were envisioned
in all of the member countries, in 1980 only
Senegal, Mali, and Burkina Faso had Food Corps
projects. The three countries happened to have
fulfilled a number of criteria set by CILCA, and
thus had project proposals which were in a more
advanced state. Niger and Gambia were to be included in the second phase of the project-test;
Mauritania, Chad, and Cape Verde made up the
final phase of the project-test.

The Food Corps project, based upon an
integrated development approach, was to carry out
activities involving market gardening, handi-
crafts, environmental protection, improvement of
village hudraulics, increased food production,
health care, rural education, livestock, and
credit facilities. The role of CILSS in the Food
Corps projects was to prepare project tests, to
supervise their implementation, to help the national governments execute the projects, and to
help in evaluating the results. The direct management of the projects fell under the jurisdiction of the national governments.

The cost of the first phase (three years)
varied according to the country, and amounted to
$1.8 million for Burkina Faso, $3.7 million for
Mali, and $1.6 million for Senegal. To help
defray the cost of the project tests, the national
governments were assessed amounts ranging from 15
to 33 percent of the project. Donations of land
and buildings from the Sahel governments and an
emphasis on peasant voluntarism aided in lowering
the cost of the project.

The Crop Protection Program

In addition to the Food Corps project, CILSS
has begun a Crop Protection Program. The annual
10 percent to 40 percent loss in crops due to

141

pests and other environmental hazards constituted a major concern to both donors and Sahelians alike. To combat crop losses, CILSS created the Unité de Gestion Régionale (UGR) to mount an integrated campaign to prevent crop loss. The work of the UGR was divided into seven components called annexes. For the most part, activities and projects were to be executed at the regional level, unlike the projects of the production and supporting services teams.

The goal of the first component, Annex A, was to reinforce the national crop protection services. Because Annex A´s activities were to be conducted on a bilateral basis, CILSS´ primary role was to evaluate the projects and follow the progress achieved.

Annex B, the Integrated Pest Management (IPM) program, constituted the major share of the work of the UGR. Estimated at a cost of $29 million, Annex B was intended to develop technically and environmentally sound production practices which would enable farmers to cut down on crop losses due to pests. Annex B comprised three parts-- applied research, outreach, and regional cooperation. Research stations in five of the states and activities in all of the member countries were to expand knowledge on the control of the principle crop enemies (locusts, crickets, and grasshoppers). Subsequently, the research results were to be integrated into Sahelian farming techniques. USAID was the primary donor for Annex B ($25 million) and the FAO was the contracting agency. Annex B respresented an unprecedented attempt to coordinate activities among three sovereign bodies, CILSS, USAID, and the FAO.

The third component, Annex C, the Regional Locust and Bird Control and Research Program, was to be implemented through the International Organization to Control the African Migratory Locust (OICMA) and the Joint Locust Control and Protection Against Grain-Eating Birds (OCLALAV). CILSS´ role in Annex C was limited to providing vehicles, pesticides, and other materials to the executing agencies. The cost of Annex C´s activities was estimated at $6.5 million.

The fight against grain-eating birds was the goal of Annex D. The first part of this program,

Annex Dl, was to provide technical assistance at
the regional level. Annex Dl maintained as its
objectives the following: the training of personnel, the preparation of self-teaching manuals for
technical staff, the evaluation of losses under
various storage conditions, the study of traditional storage methods and the development of more
appropriate methods, and the execution of projects
to combat harmful predators. The cost of Annex
Dl, $1.8 million, received some initial support
from the UNDP.

The Annex D2, the second part of the program,
was to conduct research on grain-eating birds in
order to discover improved methods of reducing
their destructiveness. The cost of funding Annex
D2 aroused the interest of the UNDP.

The fifth component of the UGR was a $2.6
million program to improve the protection of har-
vested crops. Originally designed as a five-year
program, Annex E was redesigned as a 3- 1/2 year
project to reduce expenses. Pending the redesign
to reflect the shortened operating time, the Germans expressed an interest in funding this program.

Annual crop losses in the Sahel are related
to the sizeable rodent populations. Senegal and
Niger are particularly hard hit by these predators. Annex F, the sixth component of the Crop
Protection program, concentrated its activities on
rodent control. Principally, Annex F is a four
year program to examine the ecology and biology of
rodents, to put into place an evaluation method-
ology of crop loss due to rodents, and to execute
a program to control the devastation. The estimated cost of $2.13 million dollars was labelled
excessively high by the Germans who expressed
interest in its funding. To meet German approval,
the UGR reformulated this project.

The final component of the Crop Protection
program, Annex G, contained two sub-components.
Annex Gl is the regional information and documentation unit. The Sahel Institute would be responsible for disseminating information regarding the
activities of the Crop Protection program. The
cost of Annex Gl was estimated at $2.03 million.
Annex G2, the regional training cell whose
function is to educate Sahelian officials on mat-

143

ters concerning the Crop Protection program, had an estimated cost of $2.08 million. Annex G2 has generated expressions of interest from the Dutch, the Americans, and the FED.

THE CILSS NATIONAL COMMITTEES

Since its inception, CILSS and the Club du Sahel have laid the plans for a development strategy and formulated projects which correspond to that strategy. To operate effectively the various structural components, CILSS requires considerable cooperation and support from the Sahelian governments. It is of little use if the strategies and projects designed by the sectoral teams do not complement or correspond to the activities of their counterparts at the national level. To achieve this cooperation and to promote a continuous dialogue between CILSS and the member states, the Council of Ministers created the position of the CILSS National Correspondent.

A staff member of the Ministry of Rural Development, the CILSS National Correspondent was the liaison between CILSS and the governments; his responsibility was to direct correspondence to the concerned departments and ministries. The CILSS National Correspondent also received the CILSS´ missions.

But by 1977, the activities of CILSS required a stronger link to the governments than that provided by the CILSS National Correspondent. After the Second Club du Sahel Conference in June 1977, the Council of Ministers agreed to expand the entire concept of the CILSS National Correspondent and created the CILSS National Committees.

The National Committees included respresentatives from all of the ministries and departments whose work touched upon CILSS´ activities. Membership on the Committees comprised personnel from the Ministries of Agriculture, Hydrology, Livestock, Fisheries, Nutrition, Foreign Affairs, Planning, Ecology, Transportation, Education, Training, Research, Information, Communications, and Health. The functions of the National Committees were to:

144

1) Finalize CILSS´ First Generation projects and to follow their implementation;

2) Foster integration and coherence among the CILSS projects at the national level;

3) Finalize the strategic outlines of the various sectors´ activities;

4) Undertake specific studies and works aimed at improving programming and implementation of the CILSS projects and preparing the Second and Third Generation projects and programs;

5) Gather and broadcast information relating to the activities of the Club du Sahel and CILSS (31).

As previously mandated, the CILSS National Correspondent maintained the role of primary liaison between CILSS and the Sahelian governments. The chairmanship of the National Committees would fall on the National Correspondent, but in the event that it did not, the Minister of Rural Development would hold the position.

The cost of running the CILSS National Committees (to cover the expenses of a vehicle, office materials and supplies, and a small discretionary fund) amounted to $113,000, a cost that neither donors nor Sahelians were eager to accept.

CONCLUSION

The structure of an organization may enhance or militate against its functions. The structure which CILSS has created is not without implications for the achievement of its objectives.

CILSS´ structure has features which make it readily comparable to other regional organizations. By the same token, CILSS´ close relations with the donor community helps it to circumvent some of the problems plaguing other regional efforts at cooperation.

Like CILSS, many regional organizations, have at their pinnacle an organ of the heads of state. When heads of state sit at the summit of a

145

regional organzation, a strong impetus to the
cooperative process may be present. On the other
hand, when political animosities exist between
heads of state, the lack of political will acts as
a brake on regional cooperation. The EAC saw its
work grind to a halt when conflicts emerged
between Uganda and Tanzania. In CILSS´ case, the
Heads of State declared their interest in the
organiztion and this helped to further cooperation. Even with the territorial dispute between
Burkina Faso and Mali which has on occasion led to
violence, cooperation within CILSS has not been
affected.

A structural organ common to many regional
groupings is the Council of Ministers. Other
regional organizations select the Minister of
Economic or Foreign Affairs to sit on the Council
of Ministers. The East African Community, the
Central African Customs and Economic Union
(UDEAC), and the Central American Common Market
all have Councils of Ministers dominated by their
Minister of Economic Affairs; on the other hand,
the Latin American Free Trade Association (LAFTA)
and the Association of South-East Asian Nations
have elected to appoint the Ministers of Foreign
Affairs to be the representatives on their Council
of Ministers. CILSS departs from most regional
organizations in that it is the Ministers of Rural
Development who comprise the Council. The tasks
which CILSS has selected make the Rural Development Ministers a fitting choice.

The selection of the Rural Development
Ministers on the Council has implications for
CILSS´ operations. Sidjanski finds that the lack
of contact between the ministers on any council of
ministers and other governmental ministries ham-
pers integration (32). When issues are raised
which fall outside of the expertise of the
ministers´ chosen fields, decisions entail delays
as the necessary contacts are made to the
ministries involved in the area of discussion.
The fact that the vital links between the organization and the government occur systematically at
only one ministry means that other government
channels do not regularly keep abreast of the
organization´s activities, and hence, do not always include the organization in the decision-

146

making process at the national level.

For CILSS, the implications of this are especially important since the Ministries of Rural Development are not highly placed within the governmental hierarchies. As a result, the priorities established by CILSS are not always incorporated into national priorities within other governmental ministries. Sahelian ministries make decisions and set priorities without CILSS' input. The result is that CILSS finds itself sometimes working at cross-purposes with the national governments. While CILSS presents one set of projects to donors for funding, it often finds the governments presenting donors with a different list. (See Chapter 6 for a more in-depth discussion on this point.)

To overcome the problem of coordination inherent in organizational structure, CILSS is attempting to widen its circle of contacts and to expand interaction at the national level through the CILSS National Committees. But unfortunately, the fact that the National Committees have found only limited funding and are not always viewed seriously by the governments has meant that the limitations imposed by the structure will continue to affect goal achievement.

The CILSS Executive Secretariat finds parallels in other regional organizations--UDEAC and LAFTA, to name a few. The powers invested in the Executive Secretariat vary according to organization. LAFTA has established a narrow range of actions which the Executive Secretariat may undertake. As a result, the role played by its Executive Secretariat is to help prepare for the Council of Ministers meetings. The UDEAC Executive Secretariat, on the other hand, enjoys a greater autonomy and is free to take up actions independent of the Council of Ministers (33).

The CILSS' Executive Secretariat plays a role in carrying out the resolutions of the Council of Ministers, and is able to exert influence upon the decisions made by the Council and the Conference of the Heads of State through its presentation of information from which decisions are made. In addition, through the types of projects and programs it has helped to formulate, the Secretariat has a measure of freedom in the implementation of the resolutions passed by the Council of Ministers and the Conference of the Heads of State. Furthermore, the Executive Secretariat plays an important role in presenting CILSS and Club activities to the CILSS governments, and is instrumental in getting the governments to support the decisions and activities of CILSS and the Club du Sahel (34).

One drawback to the organization of the Executive Secretariat is the lack of intersectoral coherence and cooperation. Although project components of a particular sector may involve the expertise of another sector, little effort is made to work together in the design of projects. Each sector works independently and when the expertise of another sector is called for, the solution is often to contact outsiders. This works against an integrated approach to development and contributes to a continuing reliance upon unisectoral development. Some of the experts deplored the lack of intersectoral activities and felt that as a minimum there should be intersectoral meetings to discuss the development strategy being pursued (35).

Not only does the lack of intersectoral activity reduce cooperation within CILSS, but it contributes to the very problem that the organization is attempting to reverse. Without integrated development, the Sahel risks a continuing cycle of drought. If such an approach is not undertaken within the CILSS framework, there is little likelihood that the projects implemented will address the need of integrated development.

By its very structure, CILSS´ ability to achieve its objectives are affected. The organization of the Conference of the Heads of State, the Council of Ministers, and the Executive Secretariat conditions the effectiveness. Thus, as with other regional organizations, CILSS is constrained by its own structure.

But what sets CILSS apart from other organizations is its close relationship with the donor community, enabling it to overcome some of the limits imposed by its structure. Donor agencies are closely involved in discussions and in planning at the level of the Executive Secretariat. The input provided by external actors expands

148

CILSS´ work program. In the case of the cereals policy, the donors were able to convince the CILSS´ Heads of State and the Council of Ministers to take steps to formulate a regional cereals policy by agreeing to help defray the costs of such a program.

The role played by the donors mitigates against some of the limitations caused by organizational structure. Because of donor support, CILSS has extracted greater cooperation from member states. (This point is taken up in the next two chapters.)

If the constraints of organizational structure pose less of a problem for goal attainment, it would be helpful to examine what CILSS has achieved in the way of donor and Sahelian support for its operations. In the next chapter, the impact of Sahelian and donor support for CILSS´ activities and organization is discussed.

NOTES

1. CILSS, Première Conférence des Chefs D´Etat (Ouagadougou: CILSS, 1973), p. 37.
2. Club du Sahel, The Operations of CILSS, mimeo (Paris: OECD, 1977), p. 2.
3. Ibid, p. 3.
4. Anne De Lattre and Arthur M. Fell, The Club du Sahel: An Experiment in International Cooperation (Paris: OECD, 1984), p. 44.
5. Ibid, p. 45.
6. Ibid.
7. OECD, Strategy and Program For Drought Control and Development in the Sahel (Paris: OECD, 1979).
8. De Lattre and Fell, p. 54.
9. The Operations of CILSS, pp. 4-6.
10. Ibid, pp. 6-7.
11. Ibid, p. 2.
12. Ibid, 3.
13. Ibid.
14. CILSS, Nouveau Textes Adoptés Par Le 7è Conseil Des Ministres Du CILSS Tenu A Ouagadougou

Du 25 Au 28 Avril 1977 (Ouagadougou: CILSS, 1977), p. 2.

15. CILSS, Statutes of the Regional Center for Training and Application in Operational Agrometeorology and Hydrology (Niamey: CILSS, 1976), pp. 1-2.

16. Ibid, p. 4.

17. CILSS, Second Evaluation Mission of the Programme for Strenthening the Agrometeorological and Establishment of a Centre for Training and Application of Agrometeorology/Operational Hydrology (Niamey: Agrhymet, 1980), p. 7.

18. CILSS, Meeting of Sahelian Experts in Research and Training (Ouagadougou: CILSS, 1977), p. 3.

19. Chapter II, Article 4 of the Sahel Institute statutes.

20. Chapter III, Article 8 of the Sahel Institute statutes.

21. Chapter IV, Article 12 of the Sahel Institute statutes.

22. Strategy and Program for Drought Control and Development in the Sahel, p. 29.

23. Ibid, p. 42.

24. Ibid, p. 48.

25. Ibid, p. 49.

26. Ibid, p. 58.

27. Ibid, pp. 69-70.

28. Ibid, p. 74.

29. Ibid, pp. 84-86.

30. CILSS, A Note on the State of Advancement of Pilot Projects in the Sahel, mimeo (N.D.), p. 4.

31. Boulama Manga, Memorandum to Ministers of Rural Development, Restarting the CILSS National Committees, (mimeo) September 9, 1977.

32. Dusan Sidjanski, Current Problems of Economic Integration (New York: United Nations, 1979).

33. Ibid, p. 12.

34. De Lattre and Fell, p. 87.

35. In 1980, the Chief of the DPP organized three intersectoral meetings to discuss the progress of each sector and the overall strategy. Prior to these meetings, no intersectoral meetings had been held for at least two years.

150

5

Support for CILSS'
Operations and Functions

In the previous chapter, the organizational structure of CILSS and the implications of
this structure for goal attainment were discussed.
Besides organizational structure, the achievement
of objectives is affected by Sahelian and donor
support for CILSS' operations. Chapter 5 will
measure Sahelian and donor support of CILSS' operations. The four variables selected are:
functions, financial contributions, staffing,
and the National Committees.

SAHELIAN SUPPORT FOR CILSS

Sahelian Support for Functions

What level of support has CILSS received from
member countries? To answer this question, CILSS'
functions as they relate to CILSS/government exchanges and program support must be analyzed. To
formulate policies and projects, to update the
state of advancement of the First Generation Program, and to stay abreast of the priorities and
interests of the member states, good communication
between CILSS and the national governments is
critical. Nevertheless, the record of the Sahel
states on this score has not always been positive.
Missions conducted for fact-finding purposes
are not always well received by the governments.
In one case, a CILSS mission was unable to meet
with a government minister when he refused to see
the CILSS' experts. Occasionally, CILSS experts

151

have wasted time running from ministry to ministry to get information, a job that should be executed by the CILSS National Correspondent. Cooperation, the exchange of information and ideas, is not always forthcoming from government officials.

Correspondence is not always promptly answered, if it is answered at all. One expert revealed that in two years, his unit had only received replies to one letter from a particualr Sahelian ministry. In another instance, one government minister had not signed a contract he had held for seven months. The Planning, Monitoring, and Evaluation unit reported that it had mailed out a questionnaire to member states to which only three countries responded with the requested information. Problems concerning communication and receptivity to CILSS´ experts have touched each sector (1).

In part, lack of cooperation can be explained by the priorities of the national governments. Each of the production and supporting services sectors does not have the same priority in all member states. The zeal with which national governments respond to correspondence or the support offered to CILSS´ experts relates directly to the interest of the government in the sector requesting the service.

A second reason for a lack of cooperation resides in the commitments of the Sahelian officials. A small number of staff in each government ministry or department, constantly faced with information seeking organizations, must devote attention to requests from CILSS, the CEAO, the United Nations agencies, bilateral and multilateral donors, and NGOs, in addition to fulfilling their governmental duties. In some cases, the short shrift given CILSS is due to the time constraints of individuals who face many actors demanding, most often, the same materials (2).

Although a lack of both interest and time has resulted in cooperation failures between CILSS and the national governments, it is important not to overemphasize these failures. Examples of a lack of support are the exception rather than the rule. In general, the states with limited staff and funds do cooperate with CILSS.

Support for CILSS´ functions can also be

152

measured by the national governments´ reinforcement of CILSS´ work. On this score, they have
demonstrated little cooperation. When donors
request that the Sahelian government list their
priority projects, CILSS´ projects are often not
included. If they are mentioned, the priority in
which they are listed does not match the order
drawn up by CILSS and the member states. Two
reasons may be adduced for this lack of support.

For one thing, the list of projects presented
to CILSS often includes projects for which the
Sahel governments have been unsuccessful in
finding donor funding. CILSS´ work consists of
writing up proposals for these projects so as to
attract donor interest. It could be that the
national governments feel that CILSS is devoting
attention to these projects so they are free to
focus their efforts on getting donors to fund
other projects.

A second reason suggested to me by the CILSS´
experts for this lack of support is that the
national governments have changed their own
priorities and neglected to keep CILSS informed of
their diminished interest in certain projects.
The time between the presentation of project ideas
and the date that CILSS finds a donor to finance
the project can be as long as seven years. In the
interim, governments have changed and/or their
priorities and interests have shifted. Because
CILSS is rarely notified by the governments of a
waning interest in a certain project, CILSS and
the donors are confronted by a lack of coordination between CILSS and the national governments.
Donors express concern as to which list of projects should be funded.

CILSS feels that the governments are not
supporting its efforts. Six experts cited this
behavior as an example of the lack of cooperation.
Other examples of a lack of reinforcement of
CILSS´ functions include: failure to contact interested donors about project funding (mentioned
by one person); failure to notify CILSS of the
state of advancement of projects (two people cited
this); the lack of consistency in government priorities (mentioned by three experts); and a
failure to receive missions and respond to correspondence (cited by six experts).

153

In sum, the cooperation given by the national governments is not always wholehearted, primarily due to a difference in priorities established by the Sahel governments, and a lack of resources and staff.

Can the same be true of other support variables? What has been the level of support granted to CILSS in financial contributions?

Sahelian Support for Financial Contributions

The effectiveness of any organization is determined by the financial support of its members. Like all regional organizations, CILSS relies on the timely availability of donations and fixed contributions from member states. Every year the experts at the Council of Ministers meetings decide upon the states' contributions for the coming fiscal year, and the Council of Ministers then votes on the amount set by the experts. Invariably, the amount decided upon by the ministers is lower than that proposed by the experts. The contributions are then divided into a formula fixed for each state: 1/25 for Gambia

TABLE 5.1
CILSS Budget (in CFA)

Fiscal Year	Amount Set	% Increase
1973	13,000,000	
1974	70,928,000	81
1975	87,547,000	19
1976	110,880,613	21
1977	119,004,400	6
1978	172,535,750	31
1979	227,752,176	24
1980	266,782,890	14
1981	284,794,198	7
1982	301,710,248	

154

TABLE 5.2
Unpaid Dues (in CFA)

Fiscal Year	Countries Owing Partial or Total Dues	Amount Owed
1975	All, as of 10/75 (a)	110,880,613
1976	All, as of 10/76 (b)	59,585,185(c)
1977	-	-
1978	Mauritania	3,032,036(d)
1979	Gambia, Burkina Faso, Mali, Chad, Mauritania as of June 1979 (e)	-
1980	Gambia, Burkina Faso, Mali, Chad, Mauritania Senegal as of 7/80 (f)	157,567,544
1981	Chad, Mauritania, Mali as of 1/82	92,323,855
1982	Burkina Faso, Mali, Chad, Mauritania as of 11/82	71,925,235

(a) As of 1976, Senegal and Chad alone owed 15,680,000 CFA.

(b) By October 1976, Burkina Faso, Mali, Mauritania, and Chad had made partial payments on their 1976 contributions. The other four states had made no payments.

(c) By 1978, the 1976 contributions still outstanding amounted to 10,102,627 CFA.

(d) As of 1981, Mauritania still owed a portion of its 1978 dues.

(e) Mauritania and Chad alone owed 30,000,000 CFA each for their 1979 dues as of July 1981.

(f) As of July 1982 Chad still owed 101,478,917 CFA for the fiscal years 1979-81. Mauritania had 34,664,732 CFA outstanding on its 1981 dues.

155

and Cape Verde and 23/25 for the remaining states. Contributions are expected to be received by the beginning of the year, but it is not unusual for states to owe all or part of their dues by as late as October.

The financial situation grew steadily worse in 1981 and after. At the 18th and 20th Council of Ministers meetings, the inability of member states to meet their financial obligations to the organization was a subject of much discussion. No doubt the renewed drought throughout the region and the continuing civil war in Chad were responsible for the predicament facing the governments. Yet without the member states' contributions, CILSS found it increasingly difficult to discharge its duties. At one point it could not even pay money owed for telex and telephone services (3).

Another reason for the slowness with which the governments meet their financial obligations relates to the difference in fiscal calendars of CILSS and the member countries. CILSS budgetary calendar begins in January, while that of the states does not start until later in the year. The member states are unable to make their payments at the beginning of the calendar year.

The effect of this difference impedes CILSS' work. Because it must wait until mid-year before payments arrive, CILSS must borrow from its internal funds to meet expenses. Although members are exhorted to speed up their payments, very few do. In fact each year, several members states fall behind in their payments by an entire year.

Where states face severe political or economic problems (Chad and Mauritania), it is understandable that they fall repeatedly into arrears. Also, given the different fiscal calendar dates, it is legitimate that some states are late in paying their fixed contributions. However, there does appear to be some justification for the assertion that some of the member countries fail to pay dues for other reasons. Senegal, one of the better-off states, is habitually delinquent in meeting its financial commitments. When a period of a year or more elapses before states meet their obligations, one wonders whether it is really due to financial constraints or, rather, to a failure to take CILSS and regional cooperation seriously.

These sentiments were echoed by CILSS staff members asked to identify some of the problems of regional cooperation.

In sum, financial support, on the whole, is demonstrated by the Sahel governments in their willingness to meet financial obligations. The Sahel governments although late in paying their dues, do eventually pay. Where dues are still outstanding after two years, the reasons usually can be traced to political or economic difficulties. It should be noted that the governments have provided CILSS with land and buildings.

Sahelian Support for Staffing

TABLE 5.3
Technical Experts of the DPP as of 1980

Unit	Name	Nationality
Dryland Agric.	A. Sawadogo	Burkinabe
Irrig. Agric.	R. Max	French
Hydraulics	M. Reitchelt	German
Livestock	S. Barry	Burkinabe
Fisheries	J. Janet	French
Transportation	L. Ranger	Canadian
Ecology/	M. Diallo	Malian
Forestry	J. Adam	Belgian
	R. Winterbottam	American
	L. Coulibaly	Malian
Planning/	M. Maiga	Malian
Monitoring/	A. Drabo	Burkinabe
Evaluation	D. Martinet	French
	J. Sorgho	Burkinabe
Human	A. Sall	Senegalese
Resources	M. White	American

So far, the level of Sahelian cooperation in the areas of functions and finances has been discussed. In the next section, I will analyze the extent to which the Sahel governments cooperate in sending qualified bureaucrats to staff the CILSS Secretariat.

TABLE 5.4
Breakdown by Nationality of the CILSS Secretariat Technical and Administrative Staff

	Number
Sahelian:	
Burkina Faso	11
Cape Verde	0
Chad	1
Gambia	1
Mali	7
Mauritania	1
Niger	1
Senegal	3
Total	25
Non-Sahelians:	
Belgium	1
Canada	1
France	3
Germany	1
United States	3
Sub-Total	9
Grand Total	34

As of 1980, the technical experts working under the unit of the Division of Projects and Programs were divided between eight Sahelians and eight non-Sahelians. When the Division Chiefs, the Executive Secretary, administrators, the Crop Protection Unit, and the Food Corps Project Director are included, the number of Sahelians working at CILSS´ headquarters is twenty-five; the number of non-Sahelians is nine. The breakdown is shown in Table 5.4 above.

The Sahelianization of CILSS has been a goal of the organization since its begining. Out of all the member states, Mali, Senegal, and Burkina Faso have been the most helpful as far as putting their nationals at CILSS´ disposal. Chad, Gambia, Mauritania, and Niger have sent only one national each to fill the CILSS´ administrative and technical ranks at headquarters. For Gambia, the language barrier contributes to the problem of finding qualified personnel, who in addition must have French-speaking capabilities. Mauritania, Niger, and Chad have a smaller pool from which to draw technical experts. Moreover, the few qualified personnel are desparately needed at home. Senegal and Mali possess greater numbers of available cadres because of the politics of colonial education which gave these two nations greater educational opportunites.

Cape Verde is the only Sahel nation which has placed none of its nationals within CILSS´ ranks, probably owing the the fact that it is a lusophone country. Another reason could be the fact of Cape Verde´s late admission into CILSS (in 1976). As it becomes more integrated into the organization, perhaps it will assign its nationals to CILSS.

Compared to the earlier years, the members have improved their efforts to Sahelianize the organization. In the beginning, there were only seven Sahelians working at CILSS´ headquarters: one Malian, one Chadian, and five Burkinabe. Within the DPP, of the four technical experts assigned to the unit in 1975, only one was Sahelian. As recently as 1979, there were more non-Sahelians than Sahelians staffing the administrative and technical positions.

Since the 1977 reorganization, more Sahelians have been assigned to work at the Secretariat. In

159

addition, the international recognition and resources granted to the organization forced the member states to be more conscientious about the issue. After donors increased their contributions to the region, the governments began to view CILSS in a more serious light, and were more willing to invest some of their most capable nationals in the organization (4).

Prior to this reorganization, the lack of qualified staff was a cause for concern. Comments told to me by both donors and the CILSS´ experts indicated that the governments were initially reluctant to send the most qualified (5). This initial reluctance is being overcome gradually. Respondents, both donors and Sahelians, agreed that important strides had been made by the governments in assigning their best to the organization.

Inter-Sahelian cooperation in staffing is also manifested in other ways. Often the high level positions within regional and international organizations are jealously coveted by members. CILSS does not depart from this pattern. Each nation maneuvers to get its own national selected to the prestigious position of Minister Coordinator or Executive Secretary. When it is time to select candidates for these positions, states are reluctant to compromise. The result has been that the selection of a candidate has entailed needless delays.

The selection of a new DPP Chief was put off for seven months because member states could not reach a compromise on a choice. Similarly, the selection of a new Executive Secretary, scheduled for January 1980, was postponed for six months. In the former case, there was no Chief of the DPP during the interim period, and the Executive Secretary was forced to take on some of the responsibilities until a new DPP head came on board. In short, nationalism has interfered with the smooth functioning of CILSS as these two cases demonstrate.

In conclusion, within the organization there exists room for improved cooperation in the nomination of personnel to the highest offices. National pride exerts itself, and CILSS has been affected. Yet, at the administrative and technical levels, cooperation has grown. As resources flowed into the region, most governments devoted more attention to the caliber of the personnel they sent to work at CILSS. The overall result has been to increase the quality of the staff.

Sahelian Support for CILSS National Committees

The links between CILSS and the governments are the National Committees. The Committees' purpose is to ensure a coordination of policy, to maintain a constant and effective outlet for dialogue, and to increase Sahelian support of CILSS activities.

National Committees have been established in all of the countries, but the degree to which they operate effectively varies considerably. As a CILSS expert revealed, the National Committees "...function merely as a mail box. When CILSS needs information, it depends on the Committees to furnish it" (6).

Appeals to member states to make the Committees operational have been made at each Council of Ministers meeting, beginning with the Seventh in June 1977. The failure of the governments to financially support the Committees jeopardizes CILSS' effectiveness by increasing the time spent traveling to gather information from the governments, by reducing planning and coordination between the Ministry of Rural Development and other ministries, by reducing the information upon which CILSS can evaluate its progress in implementing the projects of the FGP, by relegating CILSS to a status of marginal actor in the national planning process, and by increasing the chance that the strategies and policies pursued by CILSS will conflict with those of the national governments.

The key to CILSS' effectiveness rests in the link which must occur between CILSS and all the departments and ministries whose actions affect CILSS' operations. The Committees should increase CILSS' visibility within the ministries and augment cooperation and coordination. In the end, the most effective Committees are in those states where the National Correspondent plays an active role in promoting CILSS´ concerns and the highest government officials strongly support CILSS´ work. States which do not have a well-organized National Committee demonstrate a lack of resolve to back CILSS´ work.

Evaluation of Sahelian Support for CILSS

Overall, cooperation has failed to occur on the issue of funding and support of the National Committees. Some cooperation has been achieved in the area of support for CILSS´ functions. Sahelian governments are more willing to support CILSS in the areas of financial contributions and staffing. Due to the prominence of CILSS in the international community, staffing has achieved the most in terms of advancement.

In a question designed to tap the extent of Sahelian support, I asked respondents to analayze how seriously the national governments take CILSS. Only four respondents felt that the states took CILSS seriously. Half of the respondents cited the following as evidence of the states not taking CILSS seriously: failure to respond to memoranda, failure to show up at meetings, failure to send qualified staff, and a failure to respect the CILSS priority projects in donors´ meetings. Six respondents (27.2 percent) believed internal constraints--political and economic--prevented the governments from adequately supporting CILSS. Two staff members of CILSS believed that the lack of support shown by some nations could be explained by the fact that not all governments were equally supportive of CILSS activities. Two respondents (9 percent) felt that the states questioned the ability of CILSS to accomplish the desired results, thereby contributing to their lack of assistance.

In all, there are several variables which explain the low level of cooperation and support of CILSS: political and economic problems, nationalism, the priorities of national governments, and the structure of CILSS itself. All of these factors combine to weaken the level of cooperation achieved and the degree of cooperation possible within the CILSS framework.

National self-interest plays an important

role in the amount of cooperation attained. To the extent that the governments perceive benefits from cooperation, they will be encouraged to do so. Paradoxically, the more benefits they receive, the less likely it is that they will continue to cooooperate. Increased cooperation demands greater sacrifices that do not necessarily match the gains achieved over time. Thus, cooperation becomes more politically and economically difficult, demanding too many costs which governments may not be willing or ready to pay.

Political will greatly determines the level of cooperation achieved. Support for CILSS at the highest governmental levels has been particularly strong in the Gambia, Burkina Faso, Cape Verde and Mali. In the African context, the attitudes of political leaders impede or enhance the progress of regional organizations.

In assessing the growth of cooperation, there are several areas in which CILSS has made a difference. For example, great progress has been made in the discussion of sensitive policy issues within the CILSS/Club du Sahel framework. The Cereals Policy and Recurrent Costs Colloquia stand out as advancements in regional cooperation. Cereals policy is a sensitive, volatile topic in Africa and yet the governments were able to sit down to discuss it and to develop a framework for actions.

CILSS has enhanced cooperation in another area. The number of meetings, seminars, and conferences provide the governments an opportunity to share their problems with other nations. Many of the problems can only be solved at a regional level. Thus, by its actions CILSS helps to push forward the cause of regionalism. CILSS provides the states the wherewithal to implement solutions too costly for individual states to undertake alone. The Crop Protection program, the Agrhymet Program, and the Sahel Institute contribute to building regional cooperation.

Overall, the conclusion is that the Sahel nations have laid an important foundation upon which regionalism can grow. Cooperation has enabled problems to be discussed in a regional context, increased baseline data on the Sahel, and helped to contribute to the goal of regional self-sufficiency. Unfortunately, when it comes to giving CILSS the requisite tools for carrying out the First Generation Program, the states have been reluctant to invest. An absence of financial contributions, a lack of support for CILSS functions, and the failure to get the National Committees working effectively have continued to slow down the process of inter-Sahelian cooperation.

DONOR SUPPORT FOR CILSS

Donor Support for CILSS´ Functions

Published reports voicing Sahelian and donor concerns have emphasized the unique North-South partnership which has resulted from the creation of the Club du Sahel and CILSS. In reality, donor procedures and requirements often override Sahelian-donor agreements and undermine the meaning of North-South cooperation.

Donor country reports and Sahelian pronouncements have urged the donor community to relax certain donor requirments such as tied aid restrictions (7). These are clauses imposed by several donors, including the United States, which require the Sahelians to purchase their products or services. Convincing donors to lift these restrictions often results in a delay in the start-up of a project. For example, Cape Verde wanted a donor to purchase locally-produced cement which costs one-third the price of imported cement. Six months of negotiations were necessary before the use of local cement was agreed to by the donor.

Delays of over two years are not unusual when the governments attempt to get the donors to waive tied aid clauses. Negotiations between CILSS and USAID over a buy-American car clause contributed to a delay in the start of the regional foresty school project. Two and a half years after the project was designed and approved, a vehicle still had not been delivered.

A celebrated case of donor inflexibility on procedures has been the Integrated Pest Management (IPM) project, financed by USAID and implemented by CILSS through the FAO. Negotiations for the

164

IPM project began in December 1974, but were bogged down because of American aid procedures which conflicted with FAO policies. In this instance, USAID procedural requirements on several points (clauses for the preference of hiring Americans, "fly American" provisions, and guarantees of access to FAO books and records, to name just a few USAID regulations) necessitated two years of negotiations between it and the FAO. The resolution of the disputed requirements placed the FAO in the position of agreeing to procedures which violated its own policies and statutes. Although the United States, as a member of the FAO, is bound by international agreement to its regulations, agreement was not forthcoming in the case of the IPM.

In response to the question, "What are the principle criticisms made about the donors?", seven respondents (24.1 percent) mentioned donor rigidity on procedures and regulations. Since the creation of CILSS and the Club du Sahel, both have attempted to get donors to be more flexible in their relations with the Sahel. These efforts have not always been successful.

Recent developments within the Sahel indicate continuing rigidity on the question of procedures. The development strategy and program agreed upon by both donors and Sahelians at the Second Club du Sahel Conference stated that criteria for the selection of projects should include variables other than cost-benefit analysis. Delegates to the Conference questioned the applicability of cost-benefit analysis to the Sahel. A multi-criteria approach to the selection of projects, emphasizing food self-sufficiency, the effect on rural populations, balance of payments effects, profitability, the reduction of regional and social imbalances, and effects on the Sahelian ecology was approved of by donors and Sahelians (8). Lately, donors have increasingly advocated a return to the selection of projects based upon profitability criteria. Despite Sahelian objections, the donors, through the Club du Sahel, are urging the Sahelians to accept a greater use of profitability measurements in the selection of projects for funding. The Cereals Policy Collo-

165

quium and the Recurrent Costs study encouraged the Sahelians to increase their reliance on market mechanisms and the use of users' fees in government services.

Another criticism of the donors in this regard is their tendency to usurp CILSS' role in development planning. Six respondents (20.6 percent) made this criticism. A complaint often heard was that the donors would not accept the work done by CILSS in the design of a project proposal. Rather than go along with the feasibility studies conducted by CILSS, donors would carry out their own studies. As one expert in the Secretariat stated, "Rarely does a donor go into a country and ask what projects have been identified by the governments and CILSS. Donors will go in and decide to fund such-and-such a project. Instead of taking on faith CILSS' projects, donors go their own way in developing projects" (9).

An example of this is the Mauritania forestry project, first identified in 1976, to fix sand dunes around two cities. A project that CILSS designed as a sand dune fixation project was expanded by an interested donor to incorporate renewable energy and natural resources management components. The project involved an inventory, through the use of satellite imagery, of the southern third of Mauritania's natural resources. Three-quarters of the projects' funds received ($3.4 million) will be used up by the Remote Sensing Institute in Ouagadougou to conduct remote sensing tests and to train personnel to interpret the results. The fixation of the sand dunes will take longer than expected due to the fact that the donor altered the project.

Despite the lack of progress in getting the donors to accept CILSS' proposals or in making donor procedures more pliable, CILSS and the Club have continued in their efforts to harmonize and simplify these procedures. Sahelian complaints about donor criteria for project selection centered on the multitude and diversity of forms which the Sahel governments were required to fill out when seeking donor funding. Working jointly, CILSS and the Club devised a document for use by the governments when requesting financial resources. The Project Identification Document

166

(PID) simplifies the application forms for the governments. Donors have been reluctant to accept the PID for their own use. As one Sahelian expert told me, "...no donor accepts a schema that is not its own. Each donor has its own model for project identification documents" (10).

In sum, donor procedures and requirements, when they conflict or overlap with CILSS´ functions, are not altered. Little cooperation has been achieved in this area and CILSS often finds that it must concede to the donors´ operations if it hopes to receive funding for projects. Even when CILSS works with the Club, it is unable to influence the level of cooperation it can attain from donors on operational matters. As long as donors must justify their funding to legislatures and public opinion hostile to foreign aid, little cooperation will be achieved in the area of flexibility on procedural matters, tied aid, or support for CILSS´ operations.

Donor Support for Financial Contributions

Generally, donors have been supportive in granting resources to CILSS (for other than project assistance). In the early years, German, Dutch, American, and French aid was used to pay for offices, equipment, supplies, and other items. Through a donation provided by the Germans, CILSS was able to locate in the headquarters it now occupies.

Each year donors provide funds to the CILSS Executive Secretariat, the Sahel Institute, and the Agrhymet Center. In 1978, for example, the United States granted $862,000 to the Executive Secretariat to help pay for operational expenditures, to pay for local personnel and three Americans working in the Secretariat. USAID made available to the Sahel Institute $400,000 to set up the demography planning unit. It also provided over $1 million to cover the operating costs of the Agrhymet Center in 1978 (11).

Donor contributions also cover the expenses of the Club Secretariat. France, Germany, the Netherlands, and the United States provide major funding to finance seminars and colloquia to prepare CILSS/Club reports, to conduct missions, and to pay for Club personnel and operations. Finally, donors have payed for the costs of the periodic Club conferences. Funding for the conferences has been provided by the Italians, the Arab/OPEC groups, and the other major donors.

When it comes to funding other than the cost of projects, the donors have provided CILSS with the needed resources. Donors cooperate in making monies available for feasibility studies, but are slow to contribute to implementing projects. (Chapter 6 discusses this point in depth.) In sum, donors have assisted CILSS and the Club in paying for the publication of reports, meetings, personnel, operational costs, and the Club conferences.

Donor Support for Staffing

What degree of cooperation has been achieved in donor support of CILSS´ staff? Between 1973-78, there were few Sahelian experts to be found; consequently, many non-Sahelians from the OECD nations filled CILSS´ technical and administrative positions. In 1975, three out of the four technical experts working in the DPP unit were OECD nationals.

Efforts to Sahelianize the organization, were agreed upon after the 1977 reorganization. Since then donors have made funds available to recruit and hire Sahelians to work at the Executive Secretariat and the specialized institutions. In 1980, of the thirteen Sahelian experts assigned to the Secretariat, all were funded by bilateral or multilateral donor agencies. The salaries of the ten non-Sahelian technical experts at CILSS headquarters were also provided by various donor agencies. At the beginning of 1985, out of twenty-three middle- and high-level cadres working within the CILSS Secretariat, donors paid the salaries of fifteen (65 percent). This support also extended to the Sahel Institute where eleven out of sixteen employees were paid for out of donor contributions. In the early years, donors were willing to provide CILSS with the salaries and the personnel to staff its operations. Since 1980 they have

168

grown less desirous of footing the bill. According to donor sentiment, the member states, as an indication of their commitment to CILSS, should assume their responsibility to pay for the staff within the CILSS headquarters and the specialized insitutions.

Nevertheless, the donors have proved themselves willing to cooperate in providing personnel and funds to hire staff. Without donor support in this area, CILSS' work would have been hampered tremendously.

Donor Support for the National Committees

The lack of Sahelian support for the CILSS National Committees is paralleled by that of the donors. The Sahelian position has been that donors, if they want CILSS to function effectively, should provide the resources necessary to enable the Committees to work properly. The donors, while recognizing the importance of the Committees in the development of coordination and cooperation, have been reluctant to put much in the way of funding at the disposal of CILSS. Negotiations between the UNDP and CILSS on funding the Committees conducted in 1980 were initially slowed down by conflicts. Disagreement ensued over the question of the source of the resources for the Committees. UNDP officials wanted the funds to come from its allocations to the states; CILSS preferred that additional funds be set aside for the Committees. To generate funding for the Committees, negotiations with USAID began in 1980 and continued throughout 1981. Eventually, some donor funding of the Committees was secured. Still, at the 20th Council of Ministers meeting, the lack of activity and dynamism of the Committees was an item on the agenda.

Evaluation of Donor Support for CILSS

Donor support for CILSS, as the preceding discussion shows, is greatest in the areas of staffing and financial contributions for non-project items, weaker in the area of support for

169

functions, and virtually absent with regards to the CILSS National Committees. Unlike the Sahel governments, donors have more resources to draw on and that explains why their financial support is greater.

Where support conflicts with donor procedures or requirements, CILSS has not been able to convince the donors to modify their positions. Thus, it appears as if donor support of CILSS' functions does not include accepting modifications in the implementation of development plans.

CONCLUSION

The expansion of CILSS' activities could not have been accomplished without the support of the Sahel governments or the donors. Support from both sides exhibits some similarities: neither has done much in the way of giving life to the National Committees. On the other hand, both have given strong support to the Sahelianization of the organization.

Donor assistance in terms of financial contributions has been stronger, owing to the strength of the economies of the donors. Sahelian support of CILSS' functions, although sometimes questionable, has been greater than that offered by the donors. Donors continue to remain inflexible on matters of project selection, project procedures, and tied aid clauses. What do these levels of support imply for CILSS?

The lack of support for the CILSS National Committees affects the concept of coordinated and integrated development. Without the Committees, CILSS' strategies and activities will not necessarily complement those elaborated by the government. The inability to get the Committees functioning also ensures that CILSS is marginalized in the Sahelian development process at the national level. Without the articulation of CILSS' work at the governmental level, there is no guarantee that its goals of regional food self-sufficiency and self-sustaining economic development can be realized.

The Sahel governments might continue to promote the modern industrial sectors, leaving the development of the rural areas to CILSS and the donors. As long as a lack of coherence between government development plans and CILSS´ strategy exists, regional cooperation will be neglected. Moreover, when it comes time to implement policy changes to promote CILSS´ strategy, it is not certain that the governments will be willing to sacrifice their own national (political and economic) interests.

In a worst case scenario, the lack of coherence and coordination could impact negatively on the inhabitants if contradictory programs and projects are formulated or if the governments refuse to make the necessary policy changes to promote development within the rural areas.

Besides the failure to support the National Committees, organizational effectiveness is also hampered by a lack of government support for CILSS´ functions. By failing to respond to CILSS´ correspondence, by altering the priority of the projects, and by failing to receive CILSS´ experts, the governments render CILSS less than effective. For its part, the donors, in their unwillingness to modify their regulations and procedures, undermine the cooperation within the CILSS/Club du Sahel framework.

The immediate consequence of a lack of support for CILSS´ operations and functions is that so few of the First Generation projects, as they were originally conceived, have been financed. In the next chapter, support for the First Generation projects is taken up.

NOTES

1. Experts in every sector complained of the lack of cooperation at the national level. Problems ranged from a slowness in responding to CILSS´ requests for information to outright refusals to attend to matters.

2. This problem has been discussed in Elliott R. Morss´s article, "Institutional Destruction Resulting from Donor and Project Proliferation in Sub-Saharan African Countries," World Development,

12, No. 4 (1984), pp. 465-70.

3. Anne De Lattre and Arthur M. Fell, The Club du Sahel: An Experiment in International Co-Operation (Paris: OECD, 1984), p. 86.

4. This was mentioned to me by several persons whom I interviewed at the Club, USAID, and CILSS.

5. Five persons whom I interviewed mentioned this problem. One CILSS expert was told by a Sahel government official that now that one of their nationals was working at CILSS, they were glad to be rid of him.

6. Interview with an expert of the Fisheries unit, June 13, 1980 in Ouagadougou, Burkina Faso.

7. CILSS/OECD, Summary Record of the Fourth Conference of the Club du Sahel (Paris: OECD, 1981), p. 6; CILSS, Summary Record of the Second Conference of the Heads of State (Ouagadougou: CILSS, 1976), p. 10; David Shear, Impediments to the Realization of the Sahel Development Program, Report to the Club du Sahel, mimeo, (1979), pp. 1-5.

8. OECD, Strategy and Program for Drought Control and Development in the Sahel (Paris: OECD, 1979), pp. 115-119.

9. Interview with an expert of the Ecology and Forestry team, June 6, 1980 in Ouagadougou, Burkina Faso.

10. Interview with an expert of the Human Resources team, July 26, 1980 in Ouagadougou, Burkina Faso.

11. USAID, Sahel Development Program, Annual Report to the Congress (Washington, D.C.: USAID, 1979), p. 25.

6

Support for the
First Generation Projects

EVALUATION OF THE PROJECTS

From 1977-1982, one of the major tasks of
CILSS and the Club du Sahel, in addition to the
articulation of a coherent development strategy,
was the design of projects to which the donors
would agree to commit resources for implementation. Since 1977, these FGP projects consumed
much of the time and energy of the CILSS experts.
The result has been the identification of 714
projects for ten sectors.

Table 6.1 shows the breakdown of the projects
of the First Generation Program by sector and by
country. Senegal and Mali ranked the highest in
terms of number of proposed projects (115 and 101,
respectively); Niger and Gambia, with 60 and 55
projects identified, had the least number of projects. Of the four poorest nations, only Mali and
Burkina Faso were scheduled to receive a high
number of projects, commensurate with their need.
That Senegal, the most affluent Sahel nation, had
the highest number of proposed projects (115),
attests to a persistent phenomenon in regional
organizations--the better-off nations receive a
disproportionately greater share of the benefits.

The data in Table 6.1 also reveal the extent
to which national projects were given priority
over regional projects. Only 51 projects (7 percent) out of 714 were regional projects. National
projects continue to reap greater support and
attention by both Sahelians and donors.

By sector, the Ecology and Forestry team

TABLE 6.1
Number of Projects in First Generation Program

Sector	Country									
	BF	CV	Chad	Gamb	Mali	Maur	Niger	Sene	Reg'l	Total
Dry. Agric.	15	5	4	6	15	12	10	15	2	84
Irrig. Agric.	9	6	13	6	18	16	9	20	–	97
Hydraulics	3	5	6	5	5	9	3	10	4	50
Livestock	13	10	11	10	22	15	7	20	9	117
Fisheries	1	5	1	4	2	3	1	3	1	21
Crop Protect.	1	1	1	1	1	1	1	1	9	17
Ecol. & Forest.	22	20	14	9	23	33	16	36	15	188
P-M-S	–	–	1	2	1	1	1	1	1	8
Transport. & Infrastruc.	1	3	7	2	1	1	1	1	3	20
Human Resources	17	16	21	10	13	9	11	8	7	112
TOTAL	82	71	79	55	101	100	60	115	51	714

174

proposed the largest number of projects (188). The heavy support given by donors and Sahelians to this sector could explain why a preponderance of proposals for Ecology and Forestry existed. Three sectors (Crop Protection, Price-Marketing-Storage, and Fisheries) had the smallest number of projects scheduled for execution (17, 8, and 21 respectively). The reason for the low numbers varied for each sector: Fisheries--because this sector has a very low priority among donors and Sahelians; Price-Marketing-Storage--because there was no expert assigned to CILSS to mobilize support for projects in this sector; and Crop Protection--because only one project had been designed for each country at the national level. Another interesting finding in the table is the situation of the Dryland Agriculture sector. Although dryland agriculture is the principle means of livelihood for about 90 percent of the population, projects in this sector have been given less emphasis than those in Irrigated Agriculture. A total of 84 dryland crops projects have been designed compared to 97 irrigated crops projects.

Table 6.2 displays the estimated costs of the FGP by country and by sector. The total cost of the FGP projects, $3.268 billion, reflected the costs in 1977 dollars. When inflation is factored in, the real cost of the projects rose to $4.18 billion (in 1980 dollars).

Mauritania and Senegal were to receive the highest dollar amounts for project costs, $699 and $651 million, respectively. The lowest amounts were to go to Gambia ($188 million) and Cape Verde ($103 million) probably due to their small land and population sizes relative to the other Sahelian states.

An analysis of the FGP projects by sector reveals, not surprisingly, that the most heavily allocated sector was Irrigated Agriculture due to costly financial investments in irrigation infrastructure. The combined costs of the Irrigated and Dryland Agriculture projects attested to the will of the Sahelians to concentrate on food production projects. On the other hand, the estimated cost of Fisheries projects is not consistent with the desires expressed by the governments to increase food production. With an estimated cost

.175

TABLE 6.2
Estimated Cost of First Generation Project
(In Thousands of U.S. Dollars)

Sector	Country									
	BF	CV	Chad	Gamb	Mali	Maur	Niger	Sene	Reg'l	Total
Dry. Agric.	177,145	5,002	19,160	41,387	144,450	93,525	79,352	169,709	570	730,300
Irrig. Agric.	19,090	4,451	71,469	57,509	155,945	297,464	84,091	291,659	-	981,678
Hydraulics	5,619	2,454	4,856	11,896	14,852	17,578	3,228	18,900	4,540	83,923
Livestock	25,832	15,070	17,881	21,333	39,952	67,720	43,088	38,820	NA	269,696
Fisheries	6,596	6,136	10,927	5,200	4,934	14,404	4,127	10,881	9,500	72,705
Crop. Protect.	2,800	583	1,564	2,000	3,990	1,504	2,500	2,777	51,782	69,500
Ecol. & Forest.	50,847	40,971	9,510	10,156	48,521	78,535	14,378	90,022	20,223	363,163
P-M-S	-	-	NA	8,360	3,300	14,932	NA	NA	9,300	35,892
Transport. & Infrastruc.	51,800	17,125	30,068	14,800	32,000	104,000	34,000	11,900	706	296,399
Human Resources	138,432	11,951	23,704	15,705	45,095	10,120	73,718	16,870	29,835	365,430
TOTAL	478,161	103,743	189,139	188,346	493,039	699,782	338,482	651,538	126,456	3,268,686

of $72 million for the first phase projects, the Fisheries sector was the least considered among the production areas.

In the supporting services areas, Human Resources and Ecology and Forestry sectors were the most expensive sectors in terms of estimated project costs. Projected costs of the projects for these two sectors totaled $365.4 and $363.1 million, respectively. Not surprisingly, Price-Marketing-Storage had a total estimated project cost of $35 million, ranking it the lowest for all supporting services areas.

At first glance, the total cost of the FGP projects for the four least well-off Sahelian states seemed to contradict statements made earlier that the poorest nations receive the smallest share of gains in regional organizations. According to Table 6.2 Chad, Mali, Burkina Faso, and Niger fall in the middle range of proposed projects' dollar value. However, when per capita cost of the projects is calculated, the picture changes somewhat.

Comparing the per capita cost of the projects by country, one notices that Mauritania ranks the highest with a total per capita project cost of $492.75 followed by Gambia with $336.28 and Cape Verde with $314.35. Per capita cost figures show that Niger, Burkina Faso, and Mali were to receive the least, $67.66, $73.52, and $75.80, respectively. Senegal and Chad ranked fourth and fifth in terms of total per capita costs of the FGP projects. An examination of the mean per capita cost of projects ($175.60) places the four poorest Sahel states at a disadvantage since they all fall below the mean. Thus, under the CILSS First Generation Program, the most severely affected nations (Burkina Faso, Chad, Mali, and Niger) fared the worst in terms of per capita project costs.

By sector, the breakdown in per capita costs followed the trends for estimated project costs; in the production areas more funds were to finance the Irrigated Agriculture sector and Fisheries had the lowest per capita project costs. In the supporting services, Transportation and Infrastructure and Ecology and Forestry were scheduled to receive the most, $20.07 and $26.14, respectively. The per capita cost of the Village

TABLE 6.3
Per Capita Cost of First Generation Projects
(In U.S. Dollars)

Sector	Country									
	BF	CV	Chad	Gamb	Mali	Maur	Niger	Sene	Reg'l	Total
Dry. Agric.	27.25	15.15	4.56	73.90	22.22	65.86	15.87	31.54	.01	28.48
Irrig. Agric.	2.93	13.48	17.01	102.69	23.99	209.48	16.81	54.21	-	55.07
Hydraulics	.86	7.43	1.15	21.24	2.28	12.37	.64	3.51	.15	5.51
Livestock	3.97	45.66	4.25	38.09	6.14	47.69	8.61	7.21	NA	20.20
Fisheries	1.01	18.59	2.60	9.28	.75	10.14	.82	2.02	.31	5.06
Crop Protect.	.43	1.79	.37	3.57	.61	1.05	.50	.51	1.73	1.17
Ecol. & Forest.	7.82	124.15	2.26	18.13	7.46	55.30	2.87	16.73	.50	26.14
P-M-S	-	-	NA	14.92	.50	10.51	NA	NA	.31	6.56
Transport. & Infrastruc.	7.96	51.89	7.15	26.42	4.92	73.23	6.80	2.21	.02	20.07
Human Resources	21.29	36.21	55.64	28.04	6.93	7.12	14.74	3.13	.99	19.34
TOTAL	73.52	314.35	94.99	336.28	75.80	492.75	67.66	121.07	4.02	175.60

and Pastoral Hydraulics ($5.51) ranked this sector the lowest of all the supporting services areas.

Finally, a comparison of the per capita cost of national and regional projects reveals some patent distinctions. The total per capita cost of all regional projects ($4.02) does not begin to match that of all national projects ($175.60). Clearly, both donors and Sahelians demonstrate a bias toward national projects in their project proposals.

From 1977-1982, CILSS and the Club worked diligently to get the 714 projects funded and executed. The figures for the estimated costs and number of projects (by sector and by countries) reveal a pattern of bias toward certain sectors and countries. Did these same biases hold when amounts committed (by sectors and by countries) are analyzed? Or did donors and Sahelians fund equally all projects across all sectors? What have been the level of aid commitments to the First Generation Program? In the next section, I will examine these questions.

AID LEVELS TO THE SAHEL

To begin with, a discussion of aid to the Sahel must be placed in the context of changes in aid following the drought. An examination of aid levels before and after the drought shows profound differences. OECD data demonstrate that aid levels to the Sahel went from $196.5 million in 1971 to $1.105 billion in 1978 (1). By 1982 total ODA to the Sahel rose to $1.513 billion (2). American aid levels to six of the Sahel nations amounted to $175 million in the twelve years prior to the height of the 1968-1974 drought (3). However, between 1975 and 1979, total U.S. public assistance to the region grew to $439 million (4). Without a doubt, the work of CILSS and the Club du Sahel has been responsible for raising aid levels (in real terms) committed to the Sahel. It is doubtful the Sahel nations, acting separately and without the assistance of CILSS and the Club, could have increased total official development assistance by more than twenty percent between 1971-1981 (5).

179

Nevertheless, aggregate aid figures overstate
CILSS' accomplishments by masking the level of
donor support by sector and by type of project.
Donor support, while registering a tremendous
increase since 1975, has fallen far short of the
expectations of CILSS and the Club.

DONOR SUPPORT FOR PROJECTS

Cooperation between CILSS and the donors can
be measured by donor support of projects. The
hypothesis tested is that there are no differences
in donor funding across sectors, countries, or
projects. In general, the evidence, through the
use of interviews and statistical analysis, does
not substantiate the hypothesis. Even though the
strategy agreed upon by the donors and Sahelians
placed a priority on the selection of all 714
projects, in reality, some sectors and projects
engaged more donor interest than others.
The fact that some sectors (Dryland Agriculture in Chad, Crop Protection in Niger, and
Fisheries in Mali) had commitments of over 100
percent conceals the real state of firm donor
commitments. In none of the cases where percentage of sector funded exceeded the estimated cost
of the program did any sector receive, in actuali-
ty, total funding for all of its proposed projects. Often, donors committed funds which exceeded the cost of a project. In total, 110
(15.40 percent) projects received commitments in
excess of their estimated costs. In other cases,
the estimated costs have yet to be calculated,
distorting the percentage of funds actually
committed to the projects. Therefore, caution
must be used when interpreting the figures for
amount committed to projects.
Overall, it appears as if 62 percent of the
projects of the FGP have been financed. For two
sectors, Dryland Agriculture and Ecology and
Forestry, about one-third of the project costs
received firm donor commitments. Human Resources
and Irrigated Agriculture received commitments for
over half of their First Generation projects (59
and 53 percent, respectively). Four sectors--
Village and Pastoral Hydraulics, Fisheries, Price-

180

TABLE 6.4

Amount (and Percentage) of Firm Donor Commitments of First Generation Projects (In Thousands of U.S. Dollars)

Sector	Country									Total
	BF	CV	Chad	Gamb	Mali	Maur	Niger	Sene	Reg'l	
Dry. Agric.	58,856 (33)	3,300 (66)	39,504 (206)	14,480 (35)	39,218 (27)	8,413 (9)	71,500 (90)	21,290 (13)	300 (53)	256,861 (35)
Irrig. Agric.	8,560 (45)	9,820 (220)	20,529 (29)	800 (1)	202,820 (130)	145,258 (49)	34,760 (41)	101,250 (35)	-	523,797 (53)
Hydraulics	18,535 (329)	16,100 (656)	1,678 (35)	4,710 (40)	37,067 (249)	10,768 (61)	14,929 (462)	27,952 (147)	37 (.008)	131,776 (157)
Livestock	43,342 (168)	500 (3)	12,638 (71)	1,183 (6)	30,261 (76)	23,550 (35)	72,279 (167)	18,679 (99)	7,733 NA	210,165 (78)
Fisheries	670 (10)	17,798 (290)	1,281 (12)	3,219 (62)	7,654 (155)	5,820 (40)	350 (8)	41,910 (39)	302 (3)	81,194 (111)

181

TABLE 6.4 (continued)
Amount (and Percentage) of Firm Donor Commitments of First Generation Projects
(In Thousands of U.S. Dollars)

Sector	BF	CV	Chad	Gamb	Mali	Maur	Niger	Sene	Reg'l	Total
					Country					
Crop. Protect.	4,900 (175)	1,912 (327)	100 (6)	810 (41)	2,549 (64)	280 (19)	10,050 (402)	11,340 (408)	33,590 (65)	65,531 (94)
Ecol. & Forest.	20,572 (40)	23,960 (58)	6,060 (64)	5,420 (53)	19,280 (40)	23,117 (29)	12,377 (86)	15,887 (18)	1,317 (7)	127,990 (35)
P-M-S	—	—	1,100 NA	536 (6)	17,733 (537)	15,220 (101)	1,300 NA	8,595 NA	37 (.003)	44,521 (124)
Transport. & Infrastruc.	13,092 (25)	400 (2)	26,797 (89)	29,889 (201)	105,301 (329)	129,281 (124)	42,950 (126)	48,473 (407)	1,849 (261)	398,032 (134)
Human Resources	71,658 (52)	6,488 (67)	10,374 (44)	5,917 (38)	44,235 (98)	21,875 (216)	34,667 (47)	19,948 (118)	3,922 (13)	219,084 (60)
TOTAL	240,185 (50)	80,278 (77)	120,061 (63)	66,964 (36)	506,118 (102)	383,582 (55)	295,162 (87)	315,324 (48)	49,087 (39)	2,058,951 (62)

Marketing-Storage, and Transportation and Infra-
structure--received funding in excess of the estimated cost of their projects.

The breakdown of these four sectors by
country revealed that some countries are over
committed for firm donor assistance while other
countries have not attained the total amount of
needed project funding. Moreover, a more detailed
analysis of those countries in which sectors
received 100 percent of project costs showed that
no sector found financial backing for all of its
proposed projects. Of the 128 projects which have
received 100 percent or more funding, only 69
percent (N=88) have procured funds for all of the
projects' components. In other words, 40 projects
while appearing to be totally funded are, in fact,
not. For these projects, donor commitments have
distorted the results by over funding aspects of
projects. In other words, a project may entail
several components, but lack the firm donor assistance to execute each component. For example, one
Cape Verde project, the promotion of market-
gardening crops and banana groves, had an estimated cost of $3.043 million. The Netherlands had
committed $4.1 million to one of the project's
components. So while it appeared as if this project was totally funded, in reality, several of
the components failed to pick up firm donor commitments. For all sectors, the funding patterns
of donors have distorted the true state of advancement.

Also, from Table 6.4 the discrepancies in
amounts devoted to regional and national projects
can be seen. Not surprisingly, donor commitments
to regional projects have covered 38 percent of
project costs; on the other hand, 61 percent of
national projects have generated donor support.
Donors tend not to invest in regional projects.
As one American official said, "USAID officials do
not get brownie points for regional projects. And
where and how fast you advance in your career
depends upon your (bilateral) record. As a result, certain AID missions are hostile to regional
projects. They don't want to take the time, they
do not want to involve their personnel in regional
projects" (6).

In addition to donor preferences for certain

183

sectors and regional projects it has been noted
that certain countries receive higher donor
commitments than others. To get a better idea of
donor commitments, Table 6.5 shows per capita
project costs and per capita firm commitments by
country.

TABLE 6.5
Country Rankings by Per Capita Cost
and Per Capita Donor Commitments

Country	Per Capita Project Cost	Country	Per Capita Firm Commitment
Mauritania	$492.75	Mauritania	$270.07
Gambia	336.28	Cape Verde	243.17
Cape Verde	314.35	Gambia	119.55
Senegal	121.07	Mali	77.82
Chad	94.99	Niger	59.10
Mali	75.80	Senegal	58.54
Burkina Faso	73.52	Burkina Faso	36.91
Niger	67.66	Chad	28.54

According to the table, the top ranking
countries (in terms of highest per capita estimated project cost), Mauritania, Cape Verde, and
Gambia, are also the top ranking countries in
amounts received from the donors. Chad ranks the
lowest in terms of total per capita firm donor
commitments. The per capita estimated project
costs for Burkina Faso, Niger, and Senegal put
these countries in seventh, eighth and fourth
place. However, the per capita firm donor commitments place Burkina Faso in seventh rank, Niger in
fifth, and Senegal in sixth.
Clearly, a bias occurs when it comes to
funding projects across countries. The states
which scored highest on the PQLI index--Gambia,

184

Mauritania, and Cape Verde--are not only scheduled
to reap a larger proportion of aid dollars, but,
in fact, have received higher firm donor commitments. Donor commitments to the better-off states
parallel the results found in the Mytelka study of
UDEAC which showed that donors prefered to grant
more aid to the Cameroon rather than to the poorer
nations, Chad and the Central African Republic
(7).

The bias in funding certain sectors also
emerges when one analyzes per capita firm donor
commitments. Table 6.6 gives an analysis of per
capita firm donor commitments by sector and by
country.

Of the four production sectors, Irrigated
Agriculture has, so far, secured the highest per
capita firm donor commitments ($24.58).
Fisheries, a sector little appreciated by donors
or Sahelians, has received only $8.13 (in per
capita figures) toward the implementation of its
projects. Livestock has received the lowest total
per capita commitments of $5.85.

In the supporting services, Transportation
and Infrastructure has received more per capita
firm donor commitments ($20.87) than any other
sector. Price-Marketing-Storage has procured in
per capita dollars only $2.36 putting it in last
place for per capita firm commitments.

To test the hypothesis that donor funding
patterns for sectors are equal, analysis of
variance tests were run. In all cases, the null
hypothesis was rejected. In other words, the
evidence supported the contention that amount
committed by donors differs with respect to individual sectors (F=3.681, p < .05). The evidence
also buttresses the contention that the percentage
of project funded by donors differs according to
sector (F=5.0578, p < .05).

Confirming the analysis of variance tests
were the statements expressed by the CILSS´
experts regarding donor support of various sectors. Several experts deplored the lack of donor
interest in some sectors, particularly, Dryland
Agriculture, Fisheries, and Ecology and Forestry,
deemed crucial to the fulfillment of the Sahelian
goals of regional food self-sufficiency and self-
sustaining economic development. Sixteen res-

185

TABLE 6.6

Per Capita Firm Donor Commitments of First Generation Projects

(In U.S. Dollars)

Sector	Country									
	BF	CV	Chad	Gamb	Mali	Maur	Niger	Sene	Reg'l	Total
Dry. Agric.	9.05	10.00	9.40	25.88	6.03	5.92	14.30	3.95	.01	9.39
Irrig. Agric.	1.31	29.75	4.88	1.42	31.20	102.29	6.95	18.81	-	24.58
Hydraulics	2.85	48.78	.39	8.41	5.70	7.58	2.98	5.19	0.00	9.10
Livestock	6.66	1.51	3.00	2.11	4.65	16.58	14.45	3.47	.25	5.85
Fisheries	.10	53.93	.30	5.74	1.17	4.09	.07	7.78	.01	8.13
Crop Protect.	.75	5.79	.02	1.44	.39	.19	2.10	2.10	1.12	1.54
Ecol. & Fores.	3.16	72.60	1.44	9.67	2.96	16.27	2.47	2.95	.04	12.40
P-M-S	-	-	.26	.95	2.72	10.71	.26	1.59	0.00	2.36
Transport. & Infrastruc.	2.01	1.21	6.38	53.37	16.20	91.04	8.59	9.00	.06	20.87
Human Resources	11.02	19.60	2.47	10.56	6.80	15.40	6.93	3.70	.13	8.51
TOTAL	36.91	243.17	28.54	119.55	77.82	270.07	59.10	58.54	1.62	99.49

pondents (55 percent) mentioned the disappointing state of advancement of the projects when asked to cite major criticisms of the donors.

Nine experts criticized the use of donor interest as a criterion in selecting projects for funding. As one expert declared, "They only finance what they want--cotton and peanut projects. Donors are more interested in export crops because of their profitability" (8). Another expert postulated that the Dryland Agriculture sector failed to engage donor interests because donors could not derive large profits from the production of sorghum, millet, and other traditional food crops.

Another way in which to determine donor support of projects is to examine the types of projects within sectors for which no donor has advanced any verbal or financial commitment. Table 6.7 shows that the Ecology and Forestry team has not found any donor to support 81 (43 percent) of its projects. Although the Fisheries sector is without funds for 10 percent of its projects,

TABLE 6.7
Percentage of Projects by Sector
Having Received No Donor Commitments

Sector	Percent	N
Dryland Agriculture	18	15
Irrigated Agriculture	23	22
Village and Pastoral Hydraulics	19	9
Livestock	31	36
Fisheries	10	2
Crop Protection	11	2
Ecology and Forestry	43	81
Transportation and Infrastructure	5	1
Human Resources	21	24

187

reality belies the statistics. No Fisheries project, as originally designed by the Fisheries team, has been supported by the donors (9). Donors have funded fisheries projects which they wish to implement rather than those CILSS or the Sahel states proposed. The Livestock sector has not fared well in finding donors to support its projects; 36 (31 percent) of its projects have generated no donor interest.

Various explanations can be advanced to explain why the projects in some sectors generate little or no donor interest. In the case of Ecology and Forestry, the CILSS experts have added projects to the First Generation Program list of 1977. These projects were only proposed in 1978 and 1980, and donors had begun to lose interest in financing the FGP projects. For another reason, aspects of Irrigated Agriculture projects which entailed expensive infrastructural investment made donors reluctant to fund this sector. Whatever the reasons, there are sectors which do not receive any donor support.

For donors as a whole, the data confirm their preferences for funding specific sectors. Does the same hold true for categorizations of donors? In the following section, I will analyze project support by categories of donors.

Of the nine major donors to the Sahel, the interests lean toward projects in Livestock and Irrigated Agriculture (on the production side) and Human Resources and Ecology and Forestry (on the supporting services side).

France and the Netherlands exhibit a preference for Irrigated Agriculture projects. Projects in Human Resources account for a major share of United Nations Development Program (UNDP), USAID, and World Bank funds. Germany, the United Nations Sudano-Sahelian Office (UNSO), and the FAO share a propensity to devote more resources to the Ecology and Forestry projects. Only one donor, the FED, gave a higher percentage of its assistance to the Livestock sector. Finally, none of the major donors devoted a considerable percentage of its aid to either the Dryland Agriculture or the Fisheries sectors.

A second categorization of donors includes Donor Types. Donor Types comprises four cate-

TABLE 6.8
Number (and Percentage) of Projects Having Received Support From Major Donors

Sector	Major Donors									
	France	FAO	FED	West Germ.	Nether.	UNDP	UNSO	USAID	World Bank	Total
Dry. Agric.	37 (17.5)	8 (17.8)	7 (9.5)	15 (11.4)	8 (15.4)	7 (9.7)	4 (7.1)	34 (14.7)	17 (16.8)	137 (14.06)
Irrig. Agric.	62 (29.4)	2 (4.4)	8 (10.8)	20 (15.2)	13 (25.0)	4 (5.4)	2 (3.6)	33 (14.3)	19 (18.8)	163 (16.73)
Hydraulics	11 (5.2)	0 (-)	3 (4.1)	8 (6.1)	1 (1.9)	13 (18.1)	7 (12.5)	12 (5.2)	3 (3.0)	58 (5.95)
Livestock	28 (13.3)	5 (28.4)	21 (28.4)	25 (18.9)	10 (19.2)	3 (4.2)	4 (7.1)	40 (17.3)	14 (13.9)	150 (15.40)
Fisheries	8 (3.8)	10 (22.2)	6 (8.1)	3 (2.3)	5 (9.6)	10 (13.9)	1 (1.8)	6 (2.6)	1 (1.0)	50 (5.13)

TABLE 6.8 (continued)
Number (and Percentage) of Projects Having Received Support From Major Donors

Sector	France	FAO	FED	West Germ.	Nether.	UNDP	UNSO	USAID	World Bank	Total
Crop Protect.	7 (3.3)	3 (6.7)	5 (6.8)	5 (3.8)	2 (3.8)	7 (9.7)	3 (5.4)	9 (3.9)	0 (-)	41 (4.20)
Ecol. & Forest.	25 (11.8)	11 (24.4)	2 (2.7)	31 (23.5)	6 (11.5)	11 (15.3)	19 (33.9)	34 (14.7)	18 (17.8)	157 (16.11)
P-M-S	5 (2.4)	1 (2.2)	1 (1.4)	6 (4.5)	0 (-)	1 (1.4)	1 (1.8)	3 (1.3)	0 (-)	18 (0.10)
Transport. & Infrastruc.	7 (3.3)	0 (-)	4 (5.4)	10 (7.6)	0 (-)	0 (-)	9 (16.1)	5 (2.2)	9 (8.9)	44 (4.51)
Human Resources	21 (10.0)	5 (11.1)	17 (23.0)	9 (6.8)	7 (13.5)	16 (22.2)	6 (10.7)	55 (23.8)	20 (19.8)	156 (16.01)
TOTAL	211 (21.66)	45 (4.62)	74 (7.59)	132 (13.55)	52 (15.33)	72 (7.39)	56 (5.74)	231 (23.71)	101 (10.36)	974 (100.0)

Major Donors

gories: public bilateral (CIDA, FAC, or USAID, for example), public multilateral (the FED, UN agencies, and the World Bank), the (Sahel) national governments, and private organizations (such as Africare). Many supporters of multilateral donor organizations claim that these organizations are politically neutral and, therefore, they have different (and nobler) interests to pursue (10). The evidence presented seems to contradict the assumptions made about multilateral aid donors. Analysis of variance tests failed to reject the null hypothesis that the amounts committed and the percentage of projects funded are equal across Donor Types. In other words, donor types do not appear to account for any of the variance in project support of the ten sectors. Multilateral institutions do not support projects in a manner different from any other donor types.

A third categorization--Donor Geography--did reveal significant variance across donor geographical groupings. Donors were divided into eight categories--OECD, Arab, African, UN agencies, Eastern bloc, Third World, national governments, and private aid groups. The breakdown of the percentage of sector funded by Donor Geography is given in Table 6.9.

Divided in these eight groupings, donors tend to vary in their support for projects. Arab, Third World, OECD, and Eastern bloc donors prefer to invest in the Irrigated Agriculture sector. The UN agencies tend to back the Human Resources sector. The Sahel governments exhibit a preference for Ecology and Forestry projects. Only private organizations devote more resources to the Fisheries sector, but given their small number and budgets, it is unlikely that they are able to make an impact on the direction of support for sectors.

The analysis of variance tests measuring support for sectors by Donor Geography rejected the null hypothesis. The evidence demonstrated that the amount committed by donor geographical groups differs with respect to sectors ($F=6.6886$, $p < .05$). Likewise, the evidence also supports the contention that the percentage of projects funded by geographical groupings differs with respect to sectors ($F=2.4861$, $p < .05$).

191

TABLE 6.9
Percentage of Sectors Funded by Donor Geography

					Donors			
Sector	OECD	Arab	Afri.	U.N.	East. Bloc	Third World	Nat'l Gov't	Priv. ONG/Grps
Dry. Agric.	13.9	3.6	8.3	11.7		20.0	25.0	16.7
Irrig. Agric.	18.3	30.9	21.7	6.2	100.0	60.0	12.5	8.3
Hydraulics	5.5	14.5	25.0	14.5			12.5	
Livestock	15.5	10.9	21.7	5.5				41.7
Fisheries	4.8		5.0	7.6				
Crop. Protect.	4.2			5.5				
Ecol. & Forest.	15.2	10.9	1.7	16.9			37.5	25.0
P-M-S	1.8	3.6	1.7	1.4				
Transport. & Infrastruc.	4.5	18.2	6.7	2.8		20.00		8.3
Human Resources	16.3	7.3	8.3	27.9			12.5	
TOTAL	100.0	99.9	100.1	100.0	100.0	100.0	100.0	100.0

There are several factors which explain donors' preference to invest in certain areas as opposed to others. For one thing, donors tend to invest in sectors in which they possess a great deal of expertise. Thus, in formulating projects, they prefer to hire their own nationals upon whose advice they depend. American expertise in grains and cattle is evident by the higher percentage of American dollars invested in the Agriculture and Livestock sectors. The United Nations´ concern for women and children makes the Human Resources a targeted sector for UN funds.

Secondly, mandates chosen by legislatures become incorporated into development work. As an example of this, the concern of American legislatures in the late 1970s for projects dealing with Human Resources was adopted into USAID´s mandate. Government assessments had shown that American aid investment should move away from support of infrastructure to support for human needs where it would have a more profound impact in improving the lives of people. As a result, USAID officials increased their support to projects in this sector. Over time, lessons from past development mistakes are incorporated into legislative rules and edicts.

Finally, donors follow development fads. As one sector becomes fashionable, resources allocated to it increase. For example, a growing interest in women in development led to the formulation of projects with women in development components. In the past, the Human Resources sector benefited from this tendency to follow development fads. In addition, as a result of the energy crisis in the 1970s, a new found concern for energy resources benefitted the Ecology and Forestry sector, as donors became more interested in projects involving renewable energy sources. Under the Reagan Administration, the development shift has been to increase the role of the African private sector in development.

All of these factors contribute to donor preferences in selecting sectors in which to concentrate their funds. Not only do donors exhibit sector preferences, they also tend to finance certain types of projects within sectors.

A prime example of funding preference is the

Fisheries sector. Included in this sector are projects for maritime (coastal) and continental (land-locked) countries. Maritime projects have generated donor support while continental projects have not. Of the continental fisheries projects, only 21 percent have received donor support; whereas 72 percent of maritime projects have been funded. Donors invest in maritime fishing because they benefit from the tuna, shrimp, and oyster hauls (products which have a strong demand in the donors' home markets).

Within sectors, projects often comprise one or more components. For example, one component could involve a feasibility study. Another component of the project could entail training cadres to execute the project. Other components could involve some type of productive activity. Table 6.10 displays the degree of donor support for project components within 7 sectors. Across sectors, the results are the same. Certain types of project components receive little donor funding. In Irrigated Agriculture, 30 percent of the Production (and Crop Improvement) projects and 50 percent of the Credit projects lack donor support. In the Livestock sector, Marketing, Livestock By-Products, and Livestock Studies projects have yet to find substantial donor commitments. The Conservation and Wildlife projects within the Ecology and Forestry unit are 80 percent unfunded. Finally, in the Human Resources sector, projects drawing little donor support include those such as Community Development and Rural Communication.

Among all sectors, the CILSS experts readily identified components of projects for which they had worked without substantial results. Here again, the comments given mirrored those concerning the selectivity of donor support for sectors. As one expert mentioned, "The activities that have been financed are for the most part feasibility studies. What remains is the financing of the projects themselves" (11).

The sentiments expressed by the experts are reinforced by the analysis of variance tests measuring donors contributions to project components. For each test measuring the amount committed and the percentage of project components funded, the null hypothesis was rejected. In

194

TABLE 6.10
Project Components with No Donor Support

Sector	Project Components	Percentage Without Support
Dryland Agriculture	Infrastructure/National Services	5
	Research	18
	Studies/Planning	11
	Production	30
	Integrated Development	5
	Credit	50
	Cereal Storage	33
Irrigated Agriculture	Infrastructure/National Services	15
	Studies/Planning	31
	Production	31
	Supporting Action	7
	Agro-Industrial Products	100
Livestock	Infrastructure/National Services	27
	Research	43
	Studies/Planning	57
	Production	15
	Integrated Development	29
	Training	33
	Livestock By-Products	50
	Marketing	75
	Health Care	21
Ecology/ Forestry	Infrastructure/National Services	50
	Research	53
	Studies/Planning	30
	Wood Production	30
	Integrated Development	41
	Training	54
	Conservation/Wildlife	80

Table 6.10 (Continued)
Project Components with No Donor Support

Sector	Project Components	Percentage Without Support
Fisheries	Studies/Planning	33
	Production	50
Human	Infrastructure/National	
Resources	Services	20
	Rural Education	19
	Rural Communication	37
	Training	15
	Small Business/Credit	25
	Health Care	10
	Community Development	39
Village	Infrastructure/National	
and	Services	21
Pastoral	Studies/Planning	10
Hydraulics	Production	50
	Integrated Development	33
	Training	50
	Water Supply	12

---

other words, donors differ with respect to amount committed and the percentage of project components funded.

When donors are further divided into Donor Type and Donor Geography, two patterns emerged. For Donor Type, the test failed to reject the null hypothesis that donor types do not differ with respect to amount committed and the percentage of project funded, according to various components. In other words, there was no statistically significant difference among bilateral, multilateral, private, or national groups in their support for

196

TABLE 6.11
Mean Percentage of Project Categories Funded

Sector	Infras./ Nat'l Services	Research	Studies/ Plan/ Eval.	Produc./ Develop.	Integ. Develop.	Training
			Project Categories			
Dry. Agric.	21.80	31.00	58.14	34.35	36.61	20.00
Irrig. Agric.	27.77	11.75	46.16	30.31	61.50	28.80
Hydraulics	55.80	100.00	27.14	50.00	0.00	0.00
Livestock	32.53	3.83	10.00	27.00	10.55	25.00
Cont. Fisheries	3.00	–	50.00	18.00	9.66	–
Mari. Fisheries	64.50	100.00	0.00	–	75.50	100.00
Ecol. & Forest.	18.76	48.31	0.00	–	26.51	24.30
Transport. & Infrastruc.	–	–	45.50	–	23.00	–
Human Resources	48.273	–	63.66	–	–	46.50
x̄ Average	34.05	49.14	33.40	31.93	30.41	34.94

197

types of components within projects.

The evidence proved otherwise on tests measuring differences amoung Donor Geography. In testing the amount committed, the evidence confirmed the notion that Donor Geography is associated with types of components funded (F=6.5785, p <.05). The same holds true for percentage of component types funded (F=2.3973, p < .05). The results indicated OECD, Arab, Eastern bloc, and other Third World nations contribute more resources to irrigated agriculture; while African donors give more to hydraulics projects; and, the UN system devotes a greater percentage of its funds to human resource activities.

A comparison of the mean percentage of projects funded across the five comparable component types (Table 6.11) revealed donor preferences in project support. Donor commitments are greatest for project components involving Research ($\overline{x}$ = 49.14) and Training ($\overline{x}$ = 34.94), and least for Production ($\overline{x}$ = 31.93) and Integrated Development ($\overline{x}$ = 30.41) projects.

In effect, donors are willing to fund the research and training project components, but are not willing to commit monies to the actual implementation of the projects (production and integrated development).

Most projects contain several components and donors agree to finance either one, a few, or all of the components of a project. As long as each component eventually finds a financial backer, projects will ultimately be implemented. What has occured in many cases is that portions of a project never elicit donor support and, therefore, the projects are not completed.

An example of this funding difference was the study of the non-structured sector of secondary urban centers which included a minor component on credit for small businesses. One donor, interested only in the minor component, wanted to inject massive amounts of credit into the small business sector. Thus, donor funding worked to distort the percentage of the project financed. If a donor funds a portion of a project in excess of its estimated cost, then it appears as if the project is totally financed when, in fact, it is not. Donor backing for project components ex-

198

plains why the Fisheries sector seems to be totally financed when, in reality, many of the project
components funded do not correspond to CILSS'
proposals. In a $12 million rainfed farming pro-
ject, one donor committed $11.74 million to
develop the western region of Gambia, even though
the project proposal was designed to promote integrated rural development in the eastern region.

What does this pattern of funding mean in
terms of the development of the Sahel? The first
consequence is that CILSS' goals of food self-
sufficiency and self-sustaining economic development will probably not be realized by the target
date, the year 2000. Secondly, if donors fail to
support integrated development projects, the likelihood of recurring droughts and famines, related
to the lack of coherence among water, vegetation,
and animal resource policies, increases.
Integrated development projects, critical to the
rational balance of resources, must become an
integral part of the Sahel Development Program.

Thirdly, if donors fail to support the projects, they will be viewed by the Sahelians as not
honoring their commitments to help the region
overcome its problems. In that case, Sahelian
support for North-South cooperation in the
CILSS/Club du Sahel framework could erode and
tensions between the two sides could arise.

So it is that the priorities of the donors do
not intersect with those of CILSS. The effect is
to skew development plans away from Sahelian needs
to donor interests. Because of donor preferences
in funding national over regional projects and
certain sectors and components over others, CILSS
is far from accomplishing the goals of the First
Generation Program set in 1977. Consequently,
only about 88 of the FGP projects (12.5 percent)
have been totally financed.

Even though donor support of projects differs
according to the individual donor and donor
geographical groupings, the differences do not
ensure a random support of projects across all
sectors, all countries, all types of projects and
all the components of projects. In the end, the
record of implementation and the form development
takes reflect the funding patterns.

More and more, development in the Sahel is

shifting from a North-South cooperative blueprint for action to one in which CILSS responds to donor ideas about development. Since CILSS has staked its reputation on the implementation of the projects, it finds that it must alter its activities in order to secure higher aid awards. This pattern has made the CILSS experts reluctant to design projects which they fear will not be supported. Projects and programs have been redesigned to answer the question: "But will the donors accept it" (12).

Unfortunately, even these efforts do not always pay off. At the 1978 Ecology and Forestry donors' meeting, donors complained of the lack of economic analysis, social impact evaluation, and complete technical analysis in the project proposals. Furthermore, they requested that more projects be designed which stressed fuel conservation and efficiency instead of wood fuel production (13). Between 1978 and 1980, the Ecology and Forestry team, working closely with French and American officials, elaborated 28 projects which took account of the donors' complaints.

When the second Ecology and Forestry donors' meeting convened in July 1980, the donors were presented with the 28 new project proposals. Their complaints this time concerned the absence of a training component in the projects. Out of 28 projects presented, only two or three were considered by donors for funding consideration (14).

At the Second Club du Sahel Conference donor and recipient countries cooperated in creating a strategy for regional development and in designing projects which would fit into the strategy. However, when it came to the projects selected for funding, donor interests have prevailed. Because CILSS does not possess the resources to pick up the unwanted projects and because it cannot modify donor behavior, it is unable to exert a countervailing influence on the project selection process. It can admonish and implore, but it cannot control or direct the donors.

One solution to counterbalance the interests of the donors would be for the Sahel governments to pay for the projects left unfinanced. To some extent, the national governments have contributed to the financing of these projects.

SAHELIAN SUPPORT FOR PROJECTS

The problem in analyzing Sahelian support for projects is that there are so few projects financed by the national governments. The lack of resources contributes to the miniscule investments made by the Sahel governments. Out of 714 projects, only nine projects have been selected by the governments for financing and all are national projects. With the exception of Cape Verde, every nation is engaged in partially funding at least one project. Senegal and Niger are committed to financing two projects.

Gambia is involved in a water project costing $4.2 million of which it has donated $1.2 million (28 percent). Burkina Faso and Mali are involved in projects in the Ecology and Forestry sector estimated to cost $13.4 and $1.91 million, respectively. Mauritania, with the aid of the People's Republic of China, is financing a $22.8 million irrigated agriculture project. Niger's commitments are to projects in the areas of Livestock and Human Resources. Senegal intends to put up $110,000 for a Livestock project. In addition, Senegal has offered resources to pay part of a $5.5 million Ecology and Forestry project. Chad has decided to disburse its own funds to help support a $40 million Irrigated Agriculture project.

The areas in which the member states contribute their own resources sum up their priorities. The five sectors which have received national government support are: Human Resources (one project); Village and Pastoral Hydraulics (one project); Ecology and Forestry (three projects); Livestock (two projects); and, Irrigated Agriculture (two projects). No government interest has been registered in Dryland Agriculture, Crop Protection, Price-Marketing-Storage, Transportation and Infrastructure, or Fisheries. Of particualar importance is the fact that Dryland Agriculture, which accounts for 95 percent of all crops produced, has elicited no government support. Fisheries, a sector with a great potential as a

201

food resource for the region, has also failed to interest the national governments. Where CILSS projects coincide with the priorities of the member states, cooperation (measured by financial contributions) can be achieved.

It should also be noted that all of the projects receiving Sahelian support are national projects. So far, no regional project has generated any government contribution. Sahelian support for CILSS' projects which have an immediate impact on national priorities and interests is greater than their support for regional projects that benefit them less directly. In essence, the cooperation given by the governments is directly proportional to their perceived gains from such cooperation.

TABLE 6.12
Sahelian Commitments of Project Components

Country	Sector	Project Component
Burkina Faso	Ecology/Forestry	Integrated Development
Chad	Irrigated Agriculture	Production
Gambia	Hyraulics	Water supply/ Management
Mali	Ecology/Forestry	Wood Production
Mauritania	Irrigated Agriculture	Production
Niger	Livestock	Production
Niger	Human Resources	Cooperatives/ Community Development
Senegal	Livestock	Infrastructure
Senegal	Ecology/Forestry	Integrated Development

Comparing Tables 6.10 and 6.12, one notices the differences between donors and Sahelians in their funding of components of projects.

Almost all of the projects supported by the governments relate to production and integrated development. Senegal´s support of the construction of a cattle platform and Niger´s involvement in a project concerned with the Association of Nigerien Women depart from the the emphasis placed upon production projects. Unlike donor preferences, the Sahel governments have not committed funds to research, training, studies, or planning (Table 6.11). Instead, the interests of the Sahel governments bear upon activities designed to increase their productive capabilities.

However, the small number of projects supported by the Sahelians cannot counterbalance the funding patterns of the donors. In the end, the variety of projects selected for funding will reflect the weight of donor contributions. As the data prove, donor interests in projects has a significant effect upon the state of advancement of the First Generation Program.

THE IMPACT OF FUNDING PATTERNS

State of Advancement

The evidence indicated that contrary to the hypotheses, donors exhibit preferences in financing projects. These preferences will have an impact on the course of development in the Sahel, North-South cooperation, and the prospects for continued inter-Sahelian cooperation.

As this chapter has shown, random funding of projects has not occured. Instead, the selection of projects is such that: some sectors have received more aid than others, components of projects are sometimes financed in excess of their estimated cost, regional projects have elicited little support, and aid to countries is not always proportionate to need. What explains the differences in support for projects? What are the consequences of funding differences?

Earlier, it was said that the better-off nations, for example, Mauritania, were receiving

203

higher per capita aid than the poorer nations. Of the poorest, Mali, is scheduled to receive aid amounts in proportion to its needs. Two others, Chad and Burkina Faso, rank lowest on measurements of per capita project costs and per capita firm donor commitments. In the context of other regional organizations, the maldistribution of resources could affect the degree of regional cooperation obtained. In the future, the poorer CILSS states could become disillusioned by their perceptions that the benefits of cooperation are not worth the costs.

The preference of donors is also exhibited across sectors where Irrigated Agriculture and Transportation and Infrastructure have received high levels of donor support. Left virtually unfunded are several sectors critical to the fulfillment of CILSS' goals of food self-sufficiency and self-sustaining economic growth--Fisheries, Crop Protection, and Livestock. More importantly, per capita firm donor commitments in Dryland Agriculture ($8.59) are one-half those of Irrigated Agriculture ($17.52), despite the fact that dryland farming employs the bulk of the labor force. Several factors explain donor selectivity.

Donors are more likely to engage in activities in areas where they have considerable expertise. Donors possess a greater knowledge of irrigated agriculture, the major crops of which are cotton, rice, wheat, and peanuts. Donor expertise of millet, cowpeas, and sorghum is less extensive. In the Fisheries sector, donors have a more detailed knowledge of coastal than inland fisheries.

Donors invest in areas where their interests lie. The likelihood that they will benefit from maritime fisheries, as opposed to continental projects, propels donors to support the former. Transportation projects are easier to implement and do not always require complex planning. The results from paving a road are easier to calculate. Therefore, donors prefer to invest in projects that are simple to implement and have a direct impact on the population. For this reason, health care projects involving vaccination are far more likely to secure donor interests than projects involving the use of traditional medicine.

In addition to funding certain sectors, donors exhibit a proclivity for certain types of projects--training, research, studies--while leaving unfunded the projects bearing upon production and integrated development. Donors have been particularly interested in training projects designed to develop a cadre of African personnel to implement the Sahel Development Program. Projects entailing research and studies carry weight with the donors because of the absence of baseline data on the Sahel. It is easier to get donors to fund studies than it is to get them to implement the recommendations of such studies. Donors are reluctant to fund certain types of projects, especially integrated development projects, because of their complexity. Integrated development projects involve the coalescence of several development sectors, a complex and difficult task to carry out. Therefore, donors prefer to invest projects that do not require complex planning and intersectoral arrangements. When it comes to selecting projects for financing, donors choose: 1) projects about which they have expertise, 2) projects which fit their cost-benefit criteria; and 3) projects which are easier to design and execute.

Another finding of this chapter has been the discrepancy in the financing of regional and national projects. Neither Sahelians nor donors exhibit much enthusiasm in funding regional projects, the preference for working at the national level is dominant. In terms of both the number of projects and per capita firm commitments, national projects retain a higher priority. Donors prefer to work at the national level because the political benefits are more direct. Furthermore, the experience of the regional Crop Protection program has made donors wary of regional projects. The Crop Protection program has entailed innumerable delays due to the logistics of coordination and agreement among three sovereign bodies. Because regional projects have not had a long history, the expertise for their execution is lacking. A simple reason for the lack of implementation of regional projects is that neither donors nor Sahelians give them much backing.

Even though the data showed that differences exist among donors (Sahelians versus the international community, donor geographical groupings, and the ten major donors) in their support of projects, these differences are not random enough to offset the interests of the major donors who account for over 55 percent of the assistance committed. The weight of the major donors prevails in directing the state of advancement of First Generation Program.

What is being (or not being) funded has implications for the course of development, inter-Sahelian relations, and North-South cooperation. In the following section, the implications of funding patterns are discussed.

Implications of Funding Practices

The level of project funding will bear upon the direction that development in the Sahel will take. First, rural development increasingly diverges from the strategy jointly agreed upon by the donors and the Sahelians at the Second Club du Sahel Conference. As long as the selection of projects is restricted to those which fit into cost-benefit analysis and profitability criterion, the range of acceptable projects will be limited.

One consequence of the project selection process has been that CILSS is delayed in achieving its goals of food self-sufficiency and self-sustaining economic development. As long as the Fisheries and Dryland Agriculture sectors go unfunded, CILSS' goals cannot be achieved. Moreover, it is not certain whether the emphasis upon Irrigated Agriculture, a more costly technology, is advisable (15). The major beneficiary of Irrigated Agriculture will be export, not food crop, producers. The link between food self-sufficiency and the expansion of export crops is tenuous at best. The history of the region has shown that as export crop production expanded, peasants were not necessarily better able to feed themselves through the purchase of imported foodstuffs.

Funding patterns also impact upon inter-Sahelian relations. The dearth of regional projects which get funded works against a spirit of cooperation at the regional level. If more regional projects were selected, the CILSS countries would be obligated to work on a regional focus for development. The heavy support of national projects reinforces the bilateral approach to development.

Secondly, a funding pattern which favors the more advantaged countries runs the risk of generating conflict among member states. The potential exists that the least well-off countries will come to resent their small share of the aid. The conflicts which could surface could undermine inter-Sahelian cooperation.

Because regionalism is built upon a shaky foundation of political will, every effort should be made to reinforce inter-Sahelian cooperation. A more equitable distribution of donor aid and greater support of regional projects would help to reinforce the regional approach to development.

In addition to the impact of funding patterns upon possible South-South cooperation, North-South cooperation is also affected. If the selection of projects continues to reflect the priorities of the donors rather than the needs of the Sahelians, the governments will begin to question the usefulness of the CILSS/Club du Sahel arrangement. With only 60 percent of the FGP projects funded, the expected fruits have not been delivered. Fewer projects have actually been completed and many have yet to find any financial backing. Moreover, several of the CILSS experts expressed doubts as to whether the remainder would ever find donor support. Perhaps, in the future, the member states may begin to ask themselves: Why bother to cooperate and sacrifice when the results are so poor?

Problems of Goal Achievement

When asked why it was that only 60 percent of the FGP had firm donor commitments, several reasons were offered. Nineteen respondents (32 percent) laid the blame on the projects. The poor quality of projects and the lack of coherence and cohesion of the projects were cited frequently. The comments given by the interviewees alluded to the need to improve project dossier quality in order to overcome the low level of donor support.

The Sahel states also shared part of the blame for the lack of advancement of the FGP. Of the 29 percent (N=17) who blamed the states, opinion was divided almost equally between those who felt the governments lacked the necessary resources, personnel, and capabilities to execute the projects and those who suggested that the Sahel states failed to adequately support and reinforce CILSS' efforts (53 percent mentioned the former and 49 percent the latter). In some cases, the states failed to bring up the CILSS list of projects in their bilateral meetings with donors.

The donors were also criticized for their role in the poor state of advancement. Thirteen respondents (22 percent) cited a number of donor actions which impeded progress: the failure to fund the proposed projects; lack of donor interest in certain types of projects; donor procedures and regulations; and the donors' tendency to fund according to simple preference.

CILSS' culpability in the state of advancement was highlighted by several experts. The failure of the National Committees and the CILSS structure were factors mentioned by twelve percent of the respondents. Experts, both donor and Sahelian, felt that CILSS lacks the ability to carry out the proposed projects.

Finally, three respondents (5 percent) believed the obstacles to the completion of the FGP resulted from the dependency of CILSS on the international community. As one expert said:

> CILSS is tied to the donors...There are a
> lot of things that are not going well,
> but CILSS is not free to act. We are in
> a system, installed and invented by the
> donors and approved by the states. The
> money comes from the Club (donors). We
> cannot change, for political reasons,
> because of political choices made by CILSS
> and the Sahelians (16).

This sentiment echoed that of another expert who stated: "CILSS has chosen a development strategy (dependency) which will never lead to food self-sufficiency" (17).

208

CONCLUSION

Clearly, the blame for the poor state of advancement of the FGP projects can be shared by the donors, CILSS, and the governments. The support given to CILSS´ operations and functions by the Sahelians and the donors relates to the level of project funding and the projects selected for funding. Because the national governments fail to follow up and contact potential donors, project implementation is delayed. If the national governments do not respond to CILSS´ requests for information, the ability to design suitable projects is rendered difficult, if not impossible. If the governments do not support CILSS in fulfilling its goals, then why, ask the donors, should they?

Likewise, the donors, by their demonstrated reluctance to reinforce CILSS´ functions, contribute to the present state of achievement. Donor reliance upon profitabilitiy as the primary criterion for project selection reduces the number of projects which will be funded. Worthwhile projects, failing to accommodate quantifiable equations of cost-benefit analysis, will not be picked up by the donors. Furthermore, donor regulations and donor tendencies to select the tried-and-tested projects (tree planting as opposed to wood conservation, and vaccination as opposed to traditional medicine) restrict the variety of projects chosen. Innovative ideas or projects which require complex planning across sectors are too often overlooked or deemed too impractical.

In addition, CILSS´ role in what has been accomplished must not be ignored. The failure to institute a more systematic approach to integrated project planning impacts upon the lack of integrated projects proposed and chosen for funding.

By the end of 1982, the First Generation Program ended. With only 60 percent of the projects funded, reflection of the state of advancement took place within CILSS and the Club du Sahel. On the donor side, there was a deep sense of dissatisfaction as to CILSS´ and the Sahel government´s ability to design and execute quality projects. On the Sahelian and CILSS side, there was regret over the lack of interest in funding the rest of the projects of the FGP. In the end, the donors felt that a new strategy was needed for CILSS, one that moved away from a primary concern for development projects. Rather, it was felt CILSS most important task was reflection and analysis of regional needs. In the next chapter, this new strategy is outlined.

NOTES

    1. CILSS/Club du Sahel, Official Development Assistance to CILSS Member Countries From 1975-1979 (Paris: OECE, 1980), p. 165.
    2. OECD/CILSS/Club du Sahel, Official Development Assistance to CILSS Member Countries in 1983 (Paris: OECD, 1985), p. 7.
    3. Hal Sheets and Roger Morris, Disaster in the Desert (Washington, D.C.: The Carnegie Endowment for International Peace, 1974), p. 9.
    4. Ibid, p. 9.
    5. Anne De Lattre and Arthur M. Fell, The Club du Sahel, An Experiment in International Cooperation, (Paris: OECD, 1984), p. 80.
    6. Interview with USAID officer, June 14, 1980 in Ouagadougou, Burkina Faso.
    7. Lynn Kreiger Mytelka, "Foreign Aid and Regional Integration," Journal of Common Market Studies, 12, No. 2 (1973), pp. 138-158.
    8. Interview with an expert of the CILSS Planning, Monitoring, and Evaluation unit, July 10, 1980.
    9. Interview with the CILSS Fisheries expert, June 13, 1980 in Ouagadougou, Burkina Faso.
    10. V.H. Oppenheim, "Whose World Bank?" Foreign Policy (1975), pp. 99-108.
    11. Interview with the CILSS Irrigated Agriculture expert, July 8, 1980 in Ouagadougou, Burkina Faso.
    12. Experts in the Fisheries, Ecology and Forestry, Human Resources, Irrigated Agriculture, and Livestock units all admitted in interviews that they are tailoring their project proposals to meet donor appproval.
    13. Interview with an Ecology and Forestry expert, July 29, 1980 in Ouagadougou, Burkina Faso.

14. Ibid.

15. On the problems of irrigation projects see, Jonathan Derrick, "West Africa's Worst Year of Famine," African Affairs, 83, No. 332 (1984), pp. 296-299 and Richard W. Franke and Barbara H. Chasin, Seeds of Famine (Montclair: Allanheld, Osmun, and Co., 1980), pp. 156-57.

16. Interview with the Fisheries expert, July 30, 1980 in Ouagadougou, Burkina Faso.

17. Interview with an expert of the Planning, Monitoring, and Evaluation unit, July 10, 1980 in Ouagadougou, Burkina Faso.

7

Conclusions:
Drought and Development
in the Sahel

THE BALANCE SHEET

Positives

Although CILSS has fallen short of many of the goals which it set for itself at the Second Club du Sahel Confernce, it is not without some minor and some important victories. An important contribution of the CILSS/Club du Sahel framework has been to expand knowledge of the Sahel. Prior to the creation of these two organizations, very little was known of the socio-economic and cultural environment or the existing resource base. The myriad sectoral, regional, and country analyses have helped donors and Sahelians to orient their activities, to improve their planning, and to decide which programs and projects to support. For the governments, knowledge gained of groups such as the herders has made policy-makers more aware of the problems facing those living far from the urban centers. By the same token, donors who before the 1968-1974 drought had little information or understanding of the region and its inhabitants, have been able to use the studies carried out by the Club and CILSS to formulate their own proposals for action.

The various meetings have helped the Sahel governments realize that their situations are not unique. In the formative years, governmental representatives were often surprised by the commonalities between and among the states. As a result, they have come to understand the need to search for regional solutions to problems of drought and ecological destruction.

A second contribution of the CILSS/Club framework has been the sectoral analyses completed on a variety of rural issues. These sectoral analyses covering irrigated and dryland agriculture, livestock, ecology and forestry, and fisheries, to name a few, have enabled donors and Sahelians to understand the conditions within a number of the Sahel countries. Based on the analyses, donors and Sahelians have been able to articulate strategies for action and identify the types of programs and projects needed to improve conditions within the rural areas of the member countries. Not only have the sectoral analyses improved the data base knowledge of the region, but they have also pointed out obstacles to the attainment of the CILSS´ objectives for development. For example, prior to 1977, few donors or Sahelian countries paid much attention to the Ecology and Forestry sector. When the 1977 ecology and forestry analysis was completed, the report actually redirected donor and Sahelian thinking on the importance of ecology and forestry in stemming ecological degradation. Lastly, periodic reviews of the sectors allow donors and Sahelians to constantly upgrade the strategy and to change their activities accordingly.

Besides the sectoral analyses which improved the knowledge base within countries, a number of policy analyses have been important in pointing to the global constraints to rural development. A number of broad policy studies (new lands, cereals, and recurrent costs) brought attention to policy issues which were undermining the effectiveness of various CILSS´ programs and projects. For example, the cereals policy colloquium highlighted the need to provide an environment free of factors which distorted market conditions and caused farmers to lose their incentive to increase production. The cereals policy studies pointed to a number of specific state policy actions (pricing policy, agriculture input subsidies, and food aid) which hampered food production. Likewise, the recurrent costs study demonstrated the need to design projects which did not entail costs too burdensome for the Sahel

214

governments to assume once donor funding had
ended. Both studies made invaluable contributions
by underscoring how donor and Sahelian policies
and actions undermined the objectives established
by CILSS.

Some CILSS/Club du Sahel discussions
concerned highly sensitive subject matters. The
fact that such discussions took place under the
CILSS/Club du Sahel auspices indicates the evolution of North-South cooperation.

A further contribution of the CILSS/Club
mechanism has been the advancement of regional
institution building. The willingness to spon-
sor endeavors such as the Sahel Institute and the
Agrhymet Center encourages the regional approach
to solving development problems. The Sahel Institute has been the organ of leadership and direction in regional research efforts. The activities
of the Agrhymet Center add to regional capabilities in conducting and analyzing satellite imagery
data necessary for predicting drought and climate
conditions. Furthermore, the agro-meteorologic
and hydrologic training components provide a cadre
of technicians to aid regional and national
development. Despite setbacks within these
specialized institutions, they both have helped
governments to pursue regional approachs to problems.

Another positive aspect of the cooperative
process has been the development of very frank
dialogue between donors and Sahelians, CILSS and
the Club du Sahel, CILSS and the Sahel
governments, and the Club and donors. Given the
different vantage points and concerns of each, the
process has not always been a smooth one. Despite
disagreements from time to time among all parties,
there has been a remarkable degree of cooperation
which has advanced North-South and South-South
dialogue. The periodic meetings (regional,
sectoral, and otherwise) have been praised by both
recipients and donors for their contribution to
airing grievances and adding honesty to the discussion.

Strains have emerged between donors and
Sahelians over the role of the CILSS/Club
mechanism. Donors tended to view the organization
as a think tank; the governments saw its role as a

revenue mobilizer. With the ending of the First Generation Program, donors persuaded CILSS and the governments that CILSS should cease its involvement in project implementation. Not wanting to abandon its activities in the area of project design and implementation, CILSS agreed to an arrangment under which its involvement in projects of a regional nature would continue.

Tensions surfaced between CILSS and the member states over the level of support given to CILSS. The Secretariat complained of a lack of support and follow-up activities by the member states. This lack of support on the part of the states was clearly demonstrated by the inability to make the CILSS National Committees function smoothly. At the heart of the matter is the fact that the government's own national strategies and priorities do not always correlate with CILSS' objectives. While paying lip service to the importance of rural development, government resources and energies are directed to other sectors of the economy. Likewise, the failure of CILSS to obtain complete funding for the FGP aroused criticism and made the governments sceptical of the benefits of the CILSS/Club process.

Another set of tensions arose between CILSS and the Club Secretariats. It concerned misunderstandings over the Club's role. The resolution creating the Club du Sahel emphasized that the Club would be subordinate to CILSS. In reality, this did not occur. The Club initiated its own activities which sometimes irritated the CILSS Secretariat. For example, in January 1980, the Club Secretariat convened a series of meetings with the CILSS experts without asking or informing the CILSS Executive Secretary. This action provoked the anger of the Executive Secretary. As one CILSS expert put it, "The Club permits itself things that are not normal" (1). In response, the Club asserts, "If we wait until they tell us to do something, it would take them six months. So we just go ahead and do it" (2).

Minor irritations occured on both sides: CILSS took actions without notifying the Club, the Club did likewise. CILSS believed that the Club worked for CILSS; the Club felt it should also be responsible to the donors. As I was told by an

216

official of the Club Secretariat, "CILSS thinks that we work for them. They forget that we work for the donors, too" (3).

Finally, disgreements occured between the Club Secretariat and the donors over donor reluctance to share information and cooperate on projects and programs. The lack of sharing entailed costly duplication of effort. Because the nature of development aid is also political, donors were sometimes reluctant to coordinate their activities when this could have proved disadvantageous to a bilateral relationship with a particular Sahel state. The funding choices of donors did not always reflect the priorites established by CILSS and the Club.

One of the major contributions of the CILSS/Club effort was the rise in the level of aid resources to the Sahel. Because of the Club Secretariat, donors expressed confidence in the lending process, and were willing to augment resources to the Sahel. Donors felt that the Club ensured a wise and careful use of their money. In an era of global economic contraction, donors must justify their expenditures and the Sahel Development Program allowed them to do so. The

TABLE 7.1
Official Development Assistance to the Sahel (1975-1983)

Year	In millions of current $US
1975	$ 817
1979	1,623
1980	1,502
1981	1,972
1982	1,513
1983	1,259

Source: OECD, Official Development Assistance to CILSS Member Countries in 1983 (Paris: OECD, 1984), p. 7.

growth in aid levels to the Sahel reflected, in part, donor confidence. As De Lattre and Fell argue, this confidence increased the support given to the region by donors such as the Italians, the Dutch, and Arab regional organizations (4).

In absolute terms, ODA has grown steadily since 1975. The average yearly growth rate has been 5.6 percent. In real terms, assistance grew by an annual average rate of 0.4 percent (5). Though aid levels dropped after 1981, the region still managed to receive more per capita aid than any other Sub-Saharan African or Asian region. As the following table points out, it appears as if the NIEO demand for more aid for the poorest was answered in CILSS´ case.

In 1975, per capita aid to the Sahel stood at $23 dollars. By 1981 this figure was $44 dollars. The 1982 figure which declined to $39 dolars reflects the appreciating value of the dollar vis-à-vis the major European currencies. Nevertheless, per capita aid to the Sahel has remained higher than per capita aid to other Sub-Saharan or Asian regions.

TABLE 7.2
Per Capita Aid Disbursements   (In current $US)

	1975	1979	1980	1981	1982
Sahel	$23	$40	$39	$44	$39
Sub-Saharan Africa (excluding the Sahel)	10	17	21	20	27
Asia	6	9	10	9	5

Source: OECD, Official Development Assistance to CILSS Member Countries in 1983, (Paris: OECD, 1984), p. 51.

CILSS made it possible for the small donor to support projects without having to finance a heavy bureaucratic machinery. Small donors used the expertise provided by CILSS and the Club to ascertain regional and national needs which they wished to support. Without the CILSS/Club mechanism, small donors would have been forced to finance all aspects of project implementation. In this way, small donors added to the number of projects being supported financially.

Finally, CILSS and the Club increased donor attention to the problems of rural development in the Sahel. For the first time, donors consented to a strategy of development that pertained primarily to the rural area. The focus on rural development allowed donors to increase their activities in this domain because they were in a position to refuse those projects which did not pertain to the priority sectors.

The CILSS/Club framework contributed to Sahelian support of the CILSS Secretariat. As a result of donor support for the work of the Secretariat, the CILSS countries put more qualified staff at CILSS´ disposal. Sahelians felt that the formation of CILSS and the Club du Sahel brought them the attention and the resources needed for their development efforts. Their confidence in this cooperative endeavor made them willing to respond to CILSS´ demands and needs.

The positive aspects of North-South and South-South cooperation would lend support to those who argue for decolonization as the way to interpret North-South relations. Through ten years of dialogue and work in a compromising spirit, donors and Sahelians gave flesh to the New International Economic Order. They pointed to the possibilities for North-South cooperation which could be mutually beneficial. In sum, the CILSS/Club du Sahel framework made several contributions. First of all, the framework for cooperation created a strategy for rural development by which national and regional development efforts could be gaged. Secondly, the donors and Sahelians grew in their understanding of conditions within the productive and supportive services sectors. In the periodic donor/Sahelian meetings, data presented on livestock, ecology

219

and forestry, and agriculture were utilized in the design and implementation of projects and programs. Thirdly, donor cooperation and Sahelian cooperation grew. While still far from perfect, donors are more willing to share their knowledge and expertise with other donors. Likewise, the Sahel governments cooperated more with each other through CILSS/Club activities. The recognition of interdependence increased; consequently, the efforts to work together to solve problems of a regional nature multiplied. Fourthly, the policy advanced donor and Sahelian understanding of the constraints and obstacles to the effectiveness of the projects and programs implemented.

Negatives

One of the major disappointments has been the pattern of funding. Sectors critical to the achievement of economic growth and food self-

TABLE 7.3
Breakdown of Funding by Sector
as a Percentage of All ODA
(1975-1983)

	1975	1977	1979	1981	1983
Food Aid	12	7	8	8	14
Rainfed Crops	2	2	1	3	3
Irrigated Crops	3	8	5	7	5
Livestock	7	1	2	1	3
Fisheries	1	2	1	1	1
Hydraulics	-	-	1	3	7
Ecology/Forestry	0	1	2	3	2
All other sectors (6)	75	79	80	74	65

Source: OECD, Official Development Assistance to CILSS Member in 1983 (Paris: OECD, 1984), pp. 45-46.

sufficiency failed to receive as much support from the donors as CILSS had hoped. Over the past ten years, very little funding has gone to the productive sectors.

Overall, donors were more willing to support the irrigated crop sector than dryland farming. Donor sentiment leaned toward the former because of its "profitability." Irrigated agriculture has received, on the whole, three times more funding than Dryland Agriculture. From 1975-1983, total ODA commitments to irrigated crop projects totalled $687,779; rainfed crop project commitments totalled $211,092 (7). Yet, irrigated agriculture only accounted for 5 percent of total cereals production, the other 95 percent of cereals production employed traditional (dryland) cropping methods. To be sure, part of the explanation lies in the fact that irrigated agriculture is a costly enterprise. Some have questioned whether the cost is worth it. If not done properly, irrigation leads to the soil becoming waterlogged or the salt leaching away. Other negative effects can occur for downstream farmers when water supply drops. Scarce resources could be better used in dryland farming which contributes more to the production of traditional cereals than irrigated agriculture which has mainly been used in the production of cash crops.

The Ecology and Forestry sector, recognized as an important one, also failed to elicit substantial donor support. In total, the amount of aid devoted to this sector did not exceeded 2 percent of total aggregate aid to the Sahel (8). Though the share of total aid going to Ecology and Forestry projects grew after 1975, the levels did not correspond to the desparate need to turn back the process of deforestation and desertification taking place.

In a similar manner, the percentage of ODA allocated to the Fisheries sectors also fell below CILSS' expectations. As a percentage of all ODA granted to the region between 1975 and 1983, the amounts committed to this sector averaged no more than 1.2 percent. The Fisheries team, in describing its accomplishments, called its work program "a failure." Donor and Sahelian support of this sector's proposals proved nonexistent and

221

what projects were funded reflected donor preference. Donor and Sahelian priorites favored
different sectors. Continental fisheries was completely ignored while maritime fisheries' projects
drowned in resources.

Evidence of this lack of support can be seen
in the fact that for two years (1983-1985) there
was no expert assigned to CILSS to carry out the
work of the Fisheries team. Even Sahelian priorities lie with other sectors. In Burkina Faso, the
government elevated the importance of fisheries in
the bureaucratic structure, but did not give the
Director of Fisheries any supporting staff with
which to carry out its mandate.

In sum, the pattern of funding demonstrates a
clear bias in support of certain sectors, countries, and project components. Due to these dominant funding patterns, CILSS objectives are far
from being met.

Most importantly, the lack of support for key
development sectors has contributed to the
region's continuing reliance upon food aid and
food imports. At present, the gap between food
production and food consumption, exacerbated by
population growth rates and migration trends, has
left the region in need of more food aid and
imports than during the last drought. Despite the
return of rains after the 1968-1974 drought, the
Sahel states never stopped requesting food aid.
While food aid shipments did decline after 1974,
they never fell below their pre-drought levels.
As the following tables show, in some cases food
aid climbed even as food production increased.

The table below of cereal production
figures between 1961-1965 and 1983-1984 shows
three different trends among the Sahel states.
For Cape Verde, Chad, and Mauritania, cereals
production declined consistently through the 1970s
and the 1980s. In fact, production levels for
these three nations were much lower in the 1980s
than before the 1968-1974 drought. In the case of
Cape Verde cereal production for 1983-1984 was 81
percent below that of 1961-1965. Mauritania's
cereals production was 73 percent below that of
1961-1965. Niger and Mali show a different pattern of cereals production. During the first
drought, cereals production declined, but it re-

222

TABLE 7.4
Average Cereals Production   (in 1000 tons)

| | Year | | | | | |
	1961- 1965	1969- 1971	1974- 1976	1977- 1979	1980- 1982	1983- 1984
Burkina Faso	918	987	1150	1180	1205	1044
Cape Verde	16	2	4	4	5	3
Chad	759	685	592	640	674	472
Gambia	86	90	83	61	85	65
Mali	1055	1049	1216	1241	1128	1077
Mauri-tania	98	87	51	33	55	26
Niger	1218	1273	1119	1562	1726	1460
Senegal	617	704	826	738	795	614

Source: FAO, 1976 FAO Production Yearbook, 30 (Rome: FAO, 1976), p. 89; United Nations, 1981 Statistical Yearbook (New York: United Nations, 1983), p. 489; United Nations, 1982 United Nations Statistical Yearbook (New York: United Nations, 1985), p. 503; FAO, 1984 FAO Production Yearbook, 38 (Rome: FAO, 1984), p. 107.

bounded after 1976, only to drop again during the 1983-1984 agricultural campaign. In Senegal and Burkina Faso, production of cereals dropped as a result of the recent drought but did not drop during the 1968-1974 drought.

Despite the fact that cereals production figures improved between 1976 and 1982, the Sahel states continued to import cereals and other food aid items. During the decade after the drought, per annum food production grew by 1.75 percent; while food imports grew by 8 percent (9). Average cereals imports doubled three times during the 1970s. Now accustomed to the imports of wheat and

TABLE 7.5
Average Cereals Imports   (in tons)

Years	Amount
At the start of the 1960s	200,000
1970-71	460,000
1976-76	630,000
1977-79	890,000
1982-84	1,333,000

Source: Jacques Giri, Rétrospective De L'
Economie Sahelienne (Paris: OECD, 1984), p. 10.

TABLE 7.6
Average Annual Growth Rates of Rice Production
and Rice Imports (1974-1982)

	Rice Production (in percent)	Rice Imports (in percent)
Burkina Faso	13	86
Chad	14	62
Gambia	6	35
Mali	-3	130
Mauritania	17	12
Niger	9	203
Senegal	9	25

Source: United Nations, 1982 Statistical Yearbook
(New York: United Nations, 1985), p. 508; FAO,
1976 FAO Trade Yearbook Volume 30 (Rome: FAO,
1977), p. 114; FAO, 1979 FAO Trade Yearbook Volume
33 (Rome: FAO, 1980), p. 118; and FAO, 1982 FAO
Trade Yearbook Volume 36 (Rome: FAO, 1983), p.
118.

rice, the Sahel nations have grown dependent upon such foodstuffs.

A comparison of average annual growth rates of rice production and rice imports reveals that in spite of average annual increases in rice production (with the exception of Mali), the Sahel states showed substantial increases in rice imports. Rice import growth rates ranged from 12 percent for Mauritania to 203 percent for Niger. Rice production growth rates, on the other hand, were much more modest figures, ranging from 6 percent for Gambia to 17 percent for Mauritania. Though production on the average increased from 1974 to 1982, imports far outstripped whatever increases occured in production. There are a number of reasons why food import growth rates remained substantial.

One explanation for the continued reliance on food imports is the inability of cereals production to keep up with population growth. However, this is only part of the answer since other agricultural crops such as cotton and groundnuts have managed to register gains in production during this same period.

To understand why the Sahel governments continue to import food products, one must look at the products that are imported. Between 1966 and 1980 the major imported food items, wheat and rice, grew to be more desired items of consumption for the Sahelian populations. Consumption growth rates of wheat and rice registered 4.6 and 2 percent respectively from 1966-1980. During this same period, growth rates of the consumption of locally-grown foodstuffs (corn, millet and sorghum) declined by 1.4, 1.4, and .7 percent, respectively (10). Therefore, a taste transfer revolution is taking place in the Sahel. Urban dwellers have developed a preference for rice and wheat over millet, sorghum, and corn.

Another explanatory variable has been the governmental sale of food imports at low or absolutely no cost. In recent years, Mauritania and Senegal distributed freely 50 percent of the food aid received (11). Government distribution of food aid at low cost helped to pacify the urban populations. The long-run costs of such a policy are damaging. Low-priced food imports depress the prices paid to peasants for their locally grown crops. Hence, peasant incentives to grow more food are reduced. Yet, the governments prefer to achieve short-term political gains at the expense of long-term economic benefits.

In addition, governments find food aid useful for another reason. Though a need for food aid continued after the drought, a portion of food aid was used for budgetary and balance of payments support. The sale of food aid gave the governments funds to shore up the public and parastatal sectors. Public officials have been able to build up their political bases through the proceeds from the sale of food aid.

A third by-product of this foreign aid is the dependency which it has engendered. In effect, Sahelians have grown accustomed to foreign assistance which expanded on the average 18.6 percent between 1971-1982. Foreign aid now represents a substantial proportion of the GNPs of the Sahel e-

TABLE 7.7
Aid in the Economies of the CILSS Nations (1982)

	Aid as a % of the GNP	Per Capita Aid Amounts ($)
Burkina Faso	19	33
Cape Verde	50	183
Chad	20	14
Gambia	23	70
Mali	19	27
Mauritania	26	111
Niger	17	43
Senegal	12	47
Total Sahel	17	39

Source: OECD/CILSS/Club du Sahel, Official Development Assistance To CILSS Member Countries In 1983 (Paris: OECD, 1985), p. 50.

conomies. On the average it accounted for 17
percent of the GNPs of the states for the year
1982. Quite literally, the economies of a number
of these countries would collapse without donor
largesse. For four states--Chad, Cape Verde,
Mauritania, and Gambia--foreign aid constituted at
least 20 percent of their GNPs.
    Another unintended result of the growth in
donor assistance is the cost of repaying that aid.
Some of the aid has been given in the forms of
loans and, sooner or later, loans must be repaid.
Donor assistance creates debt burdens for the
recipient nations. Unlike the situation in many
other developing countries facing enormous debts,
the debt problems in the Sahel have resulted from
loans contracted mostly at concessional (below
market) rates through bilateral and multilateral
financial and development agencies.

TABLE 7.8
Total External Public and Private Guaranteed Debt

Year	Total debt (in $US billions)
1975	$1,090
1976	1,456
1977	1,750
1978	2,370
1979	2,785
1980	3,332
1981	3,795
1982	4,488
1983	4,900

Source: OECD/CILSS/Club du Sahel, Analysis
Of Official Development Assistance To The Sahel
(Paris: OECD, 1985), p. 9.

TABLE 7.9
Debt and Debt Service
as a Percentage of the GNP (1982)

	Total Debt as a % of GNP	Debt Service as a % of GNP
Burkina Faso	30	2
Cape Verde	55	1
Chad	56	0
Gambia	72	3
Mali	80	1
Mauritania	148	7
Niger	46	10
Senegal	54	4

Source: OECD/CILSS/Club du Sahel, Official Development Assistance To CILSS Member Countries in 1983 (Paris: OECD, 1985), p. 27.

    The burden of debt and debt service is particularly heavy for several countries-- Mauritania, Gambia, Mali, Cape Verde, and Senegal. By 1982, these five had total debts that accounted for over fifty percent of their GNPs. A more accurate indication of the degree of indebtedness of these states is their debt service payments. Senegal, Mali, and Gambia had debt service pay-ments (the amount in principle and interest paid annually) comparable to those of the most indebted Latin American nations. In the table above, debt service payments for the most heavily indebted nations ranged from 3 percent of Gambia's GNP to 10 percent of Niger's GNP.
    The use of aid for other than productive activities, the problems of food aid dependency, the growth in foreign aid dependency,and the crushing debt payments offer evidence of dependen-cy as a product of relations between the North and the South. Certainly, after ten years of joint CILSS/Club action, one can state that the Sahel is farther from achieving its goals and objectives

now than it was after the first drought. This situation did not go unnoticed by either the Sahelians or the donors. Before the end of the First Generation Program, both were assessing the reasons for the decline in conditions within the region.

THE PALIN REPORT

As the end of the First Generation Program approached, donors and the Club du Sahel were of the opinion that the project-funding activities of CILSS and the Club had reached their limits and should be discontinued. Donors felt that projects, no matter how well-suited for the Sahel, were bound to fail if the internal socio-economic-political environment was not conducive to their successful implementation. Donors began to view the constraints to Sahelian development as internal problems which no amount of massive aid could solve. A new view emerged expressing the opinion that more serious reflection, planning, and policy analysis within CILSS would help to guide the Sahel governments in their development efforts.

By 1982 major adverse trends within the region had not changed; in fact, they continued unabated. Generally, the social and economic conditions were worse, in many respects, by 1982 than they had been in 1973-1974: the terms of trade continued to function against the Sahel, per capita growth had fallen throughout the 1970s, the external debt of the region climbed to high levels, food dependency increased rather than decreased despite many gains in productivity, and general socio-economic conditions in the region contributed to continued rural-urban migration which, in turn, aggravated population pressures within the urban areas. Within the next two years, drought and famine returned once again to the Sahel.

Discussions on the need for a strategy which would go beyond the goals of regional food self-sufficiency and self-sustaining economic growth began in 1982-1984. In the fall of 1984, a new, revised strategy for drought control and development was circulated among donors and Sahelians at a donors meeting (12).

To attain the goals CILSS and the governments had established in the early years, the old strategy pursued the development of the productive sectors. Many criticisms emerged regarding this strategy. One concerned the fact that the concentration on sectoral analysis ignored the interconnectedness of development sectors. Unless a more global, multisectoral approach was employed which took cognizance of the needs of the population to survive and meet their daily needs (short- and medium-term development), while at the same time preserving the environment (long-term development), the Sahel would never be able to solve its problems.

Another criticism of the old strategy was that it remained a top-down development process which failed to include in the design process the very population groups it was designed to aid. The exclusion of the rural inhabitants in the formulation of projects was, according to some development experts in the field, the reason for the failure of so many well-designed and well-intentioned projects and programs (13).

Finally, the strategy was criticized for its concentration on the rural areas while ignoring the relationship between the rural sector and the rest of the economy and the need to create a balance between the two. In effect, while CILSS concentrated on improving the lot of the rural dweller, this group remained outside of the concern and the priorities of the national governments. Too often, the national governments relied on CILSS and the Club to generate investments for this sector while they applied their own resources to the urban areas. In addition, many government policies served to destroy the initiative within the rural sector, for example, price and investment policies placed the urban areas at a greater advantage vis-à-vis the rural sector (14).

With these critiques in mind, the new revised strategy called for a new focus to strengthen CILSS/Club efforts. The major points of the new development strategy were:

1. To make the people of the Sahel the driving

force of development;

2. To reconstruct the Sahel economy on a more solid foundation;

3. To determine a new ecological balance and to develop the region accordingly (15).

The revised strategy accepted by the CILSS Council of Ministers coincided with discussions to modify CILSS´ role. At the Fourth Conference of the Heads of State in 1982, the Sahel leaders recognized the existing gap between the promise of CILSS and the state of development in the Sahel. They mandated the creation of a "Comité de Réflexion de Haut Niveau" to analyze the effectiveness of CILSS´ work in the development of the Sahel.

The call for a study of CILSS´ work emerged at a moment when the CILSS´ states and the donors expressed misgivings as to the organization´s ability to achieve its objectives. The states questioned whether CILSS could address the needs and the problems facing its members. Many CILSS members were displeased over the work of the specialized institutes, feeling that their activities did not correspond to real needs. Donor complaints rested on doubts about CILSS´ ability to establish priorities to improve food production and to achieve ecological balance. Moreover, donors felt that CILSS had failed to work towards translating the priorities into a meaningful and workable program. Both donors and Sahelians were disappointed about CILSS´ record of project management. In fact, the Integrated Pest Management projects had been a total failure, and by 1981 control over the various Annexes had been taken away from the organization.

Added to the concerns voiced by the CILSS states and the donors, the Club and CILSS pointed out other shortcomings of the organization. The work programme of CILSS and the Club, the promotion and support of regional cooperation, was not being translated into national actions. The accords and resolutions agreed upon in the Council of Ministers meetings were missing from national strategies and activities. In effect, the member

231

states were failing to carry out CILSS´ work. One reason for this gap between CILSS´ resolutions and governmental action was the weak institutional link betweeen the organization and the member states. The CILSS National Committees really functioned only on paper. Secondly, CILSS´ links to the governments were primarily with the Ministries of Rural Development. In reality, policy decisions and national priorities were discussed and set by other ministries--Economics, Planning, or Finance. The Ministries of Rural Development were often marginal to the policy and goal setting process within their own governments. Hence, CILSS actions could not be effectively articulated at the higher policy-setting levels of the governments.

To overcome the doubts which had gripped CILSS and its supporters, the Conference of the Heads of State called for an in-house probe of CILSS. This in-house study, when it was completed, was rejected by the Heads of State. Following this rejection of the internal study, an independent study was completed. The new study, conducted by David Palin, called for a radical reorganization of CILSS through staff reductions and a redirection of CILSS´ activities. In 1984 the Palin Report was distributed to donors at their November meeting for review and discussion. In May 1985 the recommendations of the Palin report were accepted, in the main, by the CILSS Council of Ministers.

One of the changes made concerned the objectives of CILSS which in the past had not been precisely defined. The Palin report recommended that CILSS´ role be that of:

1. A center of reflection, carrying out analytical work or policies, on the way and means of assuring agricultural development, food production and socio-ecological balance in the Sahel;

2. A center of documentation, collection, and analysis and dissemination in the same areas;

3. A catalyst for agreement and coordination among member countries and between member

232

countries and donors in areas of its
expertise on the regional and national levels.
CILSS´ role would be an advisory one designed to help develop national policies and
programs consistent with the strategy, and
to encourage discusssions of these policies
and programs with interested donors;

4. A catalyst of regional programs at the request
    of member countries which will help to
    facilitate policy coordination among the
    countries (16).

The major change in CILSS´ focus is the removal of any activity having to do with the identification, development, and implementation of national projects from CILSS´ mandate. It was
agreed that such activities are the responsibility
of the member countries. Only programs of a con-
ceptual nature such as assessment and resource
monitoring, already part of CILSS activities, were
to be continued. Operational programs (such as
aspects of the Agrhymet Center and the Sahel Institute), would not be managed by CILSS beyond the
start-up period (17).
The second major change was the reorganiztion
of the CILSS system. Under the old system, CILSS
comprised three major bodies--the Conference of
the Heads of State, the Council of Ministers, and
the Executive Secretariat. The newly reorganized
system has been expanded to 6 bodies and has
added: 1) a Technical Committee of National Experts; 2) a Board of Directors; and 3) the
Specialized Institutes.
The duties of the Technical Committee of
National Experts are the following:

1. The monitoring of activities and programs of
    the CILSS system to assure close linkages
    between the member states´ programs and those
    of CILSS;

2. The review of annual activity reports and the
    evaluation of progress reports of the work
    programs undertaken by the CILSS system
    including financial reports;

3. The ordering, receiving and analyzing of policy studies and reports prepared by the
   Executive Secretariat and/or the specialized
   committees;

4. The receiving and reviewing of projects of the
   work program and the budgets provided by the
   Board of Directors (18).

Membership on the Committee includes all of
the CILSS National Correspondants and one high
official from a multidisciplinary ministry from
each CILSS state, as well as the CILSS Executive
Secretary and the heads of the Specialized Institutes. The Technical Committee is to meet once
a year (19).
The Board of Directors´ role is to assure
consistency and integration of the CILSS system
by:

1. Identifying and eliminating duplication of
   work;

2. Assuring internal consistency of the CILSS
   system;

3. Coordinating the work programs;

4. Coordinating the budget presentations;

5. Reviewing administrative and institutional
   matters (20).

Members of the Board of Directors include
the CILSS Executive Secretary and the Directors of
the specialized institutions. The Board is scheduled to conduct its business twice a year (21).
A major restructuring of the Executive Secretariat called for by the Palin report began to
take shape in the second half of 1985.
Specifically, the main function of the Executive
Secretariat is to provide coordination and
internal consistency within the CILSS system (22).
To this end, the senior staff assigned to the
Secretariat was reduced from 23 to 16. These
reductions were affected through the elimination
of the Division of Documentation and Information

(DDI), the Regional Management Unit (UGR), and the Division of Relations with Non-Governmental Organizations, NGOs, (23). The work of documentation and information as well as that of liaison with non-governmental organizations was transfered directly to the office of the Executive Secretary (24).

Changes within the organization of the Division of Project and Programs (DPP) were also implemented. No longer responsible for the identification and implementation of national projects, this unit´s revised responsibility consisted of:

1. Collaborating with the national services and donors on the preparation of regional projects and program proposals;

2. Coordinating and monitoring of the implementation of these projects and program proposals;

3. Directing the sectoral teams.

The DPP was streamlined to include just four sectoral teams: 1) Food and Animal Production; 2) Ecology/Environment; 3) Water Resources; and 4) Human Resources. Furthermore, health and nutrition were removed from the Human Resources sectoral team and were turned over to the national governments. Eliminated completely from the work activities of the DPP were the Fisheries and Transportation and Infrastructure teams. Fisheries was transfered to another regional grouping, the CEAO. Transportation and Infrastructure was returned to the national governments (25).

In addition, a new Division of Studies and Planning was created to:

1. Maintain the consistency of activities;

2. Manage and direct the reflection of such key issues as Sahelian development, drought control, desertification, and food security;

3. Plan regional projects and programs;

4. Evaluate CILSS´ projects and programs;

235

5. Strengthen linkages between the Club du Sahel
   and the CILSS National Committees;

6. Issue periodic CILSS status reports.

Under the old CILSS structure, the states
paid the salaries of eight high-level staff
members assigned to the Secretariat, and donors
paid the salaries of the remaining fifteen. Under
the new structure, the states are responsible for
seven of the high-level cadres and donors will pay
the salaries of the other nine. This change
reflects the concern of donors who have argued in
the past that Sahelian commitment to the organization should be manifested by greater governmental
support to the Executive Secretariat, including
paying the salaries of the staff.
A final modification in the CILSS structure
was to bring the Specialized Institutes under the
direct control of the Executive Secretariat.
Prior to this each institute operated more or less
autonomously, a practice which created conflicts
between the institutes and the Secretariat. Both
the Sahel Institute and the Agrhymet Center have
disbanded their Administrative Councils whose
activities have been transfered to other units
within the respective organizations. One additional modification in the Sahel Institute´s operations involved defining its role more narrowly.
After some reflection and discussion, donors and
Sahelians came to agree that the role should be
limited to the planning, facilitation, and coordination of research and to the exchange of information on research. In the past, the Institute
extended its work to the implementation of research. This duplicated the work of other research
agencies within the member countries. No longer
would the Sahel Institute actually conduct research.
The new scaled-down Secretariat includes the
following:

Table 7.10
Senior Staff Members of the Executive Secretariat

Title	Number
Executive Secretary	1
Advisor	1
Translator	1
Legal Councillor	1
Division of Administration and Finance	
Chief	1
Financial Comptroller	2
Division of Projects and Programs	
Chief	1
Food and Animal Production Expert	1
Ecology/Environment Expert	1
Water Resources Expert	1
Human Resources Expert	1
Division of Studies and Planning	
Chief	1
Studies and Strategic Reflection Expert	1
Planning and Statistics Expert	1
Monitoring and Evaluation Expert	1
Total	16

Both the revised strategy and the restructuring of CILSS are intended to ensure that meaningful and coherent development in the Sahel takes place. CILSS´ work will be brought into line with the needs of the member states. It will operate as a center for the articulation of regional priorities by playing the role of leader and catalyst. As strategic leader, CILSS will work to coordinate the policies and strategies of the member states. The second major role will be to improve and strengthen consultation between the donors and the member states. To achieve the recommendations of the Report, CILSS´ work will be restricted to the priority sectors established by the 1984 revised strategy--food production and

ecology. To fulfill the new streamlining, any
structures and functions marginal to this new
direction of the organization were eliminated or
consolidated within other units. In this regard,
sectors such as fisheries, transportation, health
and nutrition were abolished. The Crop Protection
unit has also been disbanded. The work of the
head of the unit for Relations with Non-governmental Organizations was eliminated. Activities of
the Documentation and Information unit, while not
eliminated, were consolidated under the work of
the Executive Secretary. In sum, these changes are
to guarantee that there is an environment free of
internal obstacles to the development efforts
within the region. The question remains whether
the revised strategy and the restructuring in and
of themselves will nuture and support the development process.

BEYOND THE PALIN REPORT

The restructuring of the CILSS organization,
the revised strategy, the Club Conferences, donor
missions, and sectoral and policy analysis
meetings have promoted North-South and South-South
cooperation. They have all contributed to development within the region by periodically assessing
the weaknesses of the strategy and the activities.
Additionally, they have pointed out the limitations of CILSS in achieving the goals established
by the member states. The review of CILSS´ work
carried out within the Conferences, missions, and
meetings has enabled the organiztion to make adjustments in its work program and to chart new
areas for action. This process of assessment-
adjustment-assessment could not have been possible
without the support of the member states, the
donors, and the Club. In this way, North-South
cooperation has been crucial to the results attained. Cooperation has made it easier for CILSS
to undertake the required internal reforms.
In this same way, the dialogue and discussion
generated by the Conferences, reports, missions,
and meetings have helped the member states adjust
their own actions. The work of CILSS and the Club
has been important in demonstrating how govern-

238

mental policies impede the fulfillment of the goals of food self-sufficiency and ecological balance. Furthermore, the CILSS/Club process has supported internal reform within the member states. Partly as a result of CILSS/Club persuasion, the member states have embarked upon a course of cereals policy reforms. Senegal, Mali, Burkina, and Niger have taken steps to raise producer and consumer prices, liberalize the grain market, privatize the distribution of agricultural inputs, and to implement other measures to reduce state control over the production and distribution of food crops.

In the area of internal reform (within both CILSS and the member states), the CILSS/Club du Sahel mechanism has been its most effective. By analyzing the internal constraints to production and organizational effectiveness and by providing the wherewithal to implement the recommendations, CILSS and the Club have made it easier for such changes to occur. It is doubtful that CILSS or the governments would have embarked on internal reform were it not for the cooperation received from the international community and the Club. In addition, because of the international support granted CILSS and the Club du Sahel, cooperation among the Sahel states has been strengthened. The states view CILSS as a vehicle for obtaining greater international funds. The promise of aid has enhanced South-South cooperation and national support of CILSS.

In light of the restructuring which has ended CILSS role as resource mobilizer, will the governments continue to support CILSS? The decision to eliminate CILSS' role in project activities and resource procurement was not an easy one for CILSS or the governments. The governments have always believed that, essentially, CILSS' role was to intercede on their behalf to extract more assistance from the donors. If CILSS no longer carried out this function, would Sahelian interest in the organization wane? Would the states feel obligated to grant CILSS the budgetary support needed to carry out the reforms and to strengthen the organization's operations, especially since the domestic economies of the member states had been crippled by severe economic downturns?

The restructing called for a smaller, more qualified staff within the CILSS Secretariat. It is uncertain whether this is feasible given the need to ensure simultaneously geographical diversity of the CILSS staff. In the past, the poorer states had never had the pool of qualified talent to meet both the needs of their own bureaucracies and those of the international organizations to which they were committed.

Another issue raised by the restructuring agreement relates to attempts to promote coherence between CILSS´ actions and policies made at the national level. The new direction begun by CILSS gambles on the notion that bringing representatives from the Ministries of Plan or Economics into the CILSS´ decision-making process will help to incorporate CILSS´ work into the policy decisions taken by the states. This may or may not be the case. While including such ministries may get CILSS´ proposals a fair hearing at the highest policy-making levels, other national ministries, departments, and divisions will be making counter proposals. The reconciliation of competing claims and demands will be decided by politicians and bureaucrats who often have short-term political interests which can and do conflict with other social and economic goals. No matter how well-intentioned the policy prescriptions suggested by CILSS´ analyses and reports, they are unlikely to be promoted to national policy decisions if they conflict with the goal of maintaining political stability and legitimacy. While painful and difficult economic choices may not be eliminated, their implementation by the governments could be slower than hoped for by CILSS and the Club du Sahel. In sum, the new course upon which CILSS has set its goals has not thoroughly acknowledged the political and social environment in which policy choices are made.

A final comment on the restructuring of CILSS involves the limitations of internal reform. While not disputing the need for internal reforms within CILSS and the member states, these are not the only reforms needed to bring about ecological balance and increased food production. Chapter 6 discussed donor biases which also distort the

240

development process. Yet, neither the Palin recommendations nor the revised strategy addresses
the ways in which donor funding militates against
the attainment of CILSS´ goals.

Food aid is a case in point. Delays (on the
donor side) in shipping food aid have led to
several instances in which aid arrived at or near
harvest time. The resultant food surpluses forced
down the prices paid to peasants for their products. Food aid which creates the taste transfer
for products (wheat) virtually uncultivable in
the Sahel undermines peasant incentives to grow
more traditional crops. Consumers accustomed to
purchasing cheaper food imports no longer desire
to pay for higher-priced traditional products.
Likewise, the readiness of donors to send food
aid but not the agricultural inputs to get the
region back on its feet, undermines the chances of
increasing food production. As long as donors are
more willing to fund projects that are large,
costly, and of questionable productivity, additional constraints to development remain.

BEYOND DROUGHT AND UNDERDEVELOPMENT

There is clearly a need to combine internal
reforms of CILSS and the member states with other
measures. Donors must be more cognizant of the
ways in which some of their project choices and
funding patterns impact negatively on the
development process. Though this issue has been
raised within CILSS/Club meetings, donors have
been slow to respond with policy changes. They
remain committed to funding large-scale showcase
projects as opposed to smaller ones. They continue
to fund the establishment of a hospital over a
rural preventive health care project; a
telecommunications facility over a rural radio
project.

Due to the importance of ODA to the Sahel in
the past ten years, donors are in a position to
exert leverage over the Sahel economies and
governments. The promise of aid has been used as
a stick to "encourage" the cereals policy reforms
presently being adopted in Senegal, Burkina Faso,
Niger, Gambia, and Mauritania. USAID and other

donors advocate the postion that policy reforms must occur if generous aid commitments are to continue (26).

According to the Reagan Administration, the causes of Africa´s problems are inherently internal: lack of technology, poor educational and training levels of the population, lack of infrastructure, overpopulation, and inappropriate economic policies (27). Therefore, the solutions to these internal constraints, as argued by the Administration, are also internal. The answer provided by the Administration is to unleash the private sector (African and donor) to attend to Africa´s problems. To this end, President Reagan launched his Emergency Food Aid Initiative in July 1984, the purpose of which is, among other things, the establishment of a business leaders´ group to respond to the African food crisis and to suggest an agenda for activities.

A second aspect of the Administration´s approach has been to shift the focus of development to efforts which weaken the public sector and strengthen the private sector. The answer to underdevelopment and dependency is to remove the restraints to the growth of the African private sector. In effect, the Administration has ended the basic human needs approach to development.

As an example of this, USAID´s budget report on Burkina Faso to Congress for the 1987 fiscal year states that its second support function to that country will be in the arena of "policy dialogue."

> Policy dialogue will be linked not only to
> our bilateral efforts, but also to the
> private sector, public finance, environment
> protection, and family planning...While
> bilateral projects will provide some
> leverage for gaining policy reforms, there
> is more importantly an on-going need for a
> basic policy education process which pre-
> sents private sector and government
> officials with information, alternatives
> and impacts of various decisions (28).

To provide the information lacking to the government of Burkina Faso, USAID organized private sector workshops under the auspices of the Burkinabe Chamber of Commerce in the summer of 1985. The purpose was to "educate" government and private elite groups. The aid programs which resulted from this analysis of the Sahel´s problems have changed the course of USAID´s activities. For example, in Burkina Faso, the Administration plans to limit USAID´s spending and activities to what have been defined as activities necessary to remove the internal constraints to development: support for private enterprise, the encouragement of policy reforms, resources for family planning programs, support for education and training activities, and infrastructural development. Thus, the Administration is reducing its support of sectors such as dryland agriculture, fisheries, and livestock.

This movement toward strengthening the private sector needs to be considered carefully. In the rush to develop the Sahelian private sector, the social, political, and economic implications are ignored or minimized.

In the Sahel the thrust to build up the private sector is not just an issue of capitalist versus socialist development. It is also a social issue. To reinforce the power of private traders is to lean towards certain ethnic groups who may have long-standing grievances with government officials of a rival ethnic group. In Africa, the question of who benefits from government policies can open up old ethnic wounds and initiate new areas of conflict. In the end, the reduction of public control over the production and/or distribution of grains could work to pull the political rug from underneath the governments in power.

The contraction of government involvement in agriculture involves other political costs as well. Public control over agriculture provides government elites resources with which to reward friends and punish enemies. In general, this control grants political elites the ability to build up political support. Once governmental elites can no longer manipulate this access to resources, their power and influence could decline. The results could spell political instability and/or the fall of the party or regime in power. Thus, governments are understandably

reluctant to impose changes which could eliminate
their political power. Yet, this concern has not
been adequately addressed in the new reforms
underway.

Thirdly, the economic costs of policy reforms
are another consideration. Donors have assumed
that economic reforms will place more money in
the hands of the peasant, thereby increasing food
production. This assumption may not necessarily
hold true. Acting upon World Bank advice, the
Malian government increased producer prices and
moved to eliminate public control over grain marketing. Unfortunately, the government discovered
that the prices paid to farmers by the private
traders did not increase signficantly as a result
of the reforms. More importantly, when the
drought hit in 1983, severely depleted government
stocks, left the regime unable to provide timely
emergency food assistance to the population (29).
The government was then forced to purchase grains
from private traders at higher prices.

Policy reforms geared to expanding the role
of the private sector might only replace one large
and powerful entity (the state) by another (private business groups), without providing more
money to the rural dweller. This substitution
could still leave peasants just as disadvantaged
in the market place. In periods of drought
peasants are particularly vulnerable to the economic strength of powerful traders. During such
critical periods, peasants are forced to buy back
part of the stock at very high prices. Traders
have been known to withhold stocks, contributing
to food shortages. Instances of traders diverting
stocks from certain regions or countries occured
during both droughts. In the most recent drought,
though grain shortages existed in the northern
part of Chad, traders located in the south of the
country preferred to ship their stocks to Nigeria
and the Cameroon. Increasing the price of grains
does not, in and of itself, guarantee growth in
supply or an adequate supply at a reasonable
price.

Lastly, policy reforms to support the private
sector can be manipulated by bureaucrats for their
own economic gain. As a result of drought and
famine, many peasants and herders have sold their

244

stocks and equipment to bureaucratic elites taking
advantage of the depressed agricultural conditions. Now that policy reforms are under way,
these political elites through, their knowledge of
and access to resources for the private sector,
can still maintain political power. Whereas
before they profited as political actors; now they
are profiting as newly organized and supported
private economic elites. Ultimately, the smaller
farmholders cannot compete with this more powerful group. Merely giving the private sector a
role to play may not bring the desired economic
results. The question is: Which private sector
should be strenghtened--the small, impoverised
peasant cultivating a few acres or the more
wealthy peasant on large agricultural land-
holdings?

    The point here is that policy reform can and
does have unintended consequences. Donors view
the reform process absent of a political or social
context. The assumption is that economic incentives to agricultural producers tried in Western
nations will yield the same results in Africa.
The failure to understand and to anticipate the
socio-economic-political consequences could result
in an absence of improvement in rural conditions,
or worse, the continuation of the degradation of
the Sahel economy and ecology. Attention must be
paid to the way in which reforms can alter the
balance of power between traders and producers and
between large and small producers. Moreover,
policy reforms should go beyond a restructuring of
CILSS and the internal structures of the Sahel.
There is a need to pay attention to the external
actors and external environment which affect prospects for development. While there is no denying
the need and the importance of internal reforms,
the external economic environment must also be
reformed. For several years, the Sahel has
watched while the world economic situation declined: the global recession reduced the demand
for Sahelian goods; import prices continued to
rise, causing a reduction in Sahelian purchasing
power; interest rates soared during the late
1970s, contributing to the growth in debt; and oil
prices climbed, raising the cost of fertilizer and
other products made from oil. All of the internal

245

reforms cannot change the declining volume of trade and declining terms of trade of the region resulting from the global economic crisis. What will be the use of eradicating the internal impediments to peasant production of crops when the volume and price commanded for those crops continues to drop on the world market? What is the point of expanding output when protectionist measures in the industrialized world have locked out the goods sold by the CILSS countries? In a real sense, the de-development occuring in the Sahel is abetted by the location of the Sahel within the world economy.

Compounding the problem of the declining terms of trade, the Sahel now faces a debt crisis. This crisis demands the generation of sufficient resources to pay off external creditors. Here, the Sahel is caught in a economic squeeze. Official development assistance, providing little in terms of aid that is potentially productive, has contributed to the growth in debt. Yet, the lack of economic development requires constant levels of aid. To pay these debts, the governments are forced to lean toward the production of cash crops and other raw materials favored by Western markets. Donors and creditors have stepped in to force the Sahel nations to revise fiscal and monetary policies to pay these external debts. So, any improvements in production must go directly to pay the IMF and other creditors. Like many developing nations, the debt burden threatens to choke off potential development.

Part of the answer to the recovery of the Sahelian economy is the recovery of the volume and the price of the goods it exports. Yet, it would be a mistake to assume that only a reversal of falling export prices could extricate the region from its difficulties. The recovery of the Sahelian purchasing power and export levels must not then lead to an abandonment of the internal reforms necessary to create coherence between the rural and urban sectors. In the past, internal reforms were often avoided as long as a country's exports were sufficient to generate the needed foreign exchange to pay for imports. No longer can these reforms be avoided. Donors and creditors have encircled the Sahel. The promise of continuing aid commitments is contingent upon the implementation of these policy reforms. Yet, even with policy reforms, if the economic recovery does not reach the Sahel, recovery and development will stagnate. In sum, the new strategy and restructuring are inadequate because they only address one-half of the equation--the internal half. Full recovery necessitates both internal reforms within the Sahel and external reforms of trade and aid practices within the present global order.

Not only are underdevelopment and de-development (and recovery) of the rural sector a function of the Sahel´s incorporation into the world economy, they are also a function of that sector´s relationship with the urban sector. The rural sector has never been a market for urban goods; similarly, the urban sector has been only a poor market for most rural products. The rural sector has paid dearly for the lack of economic coherence and intergration. The disarticulation of the Sahel economies and the lack of forward and backward linkages between the rural and urban areas are factors only partially addressed by the revised strategy and the restructuring underway. The strategy primarily attempts to address the economic obstacles to internal disarticulation. It overlooks the political obstacles to an integration of the rural and urban sectors.

The revised strategy calls for "making man the driving force behind development" (30). The goal of this strategy is to "ensure that men and women of the Sahel regain control of their own growth and land use...to ensure that the men and women of the Sahel once again play an active role in their own development" (31). How this is to be accomplished is never quite spelled out. Moreover, whether this is feasible given the lack of political control and decision-making authority of the rural population is another question.

Development in the Sahel over the past twenty years has been an activity done to or for the rural population. Rural inhabitants have rarely been the subjects of their own development. Citizen participation in the decision-making process has not occured at the regional, national, or international levels (32). Projects are designed in Sahelian or donor capitals and then imposed

247

upon the inhabitants. The strategy and restructuring have not altered this fact.

The estrangement of the rural populations is twofold. The cultural considerations of the ways in which participants will respond are absent from the analysis of the project design. Not consulted in the planning of projects and programs, rural inhabitants fail to respond or to get involved as planners have envisioned. There is either moderate participation or no participation of the targeted groups once the projects begin. Needless to say, many projects which neglect to incorporate the views of the rural populations do not turn out successfully. Development from the outside is destined to fail. After such failure, the rural world becomes more marginalized economically.

This economic marginalization results from the rural world's political estrangement. The rural world does not participate in meaningful economic development because it does not participate in the political decision-making process. Economic marginalization and political disenfranchisement is reinforced by actions taken by both donors and the CILSS governments. For their part, the donors do not design projects with the interest of the rural world in mind. Often, projects supported by the donors reflect donor interests and political concerns. The magnitude of outside assistance allows the donors the opportunity to direct development efforts. By the same token, the Sahel governments undermine rural initiative and seek to dominate the interests of the peasants (33). Any effort to alter these arrangements becomes a political and economic threat to the governments, a threat which must be contained.

So after ten years of cooperation, CILSS and the Club du Sahel, though a unique and important experiment, is no closer to helping the region extricate itself from underdevelopment and dependency. This cooperative endeavor has enabled the governments to stave off complete collapse. While this is certainly an important contribution because of the human costs such a collapse would entail, the Sahel has grown ever more dependent upon donor assistance. In the final analysis, the level and the impact of this assistance have reinforced the problems of the region.

248

In assessing the weaknesses of the CILSS/Club framework, one arrives at the question, "What would have worked better?" What have been the shortcomings of the program put into effect after the first drought?

Paradoxically, the weaknesses result from a combination of too little and too much cooperation. There has been too little cooperation in the linkage of programs and projects which would aid in restoring the Sahel's economic stability vis-à-vis the international market. Too little cooperation has existed in the incorporation of the affected rural population groups in the design, planning, and implementation of programs. Both donors and Sahelians have been negligent in their attention to the inclusion of rural groups. Too much cooperation is apparent in the areas of food aid and some development sectors.

In the area of food aid, donors have often been too willing to provide food aid, even when the need for such aid has been questionable. Food aid has not always been used by the governments to ward off human tragedy; it has been used to shore up the shaky economies and to maintain political stability. Food aid has now created its own demand, guaranteeing the necessity for future aid.

In the future, a reconsideration of food aid policies must occur. The use of triangular and local food aid strategies would help to avert the problems caused by the influx of donor aid. Presently, very little food aid (only 10 percent) is secured through inter-Sahel trade or from other African countries. The use of triangular food aid procurements (the purchase of food from other African nations out of donor funds) could help to get food from grain-surplus to grain-deficit countries. Triangular trade would build-up African networks of cooperation and solidarity as the OAU has envisioned in its Lagos Plan of Action. Another strategy would be to promote inter-Sahelian grain trade; for example, Senegalese or Nigerien grain surpluses could be transported to other CILSS nations. While the costs are higher due to the lack of adequate transportation facilities, improvements in rail and road networks could lower these costs measurably. Greater reliance upon the use of grains found within West Africa would help to stem the problems of taste transfer caused by Western imports. Local grains purchases would stimulate local food production.

Secondly, food aid should be strictly limited to helping those made destitute by drought and resulting famine. It is of little use to offer it to urban dwellers in exhange for political allegiance, while those without the necessary means must compete with urbanites for this food aid. The donor community and the governments need to exercise more restraint on the distribution practices of food aid.

Thirdly, efforts must be made to improve Sahelian transportation facilities. Much of the delay in getting aid to the affected regions can be traced to inadequate transportation networks. The shortage of trucks, good road and rail systems and boats exacerbates the situation. Moreover, improved transportation and infrastructure could facilitate inter- and intra-Sahelian trade. Serious funding of trans-Sahelian road and rail networks must be undertaken by the donors and the Sahelians.

Fourthly, donor aid must be monitored so that it does not lead to taste transfers and the rejection of locally-produced cereals. The Sahel cannot afford to have its food crops replaced by those which are only available through importation. If imports of rice and wheat are necessary to avoid immediate catastrophes, they must be promptly ended once the short term emergency has lifted.

Too often donors are much to eager to continue the supply of food aid. For donors, the continued exportation of wheat and other products helps to relieve the financial crisis faced by their own farmers. Once the food emergency ends, donors must redirect aid efforts to supply seeds, tools, and other agricultural implements to permit Sahelian peasants to carry out their task of producing food for the region. As United Nations reports have found, donor assistance is quick to give food aid. Mobilization of donor support for agricultural inputs seems to languish. Unless this policy can be turned around, food production will never improve within the drought-stricken areas.

250

The reluctance to fund the productive activities has been a hallmark of the past ten years of development cooperation in the Sahel. The type of aid and the direction of aid has failed to benefit the targeted population groups. The cooperation that has been achieved has more often than not helped the political fortunes of the government elites and the political and economic interests of the donors.

Rather than the reformist and piecemeal tinkering attempted within the bounds of the CILSS/Club du Sahel experiment, more profound changes and a more radical approach to cooperation must be adopted. First of all, the internal reforms being carried out must be advanced to include more democratic and thorough integration of the rural sector into the national economies. Development must procede with a view to a coherent whole, linking the production of goods and services within the rural sector to that of the urban sector and vice versa. This calls for greater reforms of educational, health, agricultural, industrial, animal, ecological and infrastructural planning. Development must be redirected to address the needs of the many rather than to satisfy the wishes of the small political and economic elite within the urban and rural sectors.

Secondly, donor/Sahelian cooperation must be pushed to add to the agenda items to untangle and resolve problems of debt, monetary reform, trade, and protectionism. Aside from discussions on the size and the seriousness of debt, no strategy has been agreed upon to reduce this burden. In the case of trade and protectionism, CILSS/Club discussions have assumed away or ignored the implications of the decline in levels of trade and the drop in Sahelian purchasing power. Solutions to the problem of trade must be seen as an important part of any strategy to render the Sahel economically viable again.

Thirdly, donors must reasses their action in the Sahel. Greater donor coordination would reduce the costly duplication that results from the hoarding of information and data. Donor cooperation needs to be advanced in the area of streamlining of requirements. Presently, most donors advocate that certain requirements be met

251

before they agree to support a project. Such requirements are based upon donor notions of what is profitable. Usually, donors are looking for quick results and are reluctant to take on long-term activities. More flexibility in what donors select for funding is needed. Otherwise, donor reliance on narrow conceptions of "profitability" eliminates sound projects which would pay off, but only in the medium- or long-term. Perhaps, those projects and programs which require medium- and long-term support could be justified if there were more multi-donor cooperation in project funding. While CILSS/Club meetings have stressed the need to lighten donor requirements, these suggestions have yet to be taken up and implemented. In fact, donors are increasingly restricting their definition of "profitiability" to select their activities in the region.

The situation in the Sahel demands far-reaching modifications in donor and Sahelian behavior. Following this, more creative solutions, involving short-, medium-, and long-term development programs and projects which integrate the rural and urban worlds, must be implemented. In the decade after the Club's creation, some attitudes and behaviors have been modified on both sides. Unless this process of cooperation becomes more extensive and more democratically inclusive of the affected peoples and the states of the region, the world can expect periodic droughts leading to more tragic famines as an entrenched feature of life in the Sahel West Africa.

NOTES

1. Interview with an expert of the Planning, Monitoring, and Evaluation Unit, July 10, 1980 in Ouagadougou, Burkina Faso.
2. Interview with the Club Secretariat, March 11, 1980 in Paris, France.
3. Interview with the Club Secretariat, March 11, 1980 in Paris, France.
4. Anne de Lattre and Arthur M. Fell, The Club du Sahel: An Experiment in International Co-

Operation (Paris: OECD, 1984), pp. 80-81.

5. Ibid, p. 80.

6. All other sectors include: mining, tourism, balance of payments support, river basin development, human resources, cultural activities, fellowship and training, research, non-project technical assistance, integrated rural development, energy, transportation and infrastructure, industry, and urban development.

7. OECD, Official Development Assistance To CILSS Member Countries In 1983 (Paris: OECD, 1985), p. 45.

8. Ibid, p. 46.

9. Jacques Giri, Rétrospective De L´Economie Sahelienne (Paris: OECD, 1984), pp. 10 and 18.

10. OECD, Aide Alimentaire Et Coopération Pour Le Développement: L´Expérience Du Sahel mimeo (Paris: OECD, 1984), p. 15.

11. USDA, Food Problems and Prospects in Sub-Saharan Africa (Washington, D.C.: USDA, 1981), p. 135.

12. OECD/CILSS/Club du Sahel, Proposals For A Revised Strategy For Drought Control And Development In The Sahel (Paris: OECD, 1984).

13. Ibid, p. 16.

14. Ibid, pp. 38-39.

15. Ibid, p. 4.

16. OECD/CILSS/Club du Sahel, Summary Record of the Donor Coordination Meeting, Review of the Operations and Organizations of The CILSS mimeo (Paris: OECD, 1985), p. 25.

17. Ibid, p. 26.

18. Club du Sahel memorandum of May 22, 1985, on the reorganization of the CILSS system, pp. 5-6.

19. Ibid, p. 6.

20. Ibid, p. 6.

21. Ibid, pp. 6-7.

22. Ibid, p. 7.

23. Ibid, p. 10-11.

24. Ibid, p. 10.

25. Ibid, p. 11.

26. This was a statement made by the USAID administrator, Peter MacPherson, U.S. Congress, Joint Committe on Foreign Affairs and the Select Committe on Hunger, Hearings on World Food and Population Issues, 98th Cong., 2nd sess.

(Washington, D.C.: GPO, 1985), p. 67.

27.   Ibid, p. 80.

28.   USAID, Annual Budget Submission FY 87
Burkina Faso, 1985, p. 8.

29.   Niger Twose,   Why the Poor Suffer Most
Drought and the Sahel (London: Oxfam, n.d.), p. 6.

30.   Proposals For A Revised Strategy For
Drought Control And Development In The Sahel, p.
4.

31   Ibid, p. 7.

32. Ibid, pp. 13-16; Adrian Adams, "The Senegal River Valley: What Kind of Change?" Review of
African Political Economy, No. 10 (1978), pp. 33-
59; and Richard W. Franke and Barbara H. Chasin,
Seeds of Famine (Montclair: Allanheld, Osmun,
1980), Part 3.

33. Adams, 57-58.

Bibliography

Abangwu, George C. "Systems Approach to Regional
    Integration in West Africa." Journal of
    Common Market Studies, 13, Nos. 1 and 2
    (1975), pp. 116-135.
Adams, Adrian. "The Senegal River Valley: What
    Kind of Change?" Review of African Political
    Economy, No. 10 (1978), pp. 33-59.
Adedeji, Adebayo. "Prospects of Regional Economic
    Cooperation in West Africa." The Journal of
    Modern African Studies, 8, No. 2 (1970),
    pp. 213-232.
_____. "Foreign Debt and Prospects for Growth in
    Africa During the 1980s." The Journal of
    Modern African Studies, 23, No. 1 (1985),
    pp. 53-74.
Africa. "Drought Next Time." Africa, No. 121
    (1981), pp. 51-52.
"Africa's Shrinking Harvest: Food and Hunger
    1985." Special issue of Africa News, 24, No.
    4 (February 25, 1985).
Afrique Agriculture. "La IVème Conférence Du Club
    Du Sahel A Koweit." Afrique Agriculture, No.
    65 (1981), pp. 38-53.
Akindele, R.A. The Organization and Promotion of
    World Peace: A Study of Universal-Regional
    Relationships. Toronto: University of Toron-
    to Press, 1976.
American Enterprise Institute. A Conversation
    with Anne de Lattre: Developing the Sahel.
    Washington, D.C. American Enterprise Insti-
    tute for Public Policy Research, 1979.
Amin, Samir. "Underdevelopment and Dependence in

255

Black Africa--Origins and Contemporary Forms." The Journal of Modern African Studies, 10, No. 4 (1972), pp. 503-524.

_____. Neo-Colonialism in West Africa. New York: Monthly Review Press, 1973.

_____. Unequal Development. New York: Monthly Review Press, 1976.

_____. "Self-Reliance and the New International Economic Order." Monthly Review, 29, No. 3 (1977), pp. 1-21.

_____. "An Alternative Strategy for Development: Industrialization in the Service of Agriculture." CERES, 14, No. 5 (1981), pp. 27-32.

Amuzegar, Jahangir. "The North-South Dialogue: From Conflict to Compromise." Foreign Affairs, 54, No. 3 (1976), pp. 547-562.

Arkhurst, F.S. "Problems of Economic Integration in Africa." Africa in the Seventies and Eighties, ed., F.S. Arkhurst. New York: Praeger Publishers, 1970.

Arnold, Guy. Aid in Africa. London: Kogan Paul, Ltd. 1979.

Audibert, Jean "Réflexion Sur Le Projet De Développement Du Sahel." Revue Juridique Et Politique, Indépendance Et Coopération, 30, No. 4 (1976), pp. 389-396.

Axline, W. Andrew. "Underdevelopment, Dependence, and Integration: The Politics of Regionalism in the Third World." International Organization, 31, No. 1 (1977), pp. 83-105.

_____. "Integration and Development in the Commonwealth Caribbean: The Politics of Regional Negotiations." International Organization, 32, No. 4 (1978), pp. 953-973.

_____ and Lynn K. Mytelka. "Sociétés Multinationales et Integration Régionale dans le Groupe Andin et Dans la Communauté des Caraibes." Etudes Internationales, 7, No. 2 (1976), pp. 163-192.

Bach, Daniel. "The Politics of West African Economic Co-operation: C.E.A.O. and E.C.O.W.A.S." The Journal of Modern African Studies, 21, No. 4 (December 1983), pp. 605-623.

Baker, Jonathan. "Oil and African Development." The Journal of Modern African Studies, 15, No. 2 (1977), pp. 175-212.

Barker, Jonathan, ed. The Politics of Agriculture
    in Tropical Africa. Beverly Hills, Califor-
    nia: Sage Publications, Inc., 1984.
Ball, Nicole. "Understanding the Causes of African
    Famine." The Journal of Modern African
    Studies, 14, No. 3 (1976), pp. 517-522.
_____. "Drought and Dependence in the Sahel."
    International Journal of Health Services, 8,
    No.2 (1978), pp. 271-298.
Bates, Robert H. Markets and States in Tropical
    Africa. Berkeley: The University of Califor-
    nia Press, 1981.
_____ and Michael F. Lofchie, eds. Agricultural
    Development in Africa. New York: Praeger
    Publishers, 1980.
Berg, Alan D. The Nutrition Factor. Washington,
    D.C.: The Brookings Institution, 1973.
Berg, Elliot. The Recent Economic Evolution of
    the Sahel. Ann Arbor: The University of
    Michigan, 1975.
Bergsten, C. Fred. "The Threat from the Third
    World." Foreign Policy, 11 (1973), pp. 102-
    124.
Bernus, E., and G. Savonnet. "Les Problèmes de la
    sécheresse dans l'Afrique de l'Ouest", Pré-
    sence Africaine, No. 88 (1973), pp. 113-138.
Berry, Leonard. Assessment of Desertification in
    the Sudano-Sahelian Region, 1978-1984 N.P.
    Clark University and United Nations Sudano-
    Sahelian Office (UNSO), January 1984.
Bhagwati, Jagdish N., ed. The New International
    Economic Order: The North-South Debate. Cam-
    bridge: The MIT Press, 1977.
Booth, David. "Andre Gunder Frank: An Introduction
    and Appreciation." in Beyond the Sociology
    of Development, ed., Ivar Oxaal, Tony Bar-
    nett, and David Booth. London: Routledge and
    Kegan Paul, 1975.
Brown, Lester R., and Edward C. Wolf. Reversing
    Africa's Decline. Washington, D.C.:
    Worldwatch Institute, 1985.
Browne, Robert S. and Robert J. Cummings. The
    Lagos Plan of Action vs. The Berg Report.
    Washington, D.C.: Howard University, African
    Studies and Research Program, 1984.
Brandt, Willy. North-South: A Programme for
    Survival. Cambridge: The MIT Press, 1980.

Brun, Thierry. "Des Famines Climatiques Aux Famines Economiques." Revue Tiers Monde, 16, No. 63 (1975), pp. 609-630.

Burley, Lawrence Anderson. "Disaster Relief Administration in the Third World." International Development Review, 15, No. 1 (1973), pp. 8-12.

Caldwell, John C. La Sécheresse dans le Sahel et ses conséquences démographiques, No. 8 Cahier: OLC, 1975.

Cantori, Louis J., and Steven L. Spiegel, eds. The International Politics of Regions. Englewood Cliffs: Prentice-Hall, Inc., 1970.

Chauleur, Pierre. "Les Plans Mis Au Point Par Les Etats Du Sahel Pour Lutter Contre La Sécheresse." Revue Juridique et Politique, Indépendence et Coopération, 30, No. 4 (1976), pp. 412-420.

Chime, Chimelu. Integration and Politics Among African States. Uppsala: The Scandanavian Institute of African Studies, 1977.

Christensen, Cheryl, and Lawrence Witucki, "An Overview of Food Policies in Sub-Saharan Africa." Paper prepared for the 1983 African Studies Association Meeting, December 7-10, 1983, Boston, Massachusetts.

Clark, John F. "Patterns of Support for International Organizations in Africa." in The Politics of Africa: Dependence and Development ed. Timothy M. Shaw and Kenneth A. Heard. London: Longman Group, Ltd. and Dalhousie University Press, 1979, pp. 319-355.

Clark, Thurston. The Last Caravan. New York: G.P. Putnam and Sons, 1978.

Club du Sahel. The Operations of CILSS. Paris: OECD, 1977.

_____. Newsletter of the Club du Sahel, No. 3 Paris: OECD, 1981.

_____. Lettre D'Information du Club du Sahel, No. 4. Paris: OECD, 1981.

_____. Strategy for Drought Control in the Sahel. Paris: OECD, 1980.

_____. Food Self-Sufficiency and Ecological Balance in the Sahel Countries. Paris: OECD, 1982.

_____ and CILSS. The Sahel Drought Control and Development Programme, 1975-1979: A Review and Analysis. Paris: OECD, 1980.

Colvin, Lucie Gallistel, et al. The Uprooted of the Western Sahel. New York: Praeger Publishers, 1981.

Comité Information Sahel. Qui se nourrit de la famine en afrique? Paris: Librairie François Maspero, 1974.

CILSS. Meeting of the Ministers on the Problems Posed by the Drought. Ouagadougou: CILSS, 1973.

_____. Summary Report of the Ministers Meeting. Ouagadougou: CILSS, 1974.

_____. Summary Report of the First Conference of the Heads of State. Ouagadougou: CILSS, 1974.

_____. Summary Report of the Third Council of Ministers Meeting. Ouagadougou: CILSS, 1975.

_____. Summary Report of the Fourth Council of Ministers Meeting. Ouagadougou: CILSS, 1976.

_____. Summary Report of the Second Conference of the Heads of State. Ouagadougou: CILSS, 1976.

_____. Status of the Regional Center for Training and Application in Operational Agrometeorology/Hydrology. Niamey: Agrhymet, 1976.

_____. Summary Report of the Fifth Council of Ministers Meeting. Ouagadougou: CILSS, 1976.

_____. Summary Report of the Sixth Council of Ministers Meeting. Ouagadougou: CILSS, 1977.

_____. Summary Report of the Seventh Council of Ministers Meeting. Ouagadougou: CILSS, 1977.

_____. Nouveaux Textes Adoptés Par Le 7ème Conseil Des Ministres Du CILSS Tenu A Ouagadougou Du 25 Au 28 Avril 1977. Ouagadougou: CILSS, 1977.

_____. Meeting of Sahelian Experts in Research and Training. Bamako: CILSS, 1977.

_____. Sahel Institute Description. N.P., 1977.

_____. Programme De Protection Des Végétation Et Des Récoltes Dans Les Pays Membres Du CILSS. Ouagadougou: CILSS, 1977.

_____. Summary Report of the Eighth Council of Ministers Meeting. Ouagadougou: CILSS, 1978.

_____. Summary Report of the Third Conference of the Heads of State. Ouagadougou: CILSS, 1978.

_____. Summary Report of the Ninth Council of Ministers Meeting. Ouagadougou: CILSS, 1978.

_____. Summary Report of the Tenth Council of Ministers Meeting. Ouagadougou: CILSS 1978.

_____. Summary Report of the Eleventh Council of Ministers Meeting. Ouagadougou: CILSS, 1978.

_____. Projet-Test De Productions Vivrières Dans La Zone de Kombissiri. Ouagadougou: CILSS, 1979.

_____. Minutes of the First Meeting of the Scientific and Technical Council and of the Advisory Board. Bamako: CILSS, 1979.

_____. Bi-Annual Progress Report, 1977-1979. Bamako: CILSS, 1979.

_____. Insah-Info, No. 1. Bamako: CILSS, 1980.

_____. Summary Report of the Twelfth Council of Ministers Meeting. Ouagadougou: CILSS, 1980.

_____. Summary Report of the Fourth Conference of the Heads of State. Ouagadougou: CILSS, 1980.

_____. Second Evaluation of the Programme for Strengthening the Sahelian Countries and Establishment of a Centre for Training and Applications of Agro-Meteorology/Operational Hydrology. N.P., 1980.

_____. Summary Report of the Thirteenth Council of Ministers Meeting. Ouagadougou: CILSS, 1980.

_____. Third Meeting of the Executive Committee of CILSS Crop Protection Program. Ouagadougou: CILSS, 1980.

_____. Sahel Institute Minutes and Recommendations of the Second Advisory Committee Meeting of the CILSS Plant Protection Program. Bamako: CILSS, 1980.

_____. Procès-Verbal De Passation De Service Entre Monsieur Seck Mane N'Diack, Secrétaire Exécutif Du CILSS Entrant Et Monsieur Aly Cisse, Secrétaire Exécutif Du CILSS Sortant. Ouagadougou: CILSS, 1980.

_____. A Note on the State of Advancement of Pilot Projects in the Sahel. Ouagadougou: CILSS, N.D.

_____. Le Centre Régional De Formation Et D'Application En Agrométéorologie Et Hydrologie Opérationelle Pour Les Pays Du Sahel. Niamey: CILSS, N.D.

_____. Summary Report of the Fourteenth Council of Ministers Meeting. Ouagadougou: CILSS, 1981.

_____. Summary Report of the Fifteenth Council of Ministers Meeting. Ouagadougou: CILSS, 1981.

_____. Summary Report of the Sixteenth Council of Ministers Meeting. Ouagadougou: CILSS, 1982.

260

_____. Summary Report of the Fifth Conference of the Heads of State. Ouagadougou: CILSS, 1982.

_____. Summary Report of the Seventeenth Council of Ministers Meeting. Ouagadougou: CILSS, 1982.

_____. Summary Report of the Eighteenth Council of Ministers Meeting. Ouagadougou: CILSS, 1982.

_____. Première Réunion Des Responsables Des Comités Nationaux Du CILSS. Ouagadougou: CILSS, 1983.

_____. Summary Report of the Nineteenth Council of Ministers Meeting. Ouagadougou: CILSS, 1983.

_____. Bilan De La Campagne Agro-Pastorale 1984/85. Ouagadougou: CILSS, 1984.

_____. Rapport Générale De La Réunion Des Experts Préparatoire Au 20ème Conseil Des Ministres Du CILSS. Ouagadougou: CILSS, 1985.

_____. Session Extraordinaire Du Conseil Des Ministres. Ouagadougou: CILSS, 1985.

CILSS and the Club du Sahel. Socio-Economic Data Book for the Sahel Countries. Paris: OECD, 1978.

_____. Deuxième Conférence Club du Sahel. N.P., 1977.

_____. Summary Record of the Third Conference of the Club du Sahel. Paris: Club du Sahel, 1979.

_____. Official Development Assistance to CILSS Member Countries from 1975-1979, Volumes I and II. Paris: OECD, 1980.

_____. Status of Financing of First Generation Programme. Paris: OECD, 1980.

_____. Termes de Référence Mission de Revision de la Stratégie de Développement de la Peche dans les Pays Membres du CILSS. Ouagadougou: CILSS, 1980.

_____. Drought Control and Development Programme for the Sahel, An Approach to Monitoring and Evaluation. Paris: OECD, 1980.

_____. Renforcement Du Reseau Pour La Prévention Des Crises Alimentaire Au Sahel. Paris: OECD, 1985.

CILSS, Club du Sahel, and the OECD. Réunion Constitutive Du "Club Des Amis Du Sahel. N.P. 1976.

_____. Demography of the Sahel Countries. Paris:

261

OECD, 1980.

_____. Summary Record of the Fourth Conference of the Club du Sahel. Paris: OECD, 1981.

_____. Work Programme of the Club du Sahel and CILSS Secretariats for 1983-1984. Paris: Club du Sahel, 1982.

_____. Assessment of the Marine Fisheries Sector. Paris: Club du Sahel, 1983.

_____. Official Development Assistance To CILSS Member Countries From 1975-1982, Volume I. Paris: OECD, 1983.

Constantin, Francois. "Régionalisme internationale et pouvoirs africains." Revue française de science politique, 26, No. 1 (1976), pp. 70-102.

Copans, Jean, ed. Sécheresse et famines du Sahel. Paris: Librairie François Maspero, 1975.

Corbett, Edward M. The French Presence in Black Africa. Washington, D.C.: Black Orpheus Press, 1972.

Corkran, Herbert Jr. Patterns of International Cooperation in the Caribbean, 1942-1969. Dallas: Southern Methodist University Press, 1970.

Cotter, William R. "How AID Fails to Aid Africa." Foreign Policy, No. 34 (1979), pp. 107-119.

Cox, Robert. "Ideologies and the New International Economic Order: Reflections on Some Recent Literature." International Organization, 33, No. 2 (1979), pp. 257-302.

Curry, Robert L. "US-AID's Southern Africa Program." Journal of Southern African Affairs, 5, No. 2 (1980), pp. 183-97.

Daddieh, Cyril Kofie. "Recovering Africa's Self-Sufficiency in Food and Agriculture." in Economic Crisis in Africa. ed. by Adebayo Adedeji and Timothy M. Shaw. Boulder: Lynne Rienner Publishers, (1985), pp. 187-200.

Dalby, David, and R. J. Harrison Church, eds. Drought in Africa. London: University of London, 1973.

De Casanova, J. Arrighi. "Demain, Le Sahel." Revue Juridique Et Politique, Indépendance Et Coopération, 30, No. 4 (1976), pp. 429-434.

De craene, Philippe. "Mali: La sécheresse, arme politique." Revue française d'études politiques africaines, No. 98 (1974), pp. 17-18.

De Lattre, Anne, and Arthur M. Fell. The Club Du
    Sahel. Paris: OECD, 1984.
Derman, William. "USAID in the Sahel: Development
    and Poverty." in The Politics of Agriculture
    in Tropical Africa, ed. Jonathan Barker.
    Beverly Hills: Sage Publications, Inc.
    (1984), pp. 77-97.
Derrick, Jonathan. "West Africa's Worst Year of
    Famine." African Affairs, 83, no. 332 (1984),
    pp. 281-299.
Dinham, Barbara, and Colin Hines. Agribusiness in
    Africa. Trenton: Africa World Press, 1984.
Dinwiddy, Bruce, ed. Aid Performance and Develop-
    ment Policies of Western Countries. New
    York: Praeger Publishers, 1973.
Dolan, Michael B., and Brian W. Tomlin. "First
    World-Third World Linkages: External Rela-
    tions and Economic Development." Interna-
    tional Organization, 34, No. 1 (1980), pp.
    41-63.
Dolman, Anthony J., and Jan van Ettinger, eds.
    Partners in Tomorrow. New York: E.P. Dutton,
    1978.
Draegne, Harold E. Arid Lands in Transition. Bal-
    timore: Horn-Shafer, 1970.
DuBois, Victor D. The Drought in West Africa, Part
    I, 15, No. 1 Washington, D.C.: American Uni-
    versity Fieldstaff Reports, 1974.
Eicher, Carl K. "Facing Up to Africa's Food Cri-
    sis." Foreign Affairs, 61, No. 1 (Fall 1982),
    pp. 154-74.
Erb, Guy F., and Valeriana Kallab, eds. Beyond
    Dependency: The Developing World Speaks Out.
    New York: Praeger Publishers, 1975.
Fagan, Stuart I. Central American Economic Inte-
    gration. Berkeley: Univeristy of California,
    1970.
Fell, Arthur M. Memorandum on the Club Du Sahel,
    No. 1856. Paris: OECD, 1979.
Foltz, William J. From French West Africa to the
    MALI Federation. New Haven: Yale University
    Press, 1965.
Food and Agriculture Organization. 1976 FAO Pro-
    duction Yearbook, Vol. 30 Rome: FAO, 1976
_____. 1976 FAO Trade Yearbook, Vol. 30 Rome:
    FAO, 1977.
_____. 1979 FAO Trade Yearbook, Vol. 33 Rome:

FAO, 1980.

_____. 1982 FAO Trade Yearbook, Vol. 36 Rome: FAO, 1983.

_____. 1984 FAO Production Yearbook, Vol 38. Rome: FAO, 1984.

Foster-Carter, Aidan. "From Rostow to Gunder Frank: Conflicting Paradigms in the Analysis of Underdevelopment." World Development, 4, No. 3 (1976), pp. 167-80.

_____. "Can We Articulate 'Articulation'?" The New Economic Anthropology, ed., John Clammer. New York: St. Martin's Press, 1978.

Frank, Andre Gunder. Latin America: Underdevelopment or Revolution. New York: Monthly Review Press, 1969.

_____. "The Development of Underdevelopment." The Political Economy of Development and Underdevelopment, ed. Charles K. Wilbur. New York: Random House, 1973.

_____. "The World Crisis: Theory and Ideology." Alternatives, 6, No. 4 (1981), pp. 497-523.

Franke, Richard W., and Barbara A. Chasin. Seeds of Famine. Montclair: Allanheld, Osmun and Company, 1980.

Fuglestad, Finn. "La grande famine de 1931 dans l'Ouest Nigérien." Revue Française d'Histoire D'Outre-Mer, 61, No. 222 (1974), pp. 18-33.

Gallais, Jean. "Les sociétés pastorales ouest-africaines face au développement." Cahiers D'Etudes Africaines, 12, No. 47 (1972), pp. 353-68.

Galtung, Johan. "A Structural Theory of Imperialism." The African Review, 1, No. 4 (1972), pp. 93-138.

_____. "Self-Reliance: Concepts, Practice and Rationale." mimeo N.P., 1976.

_____. "The Lomé Convention and Neo-Capitalism." The African Review, 6, No. 1 (1976), pp. 33-42.

Gellar, "The Ratched-McMurphy Model Revisited: A Critique of Participatory Development Models, Strategies, and Projects." Issue, 14 (1985), pp. 25-28.

George, Susan. "From the World Food Conference to 1984: a decade of failure." Third World Affairs 1985. London: Third World Foundation, 1985.

Giri, M. J. "L´Avenir A Long Terme Du Sahel."
    Revue Juridique Et Politique, Indépendance Et
    Coopération, 30, No. 4 (1976), pp. 461-90.
_____. Le Sahel Demain. Paris: Editions Karthala,
    1983.
_____. Retrospective De L´Economie Sahelienne.
    Paris: OECD, 1985.
Glantz, Michael H., ed. The Politics of Natural
    Disaster. New York: Praeger Publishers,
    1976.
Gosovic, Branislav. UNCTAD: Conflict and Compro-
    mise. Leiden: A.W. Sijthoff, 1972.
_____, and John Gerard Ruggie. "On the creation
    of a new international economic order: issue
    linkage and the Seventh Special Session of
    the UN General Assembly." International Or-
    ganization, 30, No. 2 (1976), pp. 309-45.
Green, Reginald Herbold. "The Lomé Convention:
    Updated Dependence or Departure Toward Col-
    lective Self-Reliance?" The African Review,
    6, No. 1 (1976), pp. 43-54.
_____. "Consolidation and Accelerated Development
    of African Agriculture: What Agendas For
    Action?" African Studies Review, 27, No. 4
    (1984), pp. 17-34.
_____. "From Deepening Economic Malaise Towards
    Renewed Development: An Overview." Journal of
    Development Planning, 15 (1985), pp. 9-43.
Green, Stephen. International Disaster Relief,
    Toward a Responsive System. New York:
    McGraw-Hill, 1977.
Grove, A.T. "Desertification in the African Envi-
    ronment." African Affairs, 73, No. 291
    (1974), pp. 137-51.
Gruhn, Isebill V. "The Lomé Convention: inching
    towards independence." International Organi-
    zation, 30, No. 2 (1976), pp. 241-62.
_____. "The Recolonization of Africa: Interna-
    tional Organizations on the March." Africa
    Today, 30, No. 4 (1983), pp. 37-48.
Haas, Ernst B. "The Study of Regional Integration:
    Reflections on the Joy and Anguish of Pre-
    theorizing." International Organization, 24,
    (1970), pp. 607-646.
_____. The Obsolescence of Regional Integration
    Theory. Berkeley: University of California
    Press, 1975.

_____. "Turbulent Fields and the Theory of Regional Integration." International Organization, 30, No. 2 (1976), pp. 173-212.

Hansen, Roger D. "The Poltical Economy of North-South Relations: how much change?" International Organization, 29, No. 4 (1975), pp. 921-48.

_____. Beyond the North-South Debate. New York: McGraw-Hill, 1979.

Hatem, Mervat F. "The Political Economy of International Political Organizations: The League of Nations and the United Nations." Ph.D. Dissertation. The University of Michigan, 1982.

Hayter, Teresa. Aid as Imperialism. London: Penguin Press, 1971.

Hazelwood, Arthur. Economic Integration: The East African Experience. London: Heinemann, 1975.

_____. "The End of the East African Community: What are the Lesson for Regional Integration Schemes?" Journal of Common Market Studies, 18, No. 1 (1979), pp. 40-58.

Helleiner, Gerald K. "Aid and Dependence in Africa: Issues for Recipients." in The Politics of Africa: Dependence and Development. ed. Timothy M. Shaw and Kenneth A. Heard. London: Longman Group Ltd. and Dalhousie University Press, (1979), pp. 221-45.

_____. "Aid and Liquidity: The Neglect of Sub-Saharan Africa and Others of the Poorest in the Emerging International Monetary System." Journal of Development Planning, 15 (1985), pp. 67-84.

Henry, Paul-Marc. "Le Club Des Amis Du Sahel, Un Cadre Nouveau Pour La Coopération Internationale." Revue Juridique Et Politique, Indépendance Et Coopération, 30, No. 4 (1976), pp. 397-402.

Higgott, Richard. "Structural Dependence and Decolonization in a West African Land-Locked State: Niger." Review of African Political Economy, 17 (1980), pp. 43-58.

_____ and Finn Fuglestad. "The 1974 Coup d´Etat in Niger: Towards an Explanation." The Journal of Modern African Studies, 13, No. 3 (1975), pp. 383-90.

Holly, Daniel A. "L´ONU, le système économique

international et la politique internationale." <u>International Organization</u>, 29, No.
2 (1975), pp. 469-86.

Horowitz, Michael M. "Ethnic Boundary Maintenance
Among Pastoralists and Farmers in the Western
Sudan." <u>Journal of Asian and African Studies</u>,
7, Nos. 1-2 (1972), pp. 105-14.

Imperato, Pascal J. "Nomads of the Sahel and the
Delivery of Health Services to Them." <u>Social
Science and Medicine</u>, 8, No. 8 (1974), pp.
443-57.

Independent Commission on International Humanitarian Issues. <u>Famine: A Man-Made Disaster?</u>.
New York: Random House, 1985.

International Monetary Fund. <u>Direction of Trade
Yearbook</u>. Washington, D.C.: IMF, 1980.

Jacobson, Harold K. <u>Networks of Interdependence,
International Organizations and the Global
Political System</u>. New York: Alfred A. Knopf,
1979.

Jeanneret, Charles A. <u>L´Harmonisation De La Stratégie Du CILSS/Club Du Sahel Avec Les Plans
De Développement Nationaux Des Pays Saheliens, Est-Elle Possible?</u>, Discussion Paper
No. 818. Ottawa: Ottawa University, 1981.

Johnson, G. Wesley, Jr. <u>The Emergence of Black
Politics in Senegal</u>. Stanford: Stanford
Univesity Press, 1971.

Jollah, Abdul. <u>Political Integration in French-
Speaking Africa</u>. Berkeley: University of
California Press, 1973.

Joseph, Richard. "The Gaullist Legacy: Patterns of
French Neo-Colonialism." <u>Review of African
Political Economy</u>, No. 6 (1976), pp. 4-13.

Jost, Stephane. <u>Aide Alimentaire En 1985</u>. Paris:
OECD, 1985.

Joyce, Charles L., ed. <u>Towards a Rational U.S.
Policy on River Basin Development in the
Sahel</u>. Washington, D.C.: USAID, 1978.

Kent, George. <u>The Political Economy of Hunger</u>. New
York: Praeger Publishers, 1984.

Kim, Jung-Gun. "Non-Member Participation in the
South Pacific Commission and the Caribbean
Organization." <u>Caribbean Quarterly</u>, 13, No. 4
(1967), pp. 24-30.

Kurtz, Donn M. "Political Organization in Africa:
The Mali Federation." <u>The Journal of Modern</u>

African Studies, 8, No. 3 (1970), pp. 405-24.

Labonne, Michael. "La Dégradation De La Situation Paysanne Dans Les Pays Saheliens Avant La Sécheresse." _Revue Juridique Et Politique, Indépendance Et Coopération_, 30, No. 4 (1976), pp. 442-60.

Laszlo, Ervin, Robert Baker, Jr., Elliot Eisenberg, and Venkata Roman. _The Objectives of the New International Economic Order_. New York: Pergamon Press, 1978.

Lateef, Noel V. _Crisis in the Sahel: A Case Study in Development Cooperation_. Boulder: Westview Press, 1980.

Leff, Nathaniel H. "The New Economic Order—Bad Economics, Worse Politics." _Foreign Policy_, No. 24 (1976), pp. 202-17.

Legum, Colin, ed. _The First U.N. Development Decade and its Lessons for the 1970s_. New York: Praeger Publishers, 1970.

_____, I. William Zartman, Steven Langdon, and Lynn K. Mytelka, eds. _Africa in the 1980s_. New York: McGraw-Hill, 1979.

Leys, Colin. "Underdevelopment and Dependency: Critical Notes." _Journal of Contemporary Asia_, 7, No. 1 (1977), pp. 92-107.

Lofchie, Michael F. "Political and Economic Origins of African Hunger." _The Journal of Modern African Studies_, 13, No. 4 (1975), pp. 551-67.

_____ and Stephen K. Commins, "Food Deficits and Agricultural Policies in Sub-Saharan Africa." _The Hunger Project Papers_, No. 2 (1984).

Machlup, Fritz, ed. _Economic Integration: Worldwide, Regional, Sectoral_. London: Macmillan, 1976.

Manga, Boulama. _Restarting The CILSS National Committees_. mimeo Niamey: CILSS, 1977.

Marchés Tropicaux et Méditerranéens. "Sahel: le mise en point du programme d'aide américaine." _Marchés Tropicaux et Méditerranéens_, 33, No. 1638 (1977), p. 748.

Martin, Guy. "Socialism, Economic Development and Planning in Mali, 1960-1968." _Canadian Journal of African Studies_, 9. No. 1 (1976), pp. 23-47.

Maton, Guy. "L'Irrigation, Facteur De Survie Du Sahel," _Revue Juridique Et Politique, Indé-_

pendence Et Coopération, 30, No. 4 (1976),
pp. 435-41.
Mayer, Jean. "Coping with Famine." Foreign Af-
fairs, 53, No. 1 (1974), pp. 98-120.
Mazrui, Ali A. Towards A Pax Africana. Chicago:
The University of Chicago Press, 1967.
_____. Africa's International Relations. London:
Heineman, 1977.
_____. The African Condition. London: Heineman,
1980.
Meillassoux, Claude. "Development or Exploitation:
is the Sahel famine good business?" Review
of African Political Economy, No 1 (1974),
pp. 27-33.
Michanek, Ernst. "An International Disaster Relief
Insurance." Development Dialogue, 1 (1981),
pp. 30-37.
Monod, Théodore, ed. Pastoralism in Tropical Afri-
ca. London: Oxford University Press, 1975.
Morris, David. "Some Political Dimensions of In-
ternational Relief: Two Cases." International
Organization, 28, (1974), pp. 127-40.
Morss, Elliott R. "Institutional Destruction Re-
sulting from Donor and Project Proliferation
in Sub-Saharan African Countries." World
Development, 12, No. 4 (April 1984), pp. 465-
70.
Muni, S.D. "The Paris Dialogue on International
Economic Cooperation: The North's Strategy
and the Outcome." Foreign Affair Reports, 26,
No. 10 (1977), pp. 205-23.
Mutharika, B.W.T. Toward Multinational Economic
Cooperation in Africa, New York: Praeger
Publishers, 1972.
Mytelka, Lynn K. "The Salience of Gains in Third
World Integrative Systems." World Politics,
25, No. 2 (1973), pp. 236-50.
_____. "Foreign Aid and Regional Integration: The
UDEAC Case." Journal of Common Market
Studies, 12, No. 2 (1973), pp. 138-58.
_____. "A Geneology of Francophone West and Equa-
torial African Regional Organizations." The
Journal of Modern African Studies, 12, No. 2
(1974), pp. 297-320.
_____. Regional Development in a Global Economy.
New Haven: Yale Univeristy Press, 1979.
Nabudere, D. Wadada. "The Lomé Convention and the

Consolidation of Neo-Colonialism." The African Review, No. 3 (1976), pp. 339-74.

Naw, Henry R. "From integration to interdependence: gains, losses, and continuing gaps."
International Organization, 33, No. 1 (1979),
pp. 119-47.

Nelson, Joan M. Aid, Influence, and Foreign Policy. New York: The Macmillan Company, 1968.

Newman, James L., ed. Drought, Famine and Population Movements in Africa. Syracuse: Syracuse
University, 1975.

North-South Institute. North-South Encounter: The
Third World and Canadian Performance. Ottawa: Runge Press, 1977.

Nye, Joseph S. Pan Africanism and East African
Integration. Cambridge: Harvard University
Press, 1965.

_____. International Regionalism. Boston: Little,
Brown and Company, 1968.

O'Brien, Philip J. "A critique of Latin American
theories of dependency." Beyond the Sociology
of Development, eds. Ivar Oxaal, Tony Barnett, and David Booth. London: Routledge and
Kegan Paul, 1975.

Ojo, Olatunde J.B. "Nigeria and the formation of
ECOWAS." International Organization, 34, No.
1 (1980), pp. 571-604.

Olofin, Sam. "ECOWAS and the Lomé Convention: An
Experiment in Complementary or Conflicting
Customs Union Arrangements?" Journal of
Common Market Studies, 16, No. 1 (1977), pp.
53-72.

Omolodun, J. O. "Prospects of Economic Cooperation in Sub-Saharan Africa." Foreign Affair
Reports, 27, No. 12 (1978), pp. 202-14.

OECD. The Club Des Amis Du Sahel, Proposal of
Purpose and Function. N.P., N.D.

_____. Strategy and Programme for Drought Control
and Development in the Sahel. Paris: OECD,
1979.

_____. Aide Alimentaire Et Coopération Pour Le
Développement: L'Expérience Du Sahel. Paris:
OECD, 1984.

_____. Summary Record, Donor Coordination Meeting,
Review of the Operations and Organization of
the CILSS Sahel CR (85) 49. Paris: OECD,
1985.

_____, CILSS, and the Club du Sahel. Développe-
ment Des Cultures Pluviales Au Niger. Paris:
Club du Sahel, 1982.

_____. Développement Des Cultures Pluviales En
Haute-Volta. Paris: Club du Sahel, 1982.

_____. Développement Des Cultures Pluviales Au
Mali. Paris: Club du Sahel, 1983.

_____. Développement Des Cultures Pluviales Au
Senegal. Paris: Club du Sahel, 1983.

_____. Développement Des Cultures Pluviales En
Mauritanie. Paris: Club du Sahel, 1983.

_____. Programme-Overview of Continental Fisheries
(The Gambia, Upper Volta, Mali, Mauritania,
Niger, Senegal). Paris: Club du Sahel, 1983.

_____. Development of Rainfed Agriculture in the
Sahel, Overview and Prospects. Paris: Club du
Sahel, 1983.

_____. Drought Control And Development In The
Sahel, Situation At The Start Of The 1980s.
Paris: Club du Sahel, 1983.

_____. Human Resources In the Sahel, CILSS-Club
Du Sahel Joint Action, Overview And
Prospects. Paris: Club du Sahel, 1983.

_____. Evolution of Cereals Policies. Paris: Club
du Sahel, 1983.

_____. Development Of Rainfed Agriculture In The
Gambia. Paris: OECD, 1984.

_____. Réunion Du Comité Directeur De La Concer-
tation Sur Le Développment Du Secteur Ecolo-
gie-Forets Dans Les Pays Du Sahel. Paris:
Club du Sahel, 1984.

_____. Transformation De L'Environnement Dans Le
Sahel Ouest Africain. Paris: Club du Sahel,
1984.

_____. Recurrent Costs: The Problem And Practical
Consideration For The Design Of Development
Programs. Paris: Club du Sahel, 1984.

_____. L'Aide Publique Au Développement Dans Les
Pays Membres Du CILSS En 1983. Paris:
OECD/Club du Sahel, 1984.

_____. Proposals For A Revised Strategy For
Drought Control And Development In The
Sahel. Paris: Club du Sahel, 1984.

_____. Summary Record Of The Meeting On The Coor-
dination Of Food Aid To CILSS Member Countries In 1984/85. Paris: Club du Sahel,
1984.

271

_____. Bilan-Programme Des Productions Végétales
Pluviales Et Irrigués Du Tchad. Paris: Club
du Sahel, 1984.
_____. Hydraúlique Villageoise Et Pastorale Dans
Les Pays Du Sahel. Paris: Club du Sahel,
1984.
_____. Comité Directeur Ecologie-Forets-Environne-
ment Du CILSS/Club Du Sahel Elargi Aux Repré-
sentants Des Partenaires De Coopération Bi-
laterale Et Multilaterale. Paris: Club du
Sahel, 1984.
_____. La Dette Extérieure Des Pays Du CILSS.
Paris: Club du Sahel, Sahel D(85) 259 Paris:
OECD, 1985.
_____. Summary Report of the Regional Seminar on
Desertification Sahel CR (85) 48. Paris:
OECD, 1985.
_____. Les Structures Décentralisées: La Couver-
ture Des Charges Récurrentes Et Le Dévelop-
pement En Milieu Rural Sahelien. Sahel
D(85) 258. Paris: OECD, 1985.
_____. Proposal For A Regional Strategy Of Deser-
tification Control Sahel D(85) 261. Paris:
OECD, 1985.
_____.Propositions D´Orientations Stratégiques Du
Développement Des Peches Dans Les Pays Du
Sahel Sahel D(85) 262. Paris: OECD, 1985.
_____. Planification Macroéconomique Et Dépenses
Récurrentes Au Sahel: Une Note D´Orientation.
Sahel D(85) 264 Paris: OECD, 1985.
_____. What Future For The Sahel? Sahel D(85) 276.
Paris: OECD, 1985.
_____. Analysis Of Official Development Assistance
To The Sahel. Sahel D(85) 277. Paris: OECD,
1985.
_____. Cereals Policy Reform In The Sahel. Sahel
D(85) 278. Paris: OECD, 1985.
OECD and the Club du Sahel. Chairman´s Report,
Special Meeting on the Role of the Club du
Sahel. Paris: OECD, 1983.
Osagie, Eghosa. "The Lomé Convention: An Inter-
pretation of the Trade Liberalization and Ex-
port Stabilization Provisions." The African
Review, 6, No. 3 (1976), pp. 329-37.
Ouattara, Alassane D. "Reflections on the Crisis",
Journal of Development Planning, No. 15
(1985), pp. 45-65.

Oudes, Bruce. "Crocodile Tears Over American Aid." Africa Report, 19, No. 2 (1974), pp. 52-54.

Pallangyo, E.P. and L.A. Odero-Ogwel. "The Persistence of the Food and Agriculture Crisis in Africa." in Economic Crisis in Africa. Ed. Adebayo Adedeji and Timothy M. Shaw Boulder: Lynne Rienner, 1985, pp. 169-186.

Plessz, Nicolas G. Problems and Prospects of Economic Integration in West Africa. Montreal: McGill University Press, 1968.

Poole, Bernard L. The Caribbean Commission. Columbia: University of South Carolina Press, 1951.

Puchala, Donald J. "Of Blind Men, Elephants and International Integration." Journal of Common Market Studies, 10, No. 3 (1972), pp. 267-84.

Ravenhill, John. "What is to be done for Third World commodity exporters? an evaluation of the STABEX scheme." International Organization, 38, No. 3 (1984), pp. 537-574.

Riha, Thomas J. F. "Determinants of Government Expenditure: French-Speaking Countries of Africa South of the Sahara." The Philippine Review of Business and Economics, 11, No. 1 (1974), pp. 35-59.

Robarts, Richard. French Development Assistance: A Study in Policy and Administration. Beverly Hills: Sage Publications, 1974.

Robinson, Pearl T. "The Political Context of Regional Development in the West African Sahel." The Journal of Modern African Studies, 16, No. 4 (1978), pp. 579-95.

_____. "Sahelian Regional Development in a Changing World Order." Paper presented at the African Studies Association Meeting, Philadelphia, Pennsylvania, October, 1980.

Rondinelli, Dennis A. "International Assistance Policy and Development Project Administration: The Impact of Imperious Rationality." International Organization, 30, No. 4 (1976), pp. 573-605.

Rosenbaum, H. Jon, and William G. Tyler. "South-South Relations: The Economic and Political Content of Interactions Among Developing Countries." World Politics and International Economics. Ed. C. Fred Bergsten and Lawrence

B. Krause. Washington, D.C.: The Brookings
Institution, 1975.

Rosenthal, Irving. Design and Approval of the
Sahel Integrated Pest Management Project.
Washington, D.C.: USAID, 1979.

Rosenthal, Jerry E. "The Creeping Catastrophe."
Africa Report, 18, No. 4 (1973), pp. 6-13.

Ross, Clark G. "The Deteriorating Food Grain Situa-
tion in the Sahel and a Program for Grain
Self-Sufficiency by the Year 2000." Draft.
July 1983.

_____. "A Critical Analysis Of ODA In The Sahel."
Draft. mimeo August 1985.

Rothstein, Robert L. The Weak in the World of the
Strong. New York: Columbia University Press,
1977.

_____. Global Bargaining. Princeton: Princeton
University Press, 1979.

_____. "The North-South Dialogue: The Political
Economy of Immobility." Journal of International Affairs, 34, No. 1 (1980), pp. 1-17.

Samoff, Joel. "Class, Class Conflict, and the
State: Notes on the Political Economy of
Africa." Paper presented at the African
Studies Association Meeting, Houston, Texas,
1977.

Schertz, Lyle P. "World Food: Prices and the
Poor." Foreign Affairs, 52, No.3 (1974), pp.
511-37.

Schmitter, Philippe C. Autonomy or Dependence as
Regional Integration Outcomes: Central America. Berkeley: University of California Press,
1972.

Sen Amartya. Poverty and Famines. Oxford: Clarendon Press, 1981.

Shaw, Margaret G. Administrative Structures and
Civil Service in the Sahel Countries.
Washington, D.C.: USAID, 1979.

Shaw, Timothy M. "The African Crisis: Alternative
Development Strategies for the Continent."
Alternatives, No. 9 (1983), pp. 111-27.

_____. "Debates About Africa's Future: The Brandt,
World Bank and Lagos Plan Blueprints." Third
World Quarterly, 5, No. 2 (1983), pp. 330-44.

_____ and Malcolm J. Grieve. "Dependence as an
Approach to Understanding Inequalities in
Africa." The Journal of Developing Areas, 13,

274

No. 3 (1979), pp. 229-46.

Shear, David, and Bob Clark. "International Long-Term Planning for the Sahel." International Development Review, No. 4 (1976), pp. 15-20.

Sheets, Hal, and Roger Morris. Disaster in the Desert: Failures of International Relief in the West African Drought. Washington, D.C.: The Carnegie Endowmment for International Peace, 1974.

Shepherd, Jack. The Politics of Starvation. New York: The Carnegie Endowment for International Peace, 1974.

_____. "When Foreign Aid Fails." The Atlantic Monthly. April 1985, pp. 41-46.

Sidjanski, Dusan. Current Problems of Economic Integration: The Role of Institutions in Regional Integration Among Developing Countries. New York: United Nations, 1974.

Simai, Mihály, and Katalin Garam, eds. Economic Integration: Concepts, Theories, and Problems. Budapest: Adademiai Kiado, 1977.

Singer, H.W. "The New International Economic Order: An Overview." The Journal of Modern African Studies, 16, No. 4 (1978), pp.539-48.

Sloan, John W. "The Strategy of Developmental Regionalism: Benefits, Distribution, Obstacles,and Capabilities." Journal of Common Market Studies, 10, No. 2 (1971), pp. 138-62.

Smith, Tony. "Changing Configurations of Power in North-South Relations Since 1945." International Organization, 31, No. 1 (1977), pp. 1-27.

Spero, Joan Edelman. The Politics of International Economic Relations. New York: St. Martin's Press, 1977.

Streeten, Paul. Aid to Africa. New York: Praeger Publishers, 1972.

Taylor, Phillip. Nonstate Actors in International Politics: From Transregional to Substate Organizations. Boulder: Westview Press, 1984.

Temple, R.S., and M.E.R. Thomas. "The Sahelian Drought--A Disaster for Livestock Populations." World Animal Review, No. 8 (1973), pp. 1-7.

Tendler, Judith. Inside Foreign Aid. Baltimore: The John Hopkins University Press, 1975.

Thenevin, Pierre. L'Aide Alimentaire En Céréales
Dans Les Pays Saheliens. Paris: France,
Ministère De La Coopération, 1980.

Thompson, Virginia. West Africa's Council of the
Entente. Ithaca: Cornell University Press,
1972.

Timberlake, Lloyd. Africa in crisis. London:
International Institute for Environment and
Development, Earthscan, 1985.

Todaro, Michael P. Economic Development in the
Third World. London: Longman Group, 1977.

Twose, Nigel. Behind the Weather, Why the Poor
Suffer Most, Drought and the Sahel. London:
Oxfam, N.D.

ul Haq, Mahbub. "Beyond the Slogan of South-South
Cooperation." World Development, 8, No. 10
(1980), pp. 743-51.

United Nations. 1970-1971 Yearbook of International Trade Statistics. New York: United
Nations, 1973.

_____. 1977 Yearbook of International Trade Sta-
tistics, Volume I. New York: United Nations,
1978.

_____. 1978 Yearbook of International Trade Sta-
tistics, Volume I. New York: United Nations,
1979.

_____. 1981 Statistical Yearbook. New York: United
Nations, 1983.

_____. 1982 Statistical Yearbook. New York: United
Nations, 1985.

_____. Office for Emergency Operations in Africa.
Status Report On The Emergency Situation In
Africa. New York: United Nations, 1985.

_____. Status Report On The Emergency Situation In
Africa As Of 1 August 1985. Report No.
OEOA/3/2 New York: United Nations, N.D.

_____. Status Report On The Emergency Situation In
Africa As Of 1 September 1985, Report No.
OEOA/3/3. New York: United Nations, N.D.

_____. Status Report On The Emergency Situation In
Africa As Of 1 November 1985, Report No.
OEOA/3/5. New York: United Nations, N.D.

_____. Status Report On The Emergency Situation In
Africa As Of 1 December 1985, Report No.
OEOA/3/6. New York: United Nations, N.D.

_____. Status Report On The Emergency Situation In
Africa As Of 1 January 1986, Report No.

OEOA/3/7. New York: United Nations, N. D.
_____. Special Report On The Emergency Situation
In Africa, Review of 1985 and 1986 Emergency
Needs. New York: United Nations, 1986.
_____. Office for Special Relief Operations. Bur-
kina Faso, Report of the FAO Multidonor Mis-
sion, OSRO Report No. 19/84/E. Rome: FAO,
1985.
_____. United Nations Development Program.
Drought in Africa. New York: United Na-
tions, N.D.
United States Agency for International Develop-
ment. Opportunity for Self-Reliance: An
Overview of the Sahel Development Poten-
tial.Washington, D.C. USAID, 1976.
_____.United States Response to the Sahel
Drought. Washington, D.C.: USAID, 1977.
_____. Sahel Development Program Annual Report to
the Congress. Washington, D.C.: USAID, 1978.
_____. Sahel Development Program Annual Report
to the Congress. Washington, D.C.: USAID,
1979.
_____. Sahel Development Program Annual Report to
the Congress. Washington, D.C: USAID, 1980.
_____. Sahel Development Program Annual Report to
the Congress. Washington, D.C.: USAID, 1981.
_____. Assessment of the Sahel Development Pro-
gram. Washington, D.C.: USAID, 1983.
_____. Annual Budget Submission FY 87 Burkina
Faso. Washington, D.C.: USAID, 1985.
_____. Niger Emergency Plan. mimeo Washington,
D.C.: USAID, 1985.
United States Department of Agriculture. Food
Problems and Prospects in Sub-Saharan Africa.
Washington, D.C.: USDA, 1981.
Uri, Pierre, ed. North-South: Developing a New
Relationship. Paris: The Atlantic Institute
for International Affairs, 1976.
Vaitsos, Constantine V. "Crisis in Regional Eco-
nomic Cooperation (Integration) Among Deve-
loping Countries: A Survey." World Develop-
ment, 6, No. 6 (1978), pp. 719-69.
Vengroff, Richard and Ali Farah. "State Interven-
tion and Agricultural Development in Africa:
a Cross-National Study." The Journal of
Modern African Studies, 23, No. 1 (1985),
pp. 75-85.

von Geusau, Frans A.M., ed. The Lomé Convention and a New International Economic Order. Leyden: A.W. Sijthoff International, 1977.

Wade, Nicholas. "Sahelian Drought: No Victory for Western Aid." Science, 185, No. 4147 (1974), pp. 234-37.

Waldstein, Abraham S. Government Sponsored Agricultural Intensification Schemes in the Sahel: Development for Whom?. Washington, D.C.: USAID, 1978.

Walker, Martin. "Drought." The New York Times Magazine, (June 9, 1974), pp. 12-13, 42-46.

Wallerstein, Immanuel. The Capitalist World-Economy. Cambridge: Cambridge University Press, 1979.

Weintraub, Sidney. "The New International Economic Order: The Beneficiaries." World Development, 7, No. 3 (1979), pp. 247-58.

Wessels, Wolfgang, ed. Europe and the North-South Dialogue. Paris: The Atlantic Institute for International Affairs, 1978.

Williams, Maurice J. A New Method of Cooperating with the Very Poor Countries. Paris: OECD, 1977.

_____. "National Food Strategies: A Response to Crisis." Journal of Development Planning, No. 15 (1985), pp. 85-98.

Wionczek, Miguel, ed. Economic Cooperation in Latin America, Africa, and Asia: A Handbook of Documents. Cambridge: The MIT Press, 1969.

Wodie, Francis. Les Institutions Internationales Régionales en Afrique Occidentale et Centrale. Paris: Librairie Générale de Droit et de Jurisprudence, 1970.

World Bank. Urban Growth and Economic Development in the Sahel. Working Paper No. 315. Washington, D.C.: The World Bank, 1979.

_____. Accelerated Development in Sub-Saharan Africa: an agenda for action. Washington, D.C.: World Bank, 1981.

_____. Toward Sustained Development in Sub-Saharan Africa. Washington, D.C.: World Bank, 1984.

_____. World Development Report 1985. New York: Oxford University Press, 1985.

World Health Organization. World Health Statistics Annual 1983. Geneva: World Health Organization, 1983.

278

Yansane, Aguibou Y., ed. Decolonization and Dependency: Problems of Development of African Societies. Westport: Greenwood Press, 1980.

Yondo, Marcel. Dimension Nationale et Développement Economique. Paris: Librairie Générale de Droit et de Jurisprudence, 1970.

Zartman, I. William. The Politics of Trade Negotiations Between Africa and the European Economic Community. Princeton: Princeton University Press, 1971.

_____. "Europe and Africa: Decolonization or Dependency?" Foreign Affairs, 54, No. 2 (1976), pp. 325-43.

Abbreviations

AAPC	All-African People´s Conference
ACP	African, Caribbean, and Pacific
ACCT	Agence de Coopération Culturel et Technique
ADB	African Development Bank
BCEAO	Banque Centrale Economique de l´Afrique de l´Ouest
CADA	Concerted Action for Development in Africa
CCCE	Caisse Centrale de Coopération Economique
CDC	Center for Disease Control
CDCC	Caribbean Development and Cooperation
CE	Council of the Entente
CEAO	Communauté Economique de l´Afrique de l´Ouest
CFA	Communauté Financière Africaine
CIDA	Canadian International Development Agency
CIEC	Conference on International Econo-Cooperation
CIEH	Comité Inter-Africain d´Etudes Hydrauliques
CILCA	Comité International de Liaison du Corps pour l´Alimentation
CILSS	Comité permanent Inter-états de Lutte contre la Sécheresse dans le Sahel
DAC	Development Assistance Corporation
DAF	Division of Administrative and Financial Affairs

DDI	Division of Documentation and Information
DPP	Division of Projects and Programs
ECOWAS	Economic Community of West African States
EAC	East African Community
EEC	European Economic Community
ECLA	Economic Commission for Latin America
FAC	Fonds d´Aide et de Coopération
FAO	Food and Agriculture Organization
FED	Fonds Européen de Développement
FEDOM	Fonds Européen de Développement d´Outre Mer
FGP	First Generation Program
FM	Malian Franc
GNP	Gross National Product
IGADD	Inter-Governmental Authority for Drought and Development
IPM	Integrated Pest Management
LAFTA	Latin American Free Trade Association
LCBC	Lake Chad Basin Commission
NGO	Division of Relations with Non-Governmental Organizations
NGO	Non-Governmental Organization
NIEO	New International Economic Order
OAMCA	Organisation Africaine et Malgache pour la Coopération Economique
OAU	Organization of African Unity
OCAM	Organisation Commune Africaine, Malgache et Mauricienne
OCCGE	Organisation de Coordination et de la Coopération pour la Lutte contre les Grandes Endemies
OCLALAV	Organisation Commune de Lutte Anti-Acridienne et le Lutte Anti-Aviaire
ODA	Official Development Assistance
OECD	Organization for Economic Cooperation and Development
OEOA	Office for Emergency Operations in Africa
OICMA	Organisation Internationale contre le Criquet Migrateur Africain
OMVS	Organisation pour la Mise en Valeur du Fleuve Sénégal

ONG	Division of Relations with Non-Governmental Organizations
OPEC	Organization of Petroleum Exporting States
PID	Project Identification Document
PQLI	Physical Quality of Life Index
SADCC	Southern African Development Coordination Conference
SDP	Sahel Developmetn Program
UDEAC	Union Douanière et Economic de l´ Afrique Central
UDEAO	Union Douanière et Economique de l´ Afrique de l´Ouest
UGR	Unité de Gestion Régionale
UN	United Nations
UNCTAD	United Nations Conference on Trade and Development
UNDP	United Nations Development Program
UNSO	United Nations Sudano-Sahelian Office
USAID	United States Agency for International Development
USDA	United States Department of Agriculture
USED	Unité Socio-Economique et de Démographie
WARDA	West African Rice Development Association
WHO	World Health Organization
WMO	World Meteorological Organization

Donors

Abu Dhabi Fund
Abu Dhabi Fund for Arab Economic Development
  (ADFAED)
African Development Bank (ADB)
African Development Fund (ADF)
Africare
Agence de coopération culturel et technique
  (ACCT)
Algeria
Arab Bank for Economic Development in Africa
  (ABEDA)
Australia
Austria
Bank of Brazil
Banque Centrale Economique de l´Afrique de
  l´Ouest (BCEAO)
Banque Islamique de Développement (BIslD)
Banque de l´Ouest Africaine de Développement
  (BOAD)
Belgium
Caisse Centrale de Coopération Economique (CCCE)
Canadian International Development Agency (CIDA)
Center for Overseas Pest Research (COPR)
Centre de Recherche pour le Développement Inter-
  nationale (CRDI)
Comité Inter-Africain d´Etudes Hydrauliques
  (CIEH)
Commission du Bassin du Lac Tchad (CBLT)
Communauté Economique de l´Afrique de l´Ouest
  (CEAO)
Communauté Economic de Betail et de la Viande
  (CEBV)

Denmark
Federal Republic of Germany
Finland
Fonds Arabe d´Aide Technique aux Pays Africains
  et Arabes (FAATAA)
Fonds d´Aide et de Coopération (FAC)
Fonds d´Arabe pour le Développement Economique et
  Social (FADES)
Fonds Européen de Développement (FED)
Fonds International de Développement Agricole
  (FIDA)
Fonds Saoudien de Développement (FSD)
Food and Agricultural Organization (FAO)
Inter-Governmental Maritime Consultative Organi-
  (IMCO)
International Bank for Reconstruction and
  Development/The World Bank (IBRD)
International Civil Aviation Organization
  (ICAO)
International Development Association (IDA)
International Labor Organization (ILO)
International Telecommunications Union
Iran
Iraq
Ireland
Italy
Japan
Kuwait
Kuwait Fund for Arab Economic Development (KFAED)
Lybia
Netherlands
Nigeria
North Korea
Norway
Office de Recherche Scientifique et Technique
  Outre-Mer (ORSTOM)
Office of Special Relief Operations (OSRO)
OPEC Fund for International Development (OFID)
Peace Corps
People´s Republic of China
Qatar
Saudi Arabia
Sweden
Switzerland
United Arab Emirates
United Kingdom
United Nations Capital Development Fund (UNCDF)

United Nations Children's Fund (UNICEF)
United Nations Department of Technical Coopera-
   tion for Development (UNDTCD)
United Nations Development Program (UNDP)
United Nations Educational, Scientific, and Cul-
   tural Organization (UNESCO)
United Nations Fund for Population Activities
   (UNFPA)
United Nations Industrial Development Organiza-
   tion (UNIDO)
United Nations Organization for Trade Cooperation
   (UNOTC)
United Nations Sudano-Sahelian Office (UNSO)
United Nations Volunteers (UNV)
United States Agency for International Develop-
   ment (USAID)
West African Rice Development Association
World Food Program (WFP)
World Health Organization (WHO)
World Meteorological Organization (WMO)

Index

290

Ethnic groups, 30. See
also Migration;
Refugees; Social issues
European Economic
Community (EEC), 78,
81-82, 84, 105(n40)
Executive Secretary (CILSS),
115, 147, 219, 236
and Club du Sahel, 116,
216-217
divisions, 119-121
donor support, 167-168
personnel, 158(table),
160, 168
planning, 117-118
restructuring, 234-235,
236-237, 238, 240
role, 147-148
Exports, 4, 36
demands, 3, 5(table), 6, 7
dependency, 60, 61(table)
developing states, 75, 87
economic integration, 68,
86
1968-1974 drought, 30-31
products, 55-57(table),
58
raw materials, 79, 83
stabilizing process, 79,
82, 83
See also Cash crop
production; Trade

Fact-finding missions,
151-152
Famine, 1, 3, 13, 14, 27,
32, 40, 43
FAO. See Food and Agriculture
Organization
Farmers. See Villagers
FED. See Fonds Européen
de Développement
Fertilizer production,
55-57(table)
FGP. See First Generation
Program

Financing, 73
donor support, 197-200, 205
impacts, 203-208
Sahelian support, 201-203
See also Aid; Donor aid
First Generation Program
(FGP), 95-96, 117, 118,
136, 139, 140, 151, 161,
164, 188
costs, 175-179
donor support, 180,
181-182(table), 189-190
(table), 203, 206, 207
dryland agriculture,
131-132
goals, 199, 207-208
livestock, 134-135
project evaluations, 173-179,
206-208, 209-210
termination, 209-210
Fisheries, 35, 70, 95,
130(table), 144, 214,
235, 238
donor interest, 185,
187-188, 191, 192(table),
194
donor support, 180, 185,
186(table), 196(table),
197(table), 199, 204,
210(n12), 221-222
FGP projects, 174(table),
175, 177, 178(table)
funding, 206, 220(table)
government support, 201-202
Working Group and, 116, 128,
135-136
Fonds Européen de Développement
(FED), 188
Food aid, xix, 2, 33, 222,
241
1982-1985 drought, 40,
41(table), 42, 43,
44(table), 49(n84)
politics of, 225-226,
228-229
recommendations, 249-250

296

Food and Agriculture
Organization (FAO),
130, 140, 142,
164-165, 188
Food Corps Program,
140-141, 159
Food crop production, 12,
35-36, 91, 130(table),
220(table), 235, 239,
244, 250
  availability, 21-22
  droughts, 25-27,
    38-39, 49(n84)
  protection, 141-144
  self-sufficiency, 35-36,
    43, 84, 92, 140, 199,
    204, 206, 208, 220-221
  See also Cash crop
    production; individual
    crops
Food imports, xix, 6, 31,
  223-226
Ford administration, 98
Foreign Disaster Relief
  Coordination Office
  (USAID), 32
France, 78, 188
  CILSS support, 157(table),
    158(table), 167
  trade, 59(table), 60,
    61(table), 86
Frank, Andre Gunder, 88

Gambia, 1, 36, 100, 228
  agricultural production,
    11(table), 12, 25,
    26(table), 35, 36,
    223(table), 224(table),
    225, 241
  aid levels, 226(table),
    227
  CILSS, xviii, 71(table),
    92, 111, 112(table),
    114(table), 154,
    155(table), 158(table),
    159, 163

donor support, 184,
  186(table)
FGP projects, 173,
  174(table), 175, 177,
  178(table)
GNP, 7, 8(table), 76,
  81(table), 216(table),
  228(table)
population, 8(table),
  9(table), 10
project support, 201,
  202(table)
regional cooperatives,
  71(table), 106(n46)
trade, 4, 5(tables), 6,
  59(table), 60
G-8. See Group of Eight
Germany, 143, 157(table),
  158(table), 167
Ghana, 30, 63-64, 106(n46)
Ghana-Guinea-Mali Union,
  63-64
Giscard d'Estaing, Valery, 78
G-19. See Group of Nineteen
GNP. See Gross national
  product
Goats. See Livestock
  production
Governments, African, 6
  CILSS budgeting, 154-157
  as donor, 191, 192(table)
  drought relief, 32-33
  internal reform, 243-247
  policy, 7, 12-13, 21
  project involvement, 200-203,
    209, 222
  support for CILSS,
    151-154, 159-161,
    162-164, 170-171,
    172(n5), 215-216, 231-232
Gross national product, 7,
  81(table), 30-31, 76,
  226-227, 228(table)
Groundnut production, 3, 12,
  20, 36, 82, 225

298

299

MRD (cont.)
   See also Council of
   Ministers
MNR. See Mozambique
   National Resistance
Monetary management, 76-77
Monrovia Declaration, 90
Moors, 27
Mortality rates, 9, 29.
   See also Population
   growth
Mozambique, 1-2, 52, 91
Mozambique National
   Resistance (MNR), 1-2
Multilateralization. See
   Decolonization

National Committees
   (CILSS), 144-145, 147,
   169, 236
  problems, 208, 216, 232
  Sahelian support,
   161-162, 170
National Correspondent,
   144, 145, 152, 234
Nationalism, 67, 73, 79, 91
Natural resources, 73.
   See also Ecology and
   forestry; Environmental
   impacts
N'Diack, Seck Mane, 115
Neo-functionalism, 62-63
Netherlands, the, 167,
   183, 188
New International Economic
   Order (NIEO), 72,
   73-74, 76, 77, 80,
   96, 97, 218, 219
NGOs. See Non-Governmental
   Organizations
NIEO. See New International
   Economic Order
Niger, 7, 34, 99
  agricultural production,
   11(table), 12, 20, 25,
   26(table), 31, 35, 36,

38, 222, 223(table),
   224(table), 239, 241
CILSS, xviii, 71(table),
   112(table), 114(table),
   115, 158(table), 159
disease, 27, 37
donor support, 180, 184,
   186(table)
droughts, 1, 24, 27, 31,
   33, 34, 40, 41(table),
   42, 43, 44(table)
FGP projects, 173,
   174(table), 177,
   178(table)
GNP, 7, 8(table), 76,
   81(table), 226(table),
   228(table)
malnutrition, 27, 36, 37
migration, 30, 37,
   38(table)
population, 8(table),
   9(table)
project support, 201,
   202(table), 203
regional cooperatives, 64,
   71(table), 106(n46)
trade, 4, 5(tables), 6,
   55-57(table), 58,
   59(table), 60, 61(table),
   66, 82, 83(table), 86, 87
Nigeria, 1, 29, 30, 37, 42,
   91, 106(n46), 111, 141,
   244
Nixon administration, 77, 99
Nkomati Accord, 2
Nomads. See Pastoralists
Non-Governmental Organizations
   (NGOs), 235
Nutrition, 9, 18, 128, 144,
   238. See also Malnutrition

OCAM. See Afro-Malagasy
   Common Organization
OCCGE. See Organization for
   Coordination and
   Cooperation in Combating
   Major Endemic Diseases

OCLALAV. See Joint
Organization for
Bird and Locust
Control
ODA. See Official develop-
ment assistance
OECD. See Organization for
Economic Cooperation
and Development
OEOA. See Office for
Emergency Operations
in Africa
Office for Emergency
Operations in Africa
(OEOA), 40-41
Official development
assistance (ODA),
xviii-xix, 88
levels, 179, 217(table),
218, 253(n6)
pattern, 220(table),
221, 246
OICMA. See International
Organization for
African Migratory
Locust Control
Oil. See Petroleum products
Oilseed production, 3, 20,
55-57(table), 58, 82
OMVS. See Senegal River
Basin Development
Authority
ONG. See Division of
Relations with Non-
Governmental
Organizations
OPEC. See Organization
of Petroleum Exporting
States
Organization for Coordina-
tion and Cooperation
in Combating Major
Endemic Diseases
(OCCGE), 71(table), 72
Organization for Economic
Cooperation and

Development (OECD), 52,
168, 179, 198
Club du Sahel, 93, 94, 97
donor interest, 191,
192(table)
as trade partner, 59(table),
60, 61(table), 87
Organization of African Unity
(OAU), 51, 71(table), 72,
89, 90-91
Organization of Petroleum
Exporting States (OPEC),
74, 96
Ouagadougou Programme, 92, 93

Palin, David, 232
Palin Report, 232-233, 234
Pan-African Congresses, 53
Pan-Africanism, 53-54, 63-64,
67
Pastoral-agro-sylvo projects,
134, 137
Pastoralists, 22, 23, 27, 34
agriculturalists and, 39,
134
colonial rule, 19, 20
culture change, 37-38
droughts, 17-18, 27, 29,
31, 32, 34, 37-38
Pastoral management projects,
134
Peanuts. See Groundnut
production
People's Republic of China,
201
Pereira Silva, Joao, 114(table)
Permanent Interstate Committee
to Combat Drought in the
Sahel. See Comité
permanent Inter-états de
Lutte contre la Sécheresse
dans le Sahel
Petroleum products, 3, 4, 5,
55-57(table), 77
Physical Quality of Life
Index (PQLI), 184-185

302

304

United States, 2, 32, 41, 78, 97-99, 157(table), 158(table), 164, 167, 193
United States Agency for International Development (USAID), 32, 98, 142, 167
  aid restrictions, 164, 165
  and IPM, 164-165
  project support, 183, 188, 193, 241-243
United States Department of Agriculture, 32
Unité Socio-Economique et Démographique (USED), 127-128
UNSO. See United Nations Sudano-Sahelian Office
Upper Volta, 58
Uranium, 3, 4, 58, 87
Urbanization, 10, 29-30, 31, 100
USAID. See United States Agency for International Development
USED. See Unité Socio-Economique et Démographique

Vegetable oils
  production, 3, 20, 55-57(table), 82
Venezuela, 78
Village and pastoral
  hydraulics, 131, 133, 177, 179, 180, 187(table), 196(table), 201. See also Hydraulics

Villagers, 18, 22, 29, 39, 134, 140-141

WARDA. See West African Rice Development Association
Water resources, 23, 118, 128, 133, 235
West African Customs Union (UDEAO), 64-65
West African Rice Development Association (WARDA), 51, 71(table), 72
Wheat production, 130(table), 132, 223, 225
WHO. See World Health Organization
Wildlife management, 137
William Ponty School, 53
Williams, Maurice, 93, 95
WMO. See World Meteorological Organization
Working Groups, 116, 128, 129, 131, 140
World Bank, 3-4, 23, 51, 79, 89, 90, 188
World Health Organization (WHO), 28
World Meteorological Organization (WMO), 123, 124-125

Yaoundé I, 81
Yaoundé II, 81
Young, Andrew, 140

Zaire, 78, 106(n46)
Zambia, 1, 52, 106(n46)
Zartman, William, 85-86
Zimbabwe, 1, 52